Recovery FROM AN ALCOHOLIC'S COLLATERAL DAMAGE

Recovery from an Alcoholic's Collateral Damage
Copyright © 2024 by G. Michael Sanborn

Published in the United States of America

Library of Congress Control Number: 2024904522
ISBN   Paperback: 979-8-89091-493-4
ISBN   eBook: 979-8-89091-494-1

All rights reserved. No part of this publication may be reproduced, stored in a retrieval system or transmitted in any way by any means, electronic, mechanical, photocopy, recording or otherwise without the prior permission of the author except as provided by USA copyright law.

The opinions expressed by the author are not necessarily those of ReadersMagnet, LLC.

ReadersMagnet, LLC
10620 Treena Street, Suite 230 | San Diego, California, 92131 USA
1.619. 354. 2643 | www.readersmagnet.com

Book design copyright © 2024 by ReadersMagnet, LLC. All rights reserved.

Cover design by Tifanny Curaza
Interior design by Don De Guzman

Recovery
FROM AN
ALCOHOLIC'S COLLATERAL DAMAGE

G. MICHAEL SANBORN

Contents

Introduction 1

Saint Michael's College 5

United States Army 48

City Administration 141

Teaching 152

Foster Parenting 171

Triggers and Coping 199

Recovery 211

Closing 223

For my fellow collaterals:
If anyone can do it,
If it is humanly possible,
You can do it!

Introduction

An alcoholic is always an alcoholic. When the alcoholic is no longer actively drinking, that person is an alcoholic in recovery. The harm that alcohol causes to one's life remains as emotional and physical scars. The alcoholic learns how to cope with it to mitigate these damages. Some are superficial scars that are more easily managed. Deeper scars are not so obvious or easily managed. Alcoholics can try to minimize them and even suppress them, but they remain and operate covertly. Beware, alcoholics are masters at denial especially if they are not in recovery. They deny their own condition and demand that others near them to also deny it. Those of us closest to the alcoholic may have been even more severely harmed than the alcoholic. We also learn coping mechanisms used by the alcoholic, most notably the denial.

Alcohol and drugs have continued to cause great damage to our society. Like many things, there seems to be a scale from the no effect to significant trauma. Some people have been damaged severely while others suffer lesser harm. A few who have no direct experience with an alcoholic in the family may still feel some effects without realizing it. I hope that everyone will gain understanding of the collateral harm by reading how my family suffered these damages. Perhaps even more importantly is how each of us adjusted and continued to cope with the effects. Why do some seem to escape the alcoholic's control while others fall into the same destructive path for their families? Those who escaped the alcoholic unscathed still have open wounds and/or scars. Some may have learned more successful coping strategies. No one completely escapes an alcoholic's collateral damage. Like alcoholics, we have lifelong scars that resurface when triggered. We are in recovery.

Everyone around the alcoholic is profoundly affected, whether we admit it or not. The closer one is to the alcoholic, the greater the harm. The children suffer the most. When there is one alcoholic parent, the other may be able to mitigate some of the damage. When an alcoholic is a single parent, the children are trapped directly in the most harmful zone. With no help on the inside, the only assistance is from outside the alcoholic's zone. Help is rarely forthcoming and can be extreme, such as legally removing and placing the children in another living situation. This is also very traumatic. Most likely, the help comes with a combination or series of interventions. The people providing the assistance may be totally unaware of the benefits they provide to someone suffering in silence. Conversely, there are people who could have helped but chose not to get involved.

There is a lot of literature about the common characteristics of alcoholics and the effect on their children. Situations are so varied that there is no simple list or description of characteristics for people harmed by an alcoholic family member. No one can claim to have the perfect list and/or description of effects from the alcoholic family member. The literature offers suggestions on how to cope with the complex harm the alcoholic's victim suffered. I have read many and found little that applies to me or my siblings and much that does not. I gained some awareness but little relief. Most wrote about the man being the alcoholic. In my family, my mother was the alcoholic parent. They write about domestic violence from the man. My mother was brutal to her children and to our father. I recognize that my father, like many other men, can be victims of domestic abuse. Rarely do they seek assistance. When assistance is rendered, it is a modification of the services provided to women. Society is not prepared to deal with abusive, violent, alcoholic women.

Children go through developmental stages in all families. These are rites of passages to be celebrated. Unfortunately, they are distorted or intensified in an alcoholic family. Rites of passage may not be celebrated or even recognized. Instead of celebrating a rite of passage, we were given additional responsibilities. "You're old enough now to…" or "you're too old for…" were common phrases my alcoholic mother said to avoid her obligations and place them on us.

My most effective skill was to avoid my mother, especially when she was drinking. Whenever possible, avoidance of unpleasant situations has been my go-to coping mechanism all my life. At a young age, we sought a means to counter my mother's abuse. My older sister, Cilla, especially hated the way our mother described herself as a super mother. Cilla and I decided that "Mom" was a term of endearment that we no longer felt. We revolted by calling her "Mother." She was undeniably our biological mother but not our mom. Mother never knew why we stopped calling her mom. Conversely, our two younger siblings became hopelessly conditioned in the belief that ours was a great mother while our father was the cause of our plight.

The harm done to children occurs over a long period of time and are reinforced with repetition. When all you know are lies and broken promises, it's the only thing that you can believe. There is no quick fix. No getting over it. We must cope with the harm with similar, long term, repetitive behaviors. Just like the recovering alcoholic, we suffer setbacks, too. In *"An Alcoholic's Collateral Damage,"* I wrote about the progression of the harm my mother's alcoholism caused to us. I described our family's descent from a middle-class family into this terrible world of alcoholism and extreme poverty. What was happening in our family had some characteristics common to all families with an alcoholic member. We also have some unique characteristics. It affected each of us very differently. My mother groomed each person to fill the roles she chose. For my father, she decided that he would fail and so did their marriage. My older sister and I were responsible for our younger siblings and the primary housekeepers. Mom conditioned me to be the provider, taking all the money that I earned. My older sister refused to give up her money. She earned it and refused to give it up. My younger brother learned to be irresponsible because I was held accountable for everything that he did wrong. Though my mother was grooming us all to care for her, she groomed my youngest sister to care for her personal needs directly, such as washing her feet. I also noted that alcoholism had generational connections, often skipping generations. Those who avoided alcoholism still learned some of the coping characteristics of the previous generation.

Each family and its members are unique and the circumstances also differ. I hope to show my readers how it affected us as children and how my siblings and I continue to cope with the damage throughout our adult life. Like phases in child development, adults also develop as we mature. These phases can be divided into early, middle, and late adult. In the early phase, we are developing our identity and independence. This is when we select a career and start building our family. The middle adult years are spent working to achieve and reflect on our purpose. We may reevaluate our earlier decisions and change our directions, perhaps have a mid-life crisis. During the later years, we look back on what we have accomplished and either celebrate or fall into deep depression and regret. As we cross milestones from one developmental phase to another, we find new and hopefully better coping skills. Perhaps you can identify directly with some. Most importantly, I hope that my readers understand that the effects follow a subtle path, gradually etching into our personalities over a long period of time. Healing the damage takes at least an equal amount of time and effort. I hope that considering the process provides the most applicable assistance for my fellows who have been collaterally damaged by an alcoholic. Perhaps I can be one who has a small, positive influence on you as others have done for me. I hope to help, but I humbly ask that you find some greater influences than me.

I struggled through my obsession with organization. A timeline is the easiest way to organize a biography but I realize that my readers would not be able to make the connections that I wish to demonstrate. The basic structure of this book is the chronological order of my adult life. I will describe events, accomplishments, and influences that helped me. I will explain how they helped me at that time and show how they influenced my recovery throughout my life. A few people stand out as great mentors. Most do not realize how much they helped me.

Saint Michael's College

During grade and high school, I suffered many humiliations for things such as my name. I was often called "Born in the Sand." I grew numb to it after a while and tried to ignore it. Sometimes I was called George and sometimes Michael. I developed a hatred for my name. George Henry Sanborn Jr. was my father's name. My mother explained that he wanted me to be George Henry Sanborn III. My mother wanted a son named Michael. George Michael Sanborn was the name given to me in compromise. The constant demeaning lectures from my mother and grandfather always included how horrible and irresponsible my father was. Their stated intensions were to help me to be better than my father. Their actions demonstrated that they wanted me to be like them and to serve them.

In high school, I began to accept that the Sanborn family originated from a sandy beach in England. When I was called "Born in the Sand," I simply agreed. Sometimes I retaliated by saying, "At least I know where my family was born." I asserted some control over my name> I alone decided to be called G. Michael Sanborn. I preferred Michael over Mike for many years. It seemed to be more respectful. This was the beginning of taking some control over myself, body, and mind.

No matter how terrible home is, leaving home is never easy. The fear of the unknown is worse than the known fears and chaos. I spent seventeen years learning to cope in my mother's home. I was still a minor when I started college, legally dependent upon my mother, but without her support. I knew nothing about college life and I had no mentor to ease the transition. No one in my family had ever gone to college. I left a world in which I had adjusted to the known chaos with much doubt about whether I could succeed. I felt the pressure of the expectations from the many people and organizations who trusted me with scholarships. I did not want to let them down. My math teacher, Mrs. Hronek, was most influential by assuring me that I could be successful in college, despite what my family told me. My guidance counselor, Mr. Livengood, made attending college possible by helping me to apply for scholarships and loans. I especially did not want to disappoint them. I knew that my family expected and even wished for me to fail at college and return to serve them. Throughout my childhood, my mother and grandfather told me how stupid I was.

Saint Michael's College sent instructions for my arrival on campus. I had never visited the campus. Mother drove me so she would know where I was. It was the only time she would ever go to Saint Michael's College. Temporary signs directed us to the drop off point on campus. As we stopped at the drop off location, an upper classman met us almost immediately. He showed me the entrance to Alliot Hall, assuring me that there were people inside with what I needed. I turned to Mother. She stood beside the car, wiping away some tears. I was surprised by her tears. I had only seen her cry in self-pity. I determined the tears were for her loss of my servitude to her and not my physical separation. She would have to take care of the house with only my younger sister, Debra, and brother, Gary, to help. She would also lose some welfare money as I would soon be eighteen years old. That would cut into her beer money.

The arrival sign-in, room assignment, registration, and book purchasing were well organized and went smoothly. I carried all my belongings and textbooks to my room on the fourth floor of Ryan Hall. My first roommate was unable to secure funding and left. I was moved to the first floor of Lyons Hall with a roommate from Scarsdale, New York. Bobby made certain that I understood that he was privileged and superior to me by immediately telling me that he was from Scarsdale. He pronounced Scarsdale slowly and with emphasis. He was sending a subtle message that I learned from my family. I was from a lower social class and did not belong in his world. Scarsdale and his elite stance meant nothing to me. I earned my way into college and assumed he did, too. The only benefit I saw over me is that his daddy wrote a check for his college expenses while I had to apply for scholarships and work as much as I could.

My relationship with Bobby descended quickly. He was a sociology major. His first class started at eleven o'clock. I was a science major. My classes began at eight o'clock. I had a much busier academic schedule with labs in the afternoon. Bobby stayed up late with his friends. The drinking age had been reduced to eighteen years old. It was lowered with the rationale that young men could die for their country in Vietnam but could not enter a bar in the United States. Bobby and his friends went to the bars in Burlington, returning after I was in bed. They were loud and unconcerned that I needed to sleep for my challenging curriculum. They acted like irresponsible teenagers whose parents were gone for the weekend. It seemed like they needed a better transition to act more responsibly. In contrast, I already had experience of being responsible for myself, my siblings, our home, and even my mother when she drank. I could be trusted with farm tractors and working on farms since I was eight years old.

Weekends were worse. There was a lot of alcohol, marijuana, and even some LSD. They played blackjack, gambling with cash. Some lost hundreds of dollars in one game. Cigarette and marijuana smoke were so thick that I could only see a silhouette of the person at the far end of the hall. They had water fights that flooded the whole wing of the dormitory. While I was trying to study one evening, someone spread laundry detergent, then they body-surfed the length of the hall. Annoyed by the ruckus, I opened my door just as a naked man went sliding by. I decided that my best option was to go to the library and study until it closed at two o'clock in the morning. I returned to a dormitory that was completely trashed. Debris was everywhere. Some jerks enjoyed urinating on the toilet paper in the bathroom stalls. The showers we littered with dirty, wet laundry, and trash. One shower stall was occupied with an empty beer keg. It was the first time that I had ever seen a beer keg. I noticed its tap and pump to understand how it dispensed its contents. It was in the shower because the foam often overfilled their cups and spilled on the floor. The shower floor was sticky with beer. Perhaps my ability to adapt to the chaos of my mother's home prepared me for the chaos at college. I focused on my studies. I gained satisfaction for all their ridicule by frustrating Bobby and his friends with better grades than theirs.

My first semester was rote learning. The lectures were too intense for me to do the daydreaming that I did in high school. I struggled to keep complete notes that were neat enough for later studying. I decided to get the notes as best I could then rewrite them in the evening. I read the textbooks. It took a while to feel free to mark the textbooks after twelve years of it being forbidden. I owned these books so I could underline key words and phrases. I found value in making notes in the margins, especially definitions for the words that I did not readily recognize. I struggled to memorize the facts. After a while, I started looking for some better way to connect the facts. By being persistent, I eventually reached a point when the facts seem to become logically connected. It was like a light coming on. The topic made sense when I understood the underlying concepts. It was the way subjects have been taught in high school and college. The instructor presented the facts. The successful students discovered the concepts and made their own meaningful connections.

The skills that I used trying to make sense of the crazy world Mother created to hide and perpetuate her alcoholism became an odd asset in college. I seemed to have a greater need to organize my world. I struggled to find some order in my mother's alcohol consumption. I had a keen ability to quickly determine how drunk she was with certain cues, such as her body posture, especially how she held her head. I could even determine her intoxication level in a photograph. I developed a scale with my sister. We referenced how intoxicated our mother was using a six-pack scale. It helped us cope with her changing behavior. Mother always drank sixteen-ounce Black Label beer. Her years of practice and morbid obesity turned her into a beer-drinking machine. She drank until the beer or money was gone. Rarely did she go to bed while there was still beer in the refrigerator. At one six-pack, she was happy and sometimes generous. At the second six-pack, she was getting mean and we tried to avoid her. During the third six-pack, there was no reasoning with her and we avoided her by any means. We had to leave home or she would send a younger sibling to get us to engage in an irrational argument.

I also tried to make sense of my grandfather's often irrational demands for perfection. Though he rarely drank alcohol and never to excess, he exhibited many of the same unreasonable characteristics as my mother. For instance, he demanded a particular crop be weeded a certain way. He had no tolerance for any deviation from his methods even if they produced the same or better results. Another time, he demanded a different method for the same crop. The penalty for not doing it his way was hours-long barrages of demeaning speeches, telling me how stupid I was, and how much I was worthless like my father. I cringed to shield my self-esteem as I did with my mother. I grew resentful about how he compared me to my father, who he decided was a failure. I quietly fortified my internal defense by accepting that half my genes were from my father. Even though he dropped out of college, I remember that he was a competent draftsman and skilled at math, things my grandfather could never accept or understand. I remembered all my grandfather's techniques that he called "tricks" to doing "the job" right. I could never organize and apply his ever-changing tricks to his satisfaction no matter how hard I tried. Such is typical behavior of an alcoholic but he learned it from his father, who was a hard liquor alcoholic. One of his stories he told many times was how his father downed a pint of whiskey without swallowing.

I could readily understand the unchanging concepts and methods of science and math. It demanded reasonable, justifiable quests for perfection. We conducted research and reported in a prescribed manner that was repeatable. I thrived on this consistency. I had difficulty making sense of literature and humanities. Too much was open to interpretation like my mother and grandfather's behavior. I needed concrete facts and literal word meanings. Poetry remains the worst for me.

I chose a general psychology course as an elective in my first semester. I wanted to learn about my mother's alcoholism. It was an introductory course and did not cover any abnormal psychology. I learned about child development pioneers such as Freud, Erickson, and Piaget. Piaget studied his own children but the science community accepted his findings that were done objectively. I struggled memorizing the different milestones for the tests. Piaget wrote about the transition from concrete to abstract thinking.

Oddly, I wanted a practical use of psychology to understand my mother. I was not yet ready to see how much of what I was learning applied to myself. I learned how humans continually try to make sense of the world and organize vast amounts of information. We seek consistency and symmetry in our organization of everything in our complex lives. We do our best with daily routines. I did not yet realize that I developed a keen ability to find sense in a senseless environment from my experiences during a childhood dominated by an alcoholic. I was annoyed by the asymmetry of my eyes that led others to erroneously judge me. My right eye often drifted because of the traumatic brain injury caused by my mother's alcohol-fueled temper. I hopelessly struggled to keep my eyes working together.

I struggled with chemistry. Mr. Michaels was one of the few instructors without a doctorate. He seemed to make an extraordinary effort to identify with college students but he was much too old to be one of us. I did not like how he represented a beaker of solution on the blackboard with a drawing of a martini glass. Whenever a student came in on crutches or an obviously injured arm, he accused them of falling off a barstool. These distractions conflicted with my concrete thinking and repulsion to alcohol. I struggled with the transition to the abstract, three-dimensional thought necessary to understand chemistry. Mr. Michaels left to pursue his doctorate. Dr. Gil Grady took over the class. He was a great instructor and I did much better.

I was not prepared for the levels of stress from multiple directions. I tried to stay in contact with home with weekly phone calls. I had to use the pay phones in the student center, where it was noisy. I could barely hear my mother on the phone. I got little benefit from these calls as I found that I was just trying to determine my mother's level of intoxication. Even though I knew that I was powerless to stop her from dinking, I worried about the danger in which she put herself and my siblings. I sometimes wrote letters that were never answered. Along with pressures from home, I had peer pressures in the dormitory. I refused to join in their partying lifestyle. I wanted no part of the alcohol and marijuana. I was also under great stress to achieve high academic standing for a career in medicine. I felt an obligation to the many people who trusted me with their scholarship money. The generosity of my college and community helped pay the expenses but I was left with a feeling of emptiness without my family's support. It was a very strange environment for which I was unprepared. I had to prove to my family that I was not too stupid to go to college as they told me. I was very much a loner.

When I was a child on my grandparents' farm, I found solitude by observing and exploring nature during any free time. I walked in the fields and woods. I played with grasshoppers, tomato caterpillars, birds that got caught in the chicken coop, toads, and others. Now at college, I occasionally walked about campus but found no suitable places to escape into solitude. I decided to take a walk on the streets. I went further and further with successive walks. I explored the streets, shops, and neighborhoods in Winooski and Burlington for hours. I found the federal building where I registered for the draft. I got the IIS (two-S) student deferment so that I would not be drafted during the very active Vietnam War. I found some beneficial stress relief in these walks. My mind wandered from what might be happening at home to college studies to my ultimate profession. The distraction of the activities on the streets and neighborhoods helped keep my mind working away from my homelife. I was determined to escape the lower social class into which my mother's alcoholism dragged us. I was unaware of my anxiety and depression. My father had considered suicide and spent some time at the New Hampshire State Hospital. My mother often referred to my father as being "sick" in a derogatory tone. Society in general and especially my family treated any mental illness as a severe personality defect. They practiced denial and refused to accept that someone needed help. Ironically, it was my mother who had a sickness with alcoholism. She refused to admit any problem, so no treatment would help her. I only felt relief during these walks and did not recognize how therapeutic they were.

I started college at seventeen and soon had my eighteenth birthday. There was no celebration. It was just another day. I reflected on the concept of being a legal adult. I felt no sudden wisdom, special powers, or any other magical changes. There was no difference because

I had always been responsible for myself. I was also responsible for my younger siblings. College provided the separation that relieved me of that burden. The greatest advantage for me is that I could sign my own forms and did not need my mother.

Society is released from its responsibility when a neglected child becomes eighteen years old. This includes all children in many ways. It especially includes the ones that social services identified and were under their direct and indirect supervision. It also includes all the children who needed services but were hidden from the authorities. It includes all those children who some adult saw something but did not want to get involved. It also includes the school system that could not or would not meet the child's needs in education. Suspensions and expulsions only hurt the child.

I soon learned that any organization operates by standards and procedures that benefit the organization first. They say that they have the child's best interests but theirs come first. When held into account, they may say that their continued operation is in the child's best interest. My mother had a distorted logic for her drinking. She often said that her children always came first. As my sister, Priscilla, and I grew older, we challenged my mother. We recognized how much money was spent on beer and what our new shoes would have cost. When she said that she could not afford our request for a basic need, she said the beer helped her care for us. As usual, she would blame my father for her demise but she was the one who drove him away.

I went home during the Thanksgiving holiday. I took the bus from Burlington to Charlestown. No one met me at the bus stop as I asked in a letter. I walked home. I found that my sister, Debra, had taken over the bedroom that I shared with my brother, Gary. I was displaced to the tiny back room. Gary had attempted to commit suicide by taking a whole bottle of aspirin. He was fine because he vomited it. He spent several days at the New Hampshire State Hospital, then went to live with Dad. So, it was logical for Debra to have the larger bedroom that remained unused most of the time. I did not like the extremely small bedroom in the back mostly because I had to enter it through the bedroom shared by Frank and my mother.

I had many reasons to hate my brother, but I worried about Gary, who was now fifteen years old. I knew enough biology and chemistry to know that he would not have been successful at committing suicide with aspirin. I did worry that it might have caused an ulcer that could have seriously hurt him. Mother assured me that he vomited right away so no harm was done. I then wondered what led him to such a drastic action and whether he would find a more lethal method. Again, mother put all the blame on him and his peer relationships. I knew that my mother must have pressed too hard for him to fill my role when I was gone. She wanted her children to care for her. It was too much for Gary to transition from years of little to no responsibility to taking over most of the family duties. Living with Dad was his best option. Unfortunately, he dropped out of school when he became sixteen years old.

I had not seen my father for several years. Dad married Gail, who had two daughters: Tammy and Lori. Dad adopted them, making them my sisters. Tonya and Scott were born, making them my half sister and brother. Cilla and Gary now lived with him. Dad worked many hours as a prison guard. He supported six children. Mother complained about having four. She blamed him for his inability to be a man and take care of his family. She could not credit him for his success with another family without her. She would never accept that her alcoholism was the root of our family's problems. Now, Mother had only Debra at home while Dad was providing for a family with six children.

We always went to the Thanksgiving dinner prepared by my grandmother on the farm. All my mother's family came, my aunt and uncle with their families, except Cilla and Gary this time. It was a family celebration but it did not seem right without my siblings. My grandmother was elated to have most of her family in her home to enjoy her hard work. As usual, my grandfather, Pop as we called him, pushed the adults to share a drink of brandy. Frank and Mother readily accepted his offer. I was a bit surprised because Mother usually resisted the first offer. I was confident that this would kick off a drinking binge when we got home, which it did.

Pop offered me some brandy, too, seemingly recognizing that I was an adult and eighteen was currently the legal drinking age in

Vermont. I declined his offer. Pop challenged me to "wrist wrestle" as he always did at family gatherings. He enjoyed beating everyone at arm wrestling. It was one of his ways to dominate the family physically, emotionally, and financially. This time, I almost beat him. He never challenged me again. I also felt some satisfaction that he completely avoided talking about my college. This satisfaction came after listening to him for so many years about how stupid I was. It was a bit of revenge for all those hours of being told that I was too stupid to go to college when I told him my intentions four years earlier. My grandfather had only a sixth-grade education, typical of his times. I was now studying topics he had did not know existed. My education was bringing me into a world that my grandfather could never understand. My grandfather was silent about my accomplishments because he could not dominate them. My mother was also silent. I had no family willing to celebrate my success.

My college professors taught me to evaluate the sources of my information. Accuracy and credibility were most important. Information had to be testable and proven accurate. Sources were subject to intense review by peers. Evaluators must be credible. I was beginning to use these skills with the criticism my family directed at me. I was well beyond their education even before I started college. I found comfort in realizing that members of my family were no longer qualified to criticize me.

Mother liked her beer. Since Frank moved into our home, she started drinking mixed drinks, usually whiskey and ginger ale. When she did not have beer money, she drank the hard stuff. She could get drunk much quicker, making it a little more challenging for me to anticipate her behavior. I still equated her level of drunkenness by equivalent six packs of beer. I couldn't read Frank's level of intoxication. I never saw him take a drink. He hid it well. His speech was always high pitched and raspy. He moved awkwardly all the time, which he blamed on his work-related neck injury and hip surgery. His cognitive abilities were never acute. I noticed his extreme intoxication only when he passed out, sometimes on the front lawn, under a tree.

When we went to bed, Mother and Frank made more noise than usual. They were quite intoxicated. Mother was giggling like a little girl. I was appalled that they would behave like this so close to me, like I did not matter. I was here for only a few days. They could not respect me for this short period. I could not tolerate it any longer. I stormed out of my room, through theirs and went outside. I walked as I did in college. The difference was that I did not want to go home. I walked all night. The next day, I took the bus back to college.

A few days later, I got a letter from Cilla telling me that Frank had been arrested for driving while intoxicated. I spoke with Mother by phone. She blamed it on an overzealous cop. I thought little of it and completed the semester. I dreaded returning home. The college would not let anyone remain over semester break. I also needed to take advantage of an opportunity to earn money during this period.

Dairy farmer Bob Frizzell offered my friend, Chester, and me some work cleaning the cattle stalls. I also worked as an orderly in the emergency room at Springfield Hospital on weekends. They needed help moving injured skiers.

When I got my first paycheck, I looked for my bank book to deposit it. I was stunned when I saw that there was only about eight dollars in my account. I looked in disbelief. There were pages showing many withdrawals. As I accepted that it was correct, I was so shocked that my legs weakened and I had to sit down. There was over eight-hundred dollars when I left for college. Minimum wage was one dollar forty-five cents per hour. It took over six-hundred hours of working for me to earn that money that was now gone. I looked at the withdrawals. The first one was for two hundred twenty-five dollars. It was followed by many ten and fifteen-dollar withdrawals. Sometimes twice in one day. The days without withdrawals coincided with Mother getting her welfare check. A few days after getting her check, the withdrawals continued. I realized the amounts were what Mother needed for her beer. I never thought that my mother would go so low as to take all my money this way. I had made it very clear that I did not want any of my earnings to be spent on beer since I first started earning money and giving it to her "to benefit the family." She took my savings for her beer knowing how much I opposed her drinking. I could not return to college without two hundred dollars for books and lab fees. She knew this.

I was never so angry at my mother and confronted her. She was expecting me, seemingly guilty, cowering like a child in her overstuffed chair. She explained that the first withdrawal was to repay Frenchie, the neighborhood store owner. He provided the cash to bail out Frank the night that he got arrested. Mother had to repay him the next day. Tempted with the easy access to money, she continued to make withdrawals to support he alcoholic drive.

I paced about the small house. I was overwhelmed with anger about how my mother could take my hard-earned money and literally piss it away. I yelled at my mother, "How could you do this to me?" I was vulnerable because I needed her to start that account. I was a minor when I opened the account and still a minor when I started college. It was also for my convenience when I needed to transfer money from my savings to my checking while I was at college. If you cannot trust your mother, who can you trust? Mother was making no offers to restore my money. I began to think. If the large withdrawal was to bail Frank out of jail, then maybe the police could help me get the bail money back. This would mean Frank would have to go to jail until his court hearing. When I shared this thought, Frank immediately offered his entire disability check for about that much money. At least I could go back to college if he kept his promise. I had doubts but he delivered.

I went to the bank to have my mother's name removed from the account. They explained that I would have to close it and reopen another. The teller offered a new type of account, an interest paying checking account called a Now Account. It was perfect. I closed my savings and checking accounts and opened the Now Account. I no longer needed my mother on my bank account. I was greatly relieved.

I told my mother what I had done. I emphasized that she could not withdraw any money from my account. I knew that in this small town, even if she was not on the account, she might be able to convince them, being my mother. I wanted to make it clear to her because I intended to go to the police if she did it again. Mother never repaid the rest of the money. I worked the two jobs on the farm and Springfield Hospital but was not able to replenish my account to the previous level before returning to college. At least I had enough to return to college.

This was a hard, real-life lesson for me in understanding the power of alcoholism. This "super mother" as she described herself was a lie that she repeated many times. If you hear a lie often enough, you might believe it, even if it is to convince yourself. My younger siblings fell into this trap. My mother still saw me as either an extension of herself or, worse, her lifelong servant. She succumbed to the alcoholic drive and used my money to satisfy it. Her kids did not come first as she stated many times. Her alcoholism did. Her kids coming first was a perpetuated lie to convince everyone around her. She shattered any shadow of such thoughts for me.

I also sensed that Mother secretly wanted to disrupt my education so I would return home to take care of her. Her vision for me was the same vision she had for my father. Someone to earn money to support her, including all the beer she wanted. Instead, she drove my father away. She drove me away yet I could not escape. I needed a place to go between semesters. Ordinarily, I could have gone to my grandparents' house but Aunt Alice was divorcing Uncle Beau. She and my two cousins left no room for me there.

I wondered how Pop and Gramma could have such a long-lasting marriage while all three of their children divorced. Mother and Uncle Bernie divorced twice. Aunt Alice divorced once and never remarried. I believe it was Pop's influence. I remembered the many hours working in the fields with him as he demeaned my father. No one was good enough for him. Pop's father was an alcoholic. He was not. It skipped his generation and landed squarely on my mother. It impacted my aunt and uncle. My great grandfather's alcoholism certainly had some influence on my grandfather's insatiable perfectionism. Uncle Bernie had his alcohol and marijuana parties. Aunt Alice did not drink but married an alcoholic. The influences of alcohol upon my family were complex and extensive. I wanted to understand it and was even more driven to learn more at college.

I managed semester breaks at home by spending as much time away as possible. I worked all I could. Farmer Bob Frizzell found lots of work for me in his barns. On weekends, I worked at Springfield

Hospital in the emergency room helping with skiers who broke a leg or had other injuries. I also pumped gas and did simple mechanic work at a gas station in Charlestown. I spent time with my friends. It was odd that I was the only one of my closest friends to go to college. They seemed to have stable, supportive families especially compared to mine. Perhaps I realized that college was my best or only route to escape from my childhood environment.

David was the friend with whom I spent most of my free time when I was home from college. He had a good job at Keil Lock. He bought a nice car and we rode around. We listened to his music on his eight-track player and talked about friends. We often went to the newly built McDonald's restaurant in Claremont. Neither of us spoke much about our families. I waited until Mother and Frank were asleep before coming home. David was my reliable respite from my home while on respite from college.

I returned to college as soon as the dormitories opened. I had a well-established routine that avoided the party times in the dormitory. I studied at the library. If I was caught up on my studies or was feeling particularly anxious or depressed, I went on walks. When the weather was the coldest, I limited my walks to the main and north campuses and the nearby neighborhoods. I still focused on the content of the courses that I was studying. I memorized and categorized facts and processes. Like high school, I wondered how I would ever use much of what I was studying in humanities and philosophy. The biology was more in depth and sometimes confusing. Chemistry presented by Dr. Grady and physics by Dr. Cassavant were my strongest courses.

I had stopped calling home. I was surprised when I received a letter from my paternal grandfather, George Henry Sanborn SR., in my mailbox. I had very little contact with him as I grew up. During my childhood, he sent two dollars on my birthday and ten dollars for Christmas, which my mother always took. I knew that he had divorced my grandmother and was living in Seattle, Washington. He had married his secretary, Vera. He wanted me to call him "Sandy," like she did. It seemed so wrong for me to call my grandfather by a nickname like a friend. I answered his letter with updates on my progress in college. To appease him, I began my letters with "Grandpa

Sandy." He wrote about what Vera and he did around Seattle and how it rained most of the time. He invited me to come visit him but it was not within my means and I needed to spend my time between semesters working to pay college bills. He never offered me any assistance with college.

Spring break came and I had to leave Saint Michael's College and took the bus home. A much older car than Frank's was in the driveway. I thought at first that Frank had left and felt some excitement. Mother explained that she was in an accident and this car was loaned by the dealership repairing the car. On the day that she wrecked the car, Debra was sick at school and Mother went to bring her home. It had snowed and heavy slush was on the edges of the road. She got into some slush and was unable to steer out of it. She blamed the power steering being too light for her to feel how the wheels reacted to her steering efforts. She was used to cars with no power steering. Mother always distorted events to her benefit. I called Cilla at Dad's house to discover what she might know. She confirmed Mother was getting Debra from school. It was ten thirty in the morning and she was already too drunk to drive. As usual, Mother popped Canadian Mints in her mouth before the police arrived. She always carried some along with her used tissues in the lower front shirt pockets to disguise the alcohol on her breath. With the current laws, police had to catch her behind the wheel to bring driving while intoxicated charges. She was able to get out of the car so it did not matter whether she was drinking. Cilla blamed Debra for the accident. She should have known Mother was drinking and should have stayed at school. Debra was not sick. She just wanted to go home. I did not agree with Cilla's rationale that placed the blame on someone other than the alcoholic who caused the grief.

I went to the garage where the car was awaiting repairs. It looked like the car was a total loss. The rear axle was nearly knocked out sideways. The left wheel was entirely under the car while the right wheel protruded a foot outside the right side of the car. The whole back end of the body had dents and twists in the metal. The body shop said that it was expensive but not a total loss. Mother had slid sideways into the boulders on the opposite side of the road. It was fortunate that there was no on-coming traffic.

I was just beginning to realize how many people around the alcoholic make excuses and deflect the blame to protect the alcoholic. They distort reality to protect alcoholics. I knew my mother was the sole one to blame for the accident. Mother should not have been drinking. Since she was, she should not have driven. She was drunk and incapable of driving safely. It was not the slushy roads. It was not the power steering. It was not Debra who just wanted to get out of school. It was totally my mother's fault. Fortunately, she did not crash into another car. I compared this to Frank's arrest for driving while intoxicated. He, too, would not take the blame. Instead, he blamed the overzealous cop. I can see better now with my growing science skills. Alcoholics do not accept responsibility for their alcoholism and deny its effects upon others. They find a way to blame others for their misfortune. It is unfortunate that alcoholics can manipulate people by repeating the same lie numerous times until it is believed.

When I returned to college after the break, I was even more determined to better understand how alcohol affects people. How does it affect the body? How does it become addictive? There were some things I could find in my biology and chemistry classes about nerve function but not enough. When I signed up for my sophomore

Studying Organic Chemistry

year classes. I needed to fill in an elective. A classmate, Henry, and I saw a course called Physiological Psychology. It was a required course for psychology majors. It was intense. Psychology majors dreaded it. The professor was notorious for giving only one A in his class and many failed. Henry and I were both doing well and felt up to the challenge. I hoped that I could learn more about alcohol and alcoholism with this course. I learned about the chemistry of synapses and their vulnerability. Nicotine, for instance, contributed to increasing tolerance, requiring higher doses for effects. Alcohol is a depressant that slows synaptic function. It explained the slurred speech, stumbling and awkward movements when intoxicated. It also explained the inability to accurately process information and to have a logical conversation, contributing to the unreasonableness of an intoxicated alcoholic. All psychological drugs worked by affected the function of these synapses. Surprisingly, psychiatrists did a lot of guessing when determining what psychiatric medication worked at what dose. The biochemistry of addiction and the long-term effects were not fully understood.

Continuing my studies became increasingly important for me but I was at a disadvantage from my peers. Most of their parents paid their college expenses. I had to apply for numerous scholarships each year. Each one required a separate application and essay. I had the state-of-the-art Smith Corona electric typewriter that helped me write these essays and research reports. The time for applying for scholarships came at the same time reports and exams were due in my courses. I could not bring my typewriter to the library, so I had to do all my reports, applications, and essays in my dorm room with all its distractions. I had doubts about whether I could be successful in college. I knew that I was not the only one with this disadvantage. I began reminding myself that if anyone can do it, I can, too. Some of my fellow science majors were also frustrated with the noisy dormitory. They asked me if I wanted to join them in asking for a separate wing of the dorm. I agreed but I did not expect it would be possible.

My first summer break was much like the winter and spring breaks. I worked every opportunity I had and stayed away from home with friends when I was not working. I saved my money. My sophomore year was expected to be rigorous: organic chemistry, physics, biological tutorial, humanities, theology, and philosophy. The science was intense. There were many readings in the other courses.

I was surprised that my college peers were able to coordinate with the college and we had a wing to ourselves. It was great to be able to study in the dorm room and peacefully work on reports. My roommate was Henry. Henry always got straight As. He had a very disciplined study routine. He surprised me at first when we were intently studying and his alarm went off. He closed the book he was reading, placed it on the shelf, took down another, and opened it. He then reset his alarm. He saw my confusion and explained. He had allotted that much time for that class and it was now time for the other. My study habits were quite different. I studied until I thought I knew the material, then went on to the next subject. I spent extraordinarily little time on physics. This was a time when the fastest technology was a slide rule. Texas Instruments released the TI30 about that time. It could perform logarithmic and trigonometry functions, which was revolutionary. We did not trust it for a while and checked it with our slide rules and charts. Henry expressed some frustration because I got better grades with little studying. My conceptual understanding and math skills paid off. Henry always did much better than I in the nonscience classes. We benefited as roommates, sharing mostly all the same classes. Henry was a much better roommate to me than I was to him when I felt increasing anxiety and needed a change in activity.

I was extremely disappointed with my first organic chemistry grade of sixty-four. I studied hard for it. Looking at the other posted grades, I realized that mine was the highest score. Dr. Grady scaled the grades, so I got ninety-five on the scale. I was determined to do better. On the next exam, I got an eighty-nine. I was even further ahead of most of the class. I liked Dr. Grady and how he presented the materials. He was talented at teaching the three dimensions of compounds and their reactions. It was difficult at first but I soon was able to think three dimensionally. I got ninety-eight on the next exam, making one minor mistake. I was now determined to get an A without the scale, which I did.

I liked the chemical analysis of the organic chemistry labs. We did several procedures to identify a sample that Dr. Grady gave to us. He seemed to enjoy going into the chemical supply room and closing the door while we waited outside. He emerged with a test tube with chemical in the bottom. We had three hours to tell him what it was. I became exceptionally good at this because I could imagine the compound in three dimensions. I was solving it within half an hour. I could have done it faster but I had to wait my turn in line for some of the analysis equipment. As the weeks progressed, Dr. Grady gave me a sample that was particularly challenging. I worked on it for over an hour. Finally, I looked at all the data that I collected. I was beginning to realize that the components could not fit together. I suspected that Dr. Grady had mixed two substances together. With this renewed approach, I solved it almost immediately. I still had some doubts, so I decided to bring my conclusion to Dr. Grady. He smiled and commended me. I was correct. Thank you, Dr. Grady, for challenging me!

I learned about the structure and chemistry of alcohols in organic chemistry. The biology tutorial class was about research and report writing. I decided to write about alcohol and alcoholism. A fascinating fact was how they determined the proof of distilled alcohols. Proof was twice of the actual concentration of the alcohol. If you poured whiskey on gunpowder and it smoked or burst into flames, it was one hundred percent proof that it was at least fifty percent alcohol, hence one hundred proof.

I learned about the effects of drug and how they are classified in my physiological psychology class. Biology taught us about nerve synapses. Physiological psychology explained the chemistry of synaptic conductors and inhibitors. Alcohol was a depressant. It slowed the synaptic transmission. It also had a narcotic effect in that it reduced pain and induced sleep. This explained the deteriorating coordination and why people pass out from consuming too much alcohol. Its effects on slowing motor nerve functions caused the familiar staggering and slurred speech. Its effects on the frontal lobes reduced inhibitions to behavior and the normal higher human logic functions. At low dose, alcohol can be a social lubricant. Slight suppression of inhibitions allows conversation to flow more freely. Higher doses explain the irrational arguments when the inhibitions and logical thought are mostly suppressed. The exact biochemical processes were not fully understood.

We are motivated to eat sweet things for their taste. Our bodies have adapted to reward us with brain stimulating dopamine when we eat foods our bodies need. People do not start drinking alcohol because of its taste. They drink it for the effects. We have skipped that step involving taste to recognizing something that will produce a desired effect. The effect has nothing to do with our ancestral survival like other foods. One could say that the desire for alcohol is a learned trait. One drinks alcohol for the intoxication not the nutritional effect.

I could relate what I learned to my mother. She grew increasingly clumsy as she drank more. There were several times she could hardly move. She needed to support herself with the wall and furniture. When extremely intoxicated, she could not even hold her head up straight. It also explained how unreasonable she was when she was drunk because her higher thought processes became significantly suppressed. I wondered why Mother and others wanted to argue and fight when severely intoxicated. I could not explain her need to argue in her third six-pack level of intoxication. Arguing should be a response to something in the environment. She sought us out from hiding in just to argue about something irrelevant. With higher order human reasoning suppressed, the animal-like lower brain dominated. This is where aggression originates. It gave me some insight into the mood changes as my mother consumed more and more alcohol. It also suppressed her frontal lobe rational brain so that her arguments became irrational. I could now understand why she became so angry and how alcohol affected her amygdala, the center for emotions including anger. I learned the futility of trying to reason with her at all when she was so severely intoxicated.

The liver removes the poisonous alcohol, breaking it down chemically into forms that can be metabolized. Though alcohol contributed to the total caloric intake, the bulk of calories was in the drink. Beer has a lot of carbohydrates. My mother drank sixteen-ounce Black Label beer. Each battle had two hundred twenty-five calories. On her binges, she could drink three six packs, for a total of four thousand calories. The beer alone was more than twice her required daily intake. Besides beer, she always ate huge amounts of food. Occasionally she said that it helped keep her from becoming drunk. It was faulty reasoning for me. Why drink beer if you needed to counteract it? Just drink less. She always denied ever getting drunk, boasting that she could drink any man under the table. People who got drunk passed out and slid under the table. Mother's ability to consume large amounts of alcohol and hide its effects were due mostly to her large size. She was grossly obese and continued to gain weight.

Other liver functions are delayed while it processed the large volume of alcohol. Other toxins build up in the body, which is believed to be the cause of the hangover. Alcoholics had an enlarged liver as it adapted to the extra work. Cirrhosis is when the liver replaces damaged cells with fatty tissue. Alcoholics often have a shelf-like abdominal protrusion from under their ribs from this swollen liver. Hard liquor drinkers were more affected than beer drinkers. Mother was much too fat for a protruding liver to be noticeable. She was now literally built like a refrigerator with a head, The rolls upon rolls of fat with little or no bathing harbored bacteria and fungus that caused her incessant itching she blamed on shingles. The beer and massive overeating shaped her body. Mother had always justified her large size to being big boned and said that her body "was meant to be" larger than most people. Unfortunately, my sister, Cilla, grew obese as she accepted this justification. We competed for the sweets and Cilla fought hard for her share. Again, Mother said Cilla was big boned like her and was also meant to be large. Mother groomed Cilla to justify her own obesity. Unfortunately, it had a profound impact on Cilla's quality of life.

I learned very differently during my nutrition class. Mother just made excuses about her size just as alcoholics place blame anywhere but upon themselves. Unfortunately, they believe the lies they tell themselves. Even worse, their constant repetition of lies convinces the people around them. Alcoholics can create their own world with a separate body of unsupported facts.

Marijuana was widely used on campus. I observed its effects on my peers in greater detail during my junior and senior years. There was little research on its biochemical effects since it was illegal. It seemed to dull their keen thought processing like alcohol. My marijuana intoxicated peers also seemed to be unrealistic in their expectations during my discussions with them. They expected quick solutions to the Vietnam War when none of us understood its complexities. Marijuana also made them paranoid.

Steve was my roommate during my junior and senior years. He enjoyed drinking beer and Johnny Walker Red in moderation. He had some one hundred ninety proof grain alcohol sold only in Connecticut. It is ninety-five percent alcohol, the highest possible concentration from distillation alone. I learned in my organic chemistry that ethanol with five percent water boiled at a lower temperature than pure alcohol. A hydrophilic material was necessary to remove the remaining water if one wanted pure alcohol.

I became fascinated with some of Steve's rituals for drinking and smoking marijuana. When drinking tequila, he filled a shot glass with the tequila and cut a slice of lemon, placing it beside the shot glass. He sprinkled some salt on the back of his left hand near the base of his thumb. He held his left hand with the salt at chest level, then bumped it upward with his right hand. The salt flew up in a cluster and fell on his tongue. He quickly swallowed the shot glass of tequila, then bit the lemon. He sucked on the lemon for a few seconds. It impressed me to watch him, but I had no interest in trying it.

Steve had a pot pipe made from a clear plastic tube about two inches in diameter and a foot long. On one end was a small brass bowl. He put a small amount of marijuana in the bowl. He held the pipe to his mouth with the bowl at the far end. He covered the far end of the open pipe with one hand and lit the marijuana with his other hand. I watched as smoke filled the pipe. He removed his hand from the end and the smoke rushed into his lungs. He held his breath for several seconds, then exhaled. Steve often used alcohol and marijuana in combinations. Rarely did Steve take them to excess.

We lived across from a room that hosted many marijuana parties. They had a water bong in the center of the room. It was a tall glass vase with a long, narrow neck. On the top was the bowl for the marijuana. Under the bowl was a tube that extended into the water in the bottom round vase-like structure. Several tubes extended radially from above the water at the bottom of the jar. Partiers sat cross-legged in a circle around this bong as they smoked from it. Smoke from the bowl on the top traveled through the center tube into the water. The water bubbled as they inhaled, drawing the smoke through the water and into their individual tubes. It took their cooperation, which became more difficult as they felt the effects of the marijuana.

These partiers covered the windows to darken the room. They usually locked the door, though admittance could be gained by knocking. Their parties began quietly. After a while, we heard laughing and giggling. People quietly came and left. One time, Steve and I noticed the door was not completely closed after someone entered the room. We decided to play a prank on them. We took my can of Lysol spray and his lighter. By spraying Lysol over the top of the flame, we could ignite the spray, making a small flame thrower. It worked well to burn the wings off annoying flies. We cracked open the door to the pot party and just enough to spray the flame into the room. We expected some surprise but we got far more than I expected. They all screamed and started jumping out the window. We lived on the first floor but it was still eight feet off the ground. Fortunately, no one was hurt. I felt bad about it and asked one of the partiers later. He said it appeared that the whole room had burst into flames. It penetrated less than two feet into the room. This was a vivid example to me of how marijuana distorts perception.

I observed another pot party. They grew silly and were talking about aliens. I thought I would joke with my friend and underclassman, Jerry. I walked over to him, holding my hand high. I said, "A giant hand is going to come down to earth and snatch you into space." As I said it, I brought my hand down and quickly swept it beside his head. He jumped up and ran out of the room and screamed down the hall. I thought, at first, that he was playing along with my game. He stopped at the end of the hall and paced back and forth, breathing hard and looking back down the hall towards me. I saw that he was genuinely scared. I had no idea that marijuana enhances paranoia to such a level that imaginary silliness could seem so real. I learned how it distorts one's perceptions from a small flame that filled a room and fictitious hands capable of pulling someone into space. To me, this was nonsense. To a stoned person, these things were real. These examples ended without injury but I worried about other circumstances especially since some people drove their car while stoned. Mother couldn't control the family car well with her alcohol induced discoordination. Perhaps marijuana did not affect coordination as much as alcohol. I could not be certain. I am certain that the extreme distortion of reality from marijuana is extremely dangerous.

A classmate, Malcolm, patrolled the halls, especially on weekends. The dormitories were all unlocked so he was free to patrol all of them. I heard him before I saw him. He always wore large, loosely laced boots and he set his feet far forward and down hard. This made a stomping sound that preceded his arrival. When I greeted him, he sometimes stopped and stared at me without saying anything. Other times he just kept moving, completely ignoring me. Only when Malcolm found a pot party did he respond. He sniffed it out like a bloodhound. He hunted these parties and when he found one, he stood at the doorway or knocked on the door until they invited him to join them. Malcolm participated in nonsense conversation while they smoked. It's the only time I heard his voice. He left when they stopped smoking. We realized that Malcolm was a drug burnout. Classmates explained that he did other drugs, including LSD. He had great difficulties processing simple information even when he was not stoned. We wondered how he was able to remain in college. My suspicions were confirmed when he flunked out at the end of the semester and did not return.

I wanted to study the addictive nature of alcohol and wondered about marijuana. Many believe that marijuana is not addictive. There were no conclusive studies with the limited research. I am confident that Malcolm was addicted. If not physiologically, he was emotionally addicted to it. It had an undeniable negative impact on his life, a key element of addiction. I cannot be certain if Malcolm's burnout was from his heavy use of marijuana or the other drugs or their combined effect. I wonder whether his cognitive abilities would improve if he stopped using the drugs. My studies of brain chemistry indicated such neurological damages were permanent. I also learned that the human mind is very adaptable and Malcolm may be able to restore some of his cognition by training new brain pathways.

Alcoholics seem to recover some cognition when they are in recovery. I wondered if their progress was from being freed from the intense compulsion towards intoxication that preoccupied their thoughts.

LSD was used by only a few. They always isolated themselves in their rooms. The user I knew once told me, "I'm going on a trip tonight." In my naiveté, I was puzzled at first. It was the weekend but few people went on trips. I asked him where he was going. He said that he would be in his room. It took a minute for me to realize that he was going on an LSD trip that I heard about from the hippies on the television news. This LSD user's room was very dark. He had several blankets over the windows. He disassembled the beds and the mattresses were on the floor. The floor was covered with rugs and blankets. The light switch was covered. The only light was from two lava lamps. He had a guitar in the corner of the room.

This LSD user also told me about how he gets flashbacks. These were unpredictable hallucinations that he got even when he was not using LSD. He called them free trips but warned that they can also be scary. They sometimes came at intrusive times, such as during class. I heard about an LSD user in another dorm. He ran the length of the top floor and jumped out the window at the end of the hall. He thought that he could fly. He crashed in the parking lot and died a few days later. I could not understand why anyone would want to subject themselves to such dangers and risk permanent brain injury. What is it about the human psychology that seeks chemicals to distort reality?

Some did speed. They took stimulants to help them study. These students usually did very little study during the semester and tried to "crash the course" at the end. They took stimulants to stay awake for "all-nighters." Sometimes for several nights at a time. One user described the "crash" when the speed wore off. A friend crashed during the final exam. He wrote several pages of an essay on one line, over the top of the previous words. It left one very dark line of scribble. He failed.

From my physiological psychology class, I could understand some of what LSD did to the brain. Alcohol and other drugs slow down transmissions across the nerve synapses. LSD accelerated and randomized them. It initiated nerve impulses from any synapse in the brain, one area or many simultaneously. The body does not readily break down the LSD molecule, like the natural neurotransmitters. So, it can cause the nerve to fire an impulse and continue to fire until the nerve is exhausted. It may refire the neuron immediately upon the nerve's recharging, completely disabling that nerve circuit until the LSD metabolizes. The cause of the flashbacks was not understood. Their dangers were of great concern.

There were many discussions about the drug culture at college and throughout society. I learned that there were many subcultures. Beer drinkers could be separated into age and interests subcultures. Each had their drinking rituals of times, place, and occasions. Some were proud and boisterous. There was a group who frequented bars. Others preferred to get together for an activity such as a sporting event or a fishing trip. Some belonged to more than one group. For instance, one could regularly attend a bar night and occasionally go to sporting events with a different group.

My mother would never admit to being in a culture defined with alcohol use. My mother's time and place were at home, alone, and whenever there was enough money. In my last semester, I joined a few keg parties, mostly curious about experiencing the comradery that my friends seem to enjoy from it. Keg parties were well planned and only close friends participated. I did not like being intoxicated. I did not like losing the slightest control of any aspect of my life and certainly not any loss of control over my body. I felt these effects with only two beers. I could not imagine what my mother felt after three six packs.

Treating alcoholics in recovery is difficult and varied. First, one must be determined to overcome the addiction. Medications treat many different symptoms including depression, anxiety, cravings, and impulsiveness. There are no magic pills. Some seem to be only substitutes for alcohol, creating a level of intoxication. Since I believed alcoholism resulted from a learned behavior that became addictive, I compared it to other learned behaviors. Someone who wishes to reduce their weight and remain at a desired weight, they must change something in their lifestyle. I believe that alcoholics must also change their behavior to remain free from alcohol.

Considering my mother's denial and strong personality, I realized that changing one's psychology is difficult and perhaps impossible for some. It seemed comparable to the effects a cult has on its members. Deprogramming is a term often used to recover from the effects of cult indoctrination. Recovering alcoholics must also go through a form of deprogramming with a profound change in lifestyle. The recovery is fragile and can be easily broken at any time for many or no reason.

Those of us suffering from the alcoholic's collateral harm must go through some reprogramming. My siblings and I learned throughout our childhood ways to protect our alcoholic mother. We accepted blame and placed the blame on others. It is very difficult to realize the alcoholic is responsible. We must break the comfort of distortion and reprogram our thoughts and values.

At college, the alcohol, drugs, noise, and party culture were distractors that I could ignore if I had a quiet place for temporary relief. I was well-conditioned to ignore irrational behavior and noise. My mother's home had no quiet place for studying. I did my homework and studying during study halls and the long bus ride to school. I had the library, now. I was also free to go for stress relief walks without anyone questioning where I was or what I was doing. I was not burdened with caring for my intoxicated mother, younger siblings, and the home. Living with the chaos in an alcoholic home prepared me for adapting to college. It was a difficult transition because I still felt responsible for restoring peace from the chaos when I returned home. I could have done so much better at college if I had been free from my mother's influence.

I wanted to get more involved with social connections at college. The Biological Society seemed much too formal and elitist for me. The college radio station was being revived. Its call sign was WWPV, which stood for Winooski Park Vermont. They could not use WSMC because it had been used before and the regulators would not allow its reuse. Radio stations east of the Mississippi River began with W. Those in the west began with R. My friend and fellow student Ed Bolin recruited us. I liked learning and operating the technology in the control booth. He brought several of us to Boston to take our exam for the broadcaster's license.

I enjoyed my broadcasting shifts. Cueing up records, public service announcements, answering the phones, and maintaining the log kept me busy. It seemed strange to speak to an audience that I could not see. There is no visual feedback from listeners and only an occasional phone request. I was isolated in my broadcast booth while I was playing music and talking to an audience that I could only imagine.

I needed to have a hernia repaired. It likely developed from a collision injury while playing football during high school gym class or maybe when my grandfather pushed me to lift something too heavy. The surgery required me to spend three days in the hospital where I worked. I arranged it all myself. It seemed strange that I would be cared for by friends with whom I worked. After surgery, I refused all pain medication. I learned to deal with the pain inflicted many times upon me by my mother during my childhood. I could tolerate my mother's strong blows to the head, pulled hair, pinching, neglected ear infections, the delayed treatment of pneumonia, and stepping on nails. My greatest concern was that my drunken mother would visit and embarrass me in front of my friends and coworkers. I told her not to come if she was drinking. Unsurprising but still very disappointing, she showed up drunk ignoring my firm insistence to stay away. I could immediately recognize her level of intoxication by the way she moved. She had finished one six pack and was working on her second, well over the legal limit to drive. She would never admit to being that drunk. I said, "I told you not to come when you are drinking." She said, "I know," then did her typical deep throat rumble clearing her throat, plucked at the top of her shirt, and sat in the chair. Saying "I know" was an unusual admission. I expected her to immediately deny drinking. I turned away and ignored her. She eventually left without saying goodbye and did not visit again. I realized that I was being rude to my mother. I had been powerless all my life. Now, I wanted to exert my individuality and independence. The beer meant more to her than my wellbeing and importance. I so very much wanted to escape her alcoholism but it followed me no matter how hard I tried. The one place it did not physically follow me was college. However, it still resided firmly in my thoughts, haunting me every day during my studies.

I connected with several professors. The science instructors taught more than just the collection of facts characteristic of my high school teachers. They challenged me to research and conduct tests to verify facts. It is the very foundation of science and the method in which humanity grows its knowledge base. They taught me how to do a literary research paper. Choose only credible sources such as professional journals. Collect the information relevant to my research from each article and draw my own conclusions. Then go to the references cited by my primary sources, then to those references, and continue until I have exhausted all possible sources of information. I would then have all the known information available for this topic. Once this is done, I could better evaluate the original author's conclusions.

Writing the paper was a challenge in organization. I felt stressed until II could find order and symmetry in the information that I collected. Continually trying to make sense in an alcoholic environment helped prepare me through this uncomfortable period. In an alcoholic home, I was trapped in my surroundings and given distorted information to protect the alcoholic. With no escape, I had to learn to make sense where there was none. Trying to make sense in an alcoholic's senseless world sharpened my skills to organize the sensible data in a college paper. I had a stack of notes from various articles. I learned how to sort and categorize my notes in a semicircle around me as I wrote the report. My notes extended beyond the desk beside me to the chairs and on the floor. I felt great satisfaction in putting all this information into a final, comprehensive document. I also realized that no one in the world knew more about the topic than I do now. It was a great confidence builder. My mother and grandfather had told me how stupid I was while growing up. I got a sense of retaliation for the harm they caused to my fragile developing ego every time I completed one of these reports. Writing such a paper was not only well beyond their ability, but it was also a topic that they could never understand.

I was surprised once when I saw an experiment that my grandfather was doing when I was home during a semester break. He had placed a certain number of corn seeds in a towel, wetted it and placed it under the woodstove. He questioned the viability of these seeds and he wanted to see how many sprouted. Mathematical percentages and ratios were far beyond his ability. He would take his results and judge how closely he should plant the corn seeds in the rows.

My mother learned my grandfather's set ways of planting seeds. Once, during a televised gardening program, the demonstrator placed the seeds on the surface of the soil, then sifted a light coating of soil over the top. Mother immediately said, "That's cheating!" My mother and grandfather saw only one way to plant seeds. They created a hole into which to place the seed, then covered it with the soil removed from the hole. They judged any deviation from this method to be unfair. I recognized this different skill as a potential asset, not something immoral. My mother learned from my grandfather that deviations from his expectations were not allowed. They discouraged any initiative, experimentation, or attempts to improve. I remember my grandfather's expectations in every part of our lives. He totally dominated his family. Unfortunately, most of the family complied, which profoundly limited their success. His dominance contributed to my mother's need for denial and secrecy of her beer consumption.

My grandfather had many misconceptions. One I remember well because he nagged so much about it. I did not like wearing a hat, which he always did. He had a dark tan every summer but had a bright white tan line on his forehead every summer. He warned me that the sun would cause me to go bald. Maybe he was correct. I was OK with that. I preferred to go bald rather than wear a hat. I developed the same male pattern baldness as his. Our differences were that I did not mind it. I did not share his vanity, or was it insecurity? He had a significant comb-over that looked odd or even comical when he took off his hat in the wind as he entered church. Of course, he took his hat off in his home as expected of gentlemen. He always went immediately into the bathroom to fix his hair so that the comb-over was not so noticeable.

My grandfather's vanity extended into his strength from working hard. He often said that he would live to be one hundred. He attributed it to his hard, outside work on the farm. He did not consider or understand his terrible diet of red meat and large amounts of animal fat. He died from a heart attack when he was eighty-five.

I saw other people's vanity in the way they dressed. Beards and special haircuts can be indicators of vanity in men. One's personal identity can be dependent on such trivial things as a favorite hat or shoes. Messing with a person's favorite hat or scuffing their shoes could quickly end in extreme violence. It was interpreted as a direct assault on one's personal identity. We worry far too much about our appearance and personal objects. It obscures the more important character.

Even though my mother and grandfather worried about their appearance in public, they did not seem very concerned about my clothes and shoes. My clothes had tears and patches. My shirts and pants were either hand-me-downs or used clothes that were too large or small. My shoes often falling apart. Some people called them "laughing shoes." The soles were separated at the front so that they dropped when I lifted my foot, exposing my toes. If I complained to my mother, she told me to go barefoot, like she did.

Dr. Dominic Cassavant's presentations in physics were easy for me to understand. He broke down complex topics into logical, concrete parts, then showed how the mathematical formulas worked. He was also the mayor of Winooski, Vermont. Since I was doing well, Dr. Cassavant encouraged me to lead a study group in the evening. I soon learned how true the statement was about teaching a topic that required a higher level of understanding than just learning it. There is a hierarchy of knowledge from knowing the topic, to being able to perform the skill, to teaching the topic. I was able to help my peers with their physics. I also had some upperclassmen physics majors come to my group. When I encountered a problem that I could not solve, I met with Dr. Cassavant in his office the next day. He always explained it well and I quickly understood it. I gained confidence in my abilities especially when I could help physics majors with their challenges. Dr. Cassavant encouraged me to change my major to physics but I wanted to remain consistent with my goal as a biology major. Alcoholics broke promises, found excuses, and abandoned goals. I was determined to achieve my goals. If anyone could do it, I could, too. Dr. Cassavant's recognition helped improve my self-image.

I soon realized that the Bible and other religious writings were documentation of human history. Father Couture turned my hatred of history lessons into fascination. He impressed me with his knowledge of ancient religions. It began with the obvious. Jesus was a Hebrew, which many people seem to forget. Jesus was just one of many prophets of the times. Other prophets called themselves "Son of God." Jesus distinguished himself by calling himself "Son of Man." Jesus did not intend to start a Christian religion. The title Christ had its origins in Greek and Latin. It translated into Messiah or anointed one. His teachings were to serve God, not any prophet, organized religion, idols, or the temples.

Father Couture reminded us that there was no direct translation from the ancient scrolls that were compiled into the Bible. Few people could read the ancient Hebrew but Father Couture could. Translations could not be word-for-word from the hierographic-like images that were susceptible to interpretation. He also explained how these prophets spoke in metaphors applicable to those times. It was typically the way prophets and religious leaders spoke to groups. Modern times are very different. Our language is much more complex, direct, and metaphors are infrequent. We may use examples, not vague metaphors.

My grandmother was the strongest force in my Catholic heritage. She had a clear distinction between right and wrong. Everything wrong was a sin. Not all sins were listed in the Ten Commandments. She also held priests in high regard as direct representatives of God's will. She followed the Catholic tradition of eating fish on Friday. She often mentioned how Jesus blessed a fish so that it fed a whole crowd and equated the fish requirement to this story. I thought that this was the reason for fish on Friday. Father Couture explained the evolution of the tradition. Worshipers were expected to donate to the poor every Sunday. There was a special collection during Mass. Father Couture explained that fish was a cheaper form of meat. The difference in the cost could be donated to the poor. This basic understanding became lost as the cost of fish increased.

These theology courses required a lot of reading that supported Father Couture's teaching. I had a great deal of respect for my grandmother but she entrenched my beliefs in Catholicism that required me to reject anything contrary. One person, even one like Father Couture, cannot help another change well-established concepts or beliefs. The repetition of the former concepts and beliefs through my childhood were deeply rooted in my psyche. It was like my mother's constant repetition that she was a good mother. The relationship one has with that person is even more relevant. I loved my grandmother and no one in this world was more trustworthy. However, she had an eighth-grade education and a value system based on her religion and how hard one worked on the farm. It takes a great instructor like Father Couture to show patiently, persistently, logically, and competently how to reflect upon and reevaluate these previously learned misconceptions. The change must come within the person and only through the person's own processing of the conflicting information. The greatest teacher is only effective when the student is open to challenges to gain a broader understanding.

The discussion we had with Father Couture remains foremost in my thoughts. It was a passage when Abraham was speaking with God. Abraham wanted to know his name. God answered that he was "Yahweh." Father explained that it translated from the ancient Hebrew to "I am who I am." God was refusing to give a name to Abraham. This frustrated Abraham who repeatedly asked for His name yet got the same response. Father Couture further explained that if someone knew your name, he or she had some control over you. During these times, humans had some influence over their pagan gods by commanding their name. Yahweh would give no such power to humans. Father Couture pointed out that this was somewhat true in modern times. I struggled with it for a while but eventually had to agree. To find someone, knowing their name was most helpful. If I wanted to call someone from a crowd, I would need to know their name. Similarly, ancient people believed that they could summon their gods by chanting their names. The Hebrew God refused to allow any such control over Him.

Father Couture became one of my great mentors. He helped me transition from my grandmother's literal interpretations of the Catholic faith to a more realistic and practical application. I learned to interpret Bible passages more meaningfully as I considered the lifestyle and metaphors of the times. Only with this understanding could I make useful connections to modern times. Religion helped people make sense of a confusing world. It provided a level of comfort and safety with its rituals and routines. Civilization changes over time and religions must adapt to remain relevant. Many natural events previously explained by religion could be explained with science. Understanding these changes is a skill few people develop.

My growing science skills extended into other areas. I learned to better evaluate the source of information or criticism. We all have our own interpretations of things and events. The person who could see another's perspective could achieve the best outcome. Later, I read a book by Robert Wringer, "*Winning through Intimidation.*" Though I did not care for most of his practices, I learned a very useful point. He did not waste his time with receptionists who had no authority to meet his demands. Do not argue with the person who has no power to make the decision for which you seek. I also learned to evaluate the other person's perspective, education, and willingness to compromise. I do not waste time and effort on someone unable or unwilling to understand another perspective.

I hated history in high school. It became immediately obvious that the humanities courses were not just history, it was European history. I had never seen much value in learning dates and events of things long ago. Sister Gamache taught the history but she also helped us explore the cultures and lifestyles of those times. The culture included the language, food, art, and religion. More importantly for me, she showed how modern knowledge of religion and science developed during these times. Events were recorded by story tellers for the primary purpose of entertainment, but it provided a means to learn from ancient cultures. Sister Gamache gave me a meaningful connection to the body of knowledge that interested me. Science was much more relevant and easier to understand from a historical perspective.

Father Couture and Sister Gamache taught about humanity. I could compare it to the psychology and physiology that I was learning in science. Animals can be conditioned to learn some complex tasks without any understanding of the underlying concepts, beliefs, and motivation. Humans can be conditioned like mindless animals but we can also recognize and value our collective humanity that contributes to the survival of our species. In biological classification, we are one species. There are minor variations in the species such as height, weight, eye, and hair color. Science and religion both explain that we have isolated groups that developed different minor variations but we all share one common ancestor. Religion and biology align with a concept that something influenced the course of humanity. Religion describes creating while science describes a common evolutionary ancestor. All human cultures believe in something greater than any individual. The single most common belief is the influence that religion has in our various cultures. An educated person understands his or her role and its contribution to the greater humanity.

I am most fascinated with our cultural differences when I can engage in meaningful conversation with someone from a different culture. I was most impressed with an exchange student from Palestine. We found far more similarities than differences, even in our religious texts. He surprised me when he agreed that both our texts were ancient and open to interpretation. He agreed that both could contain inaccuracies and defects from human history. We discussed how there is greater hatred between Sunni and Shiite Muslims than between Muslims and Christians. I told him that my grandmother was the most tolerant person in my family and that she would pray that he would eventually see her religion as the best way to get to heaven. He responded, "As I pray for her." It is one of the most profound statements I have heard from a teenager. Our common humanity is great when we can recognize it.

All during my childhood, my grandmother, the priests, and nuns all taught me that the Catholic religion was the only correct belief. The Bible was the word of God. A priest's authority was not to be questioned. Priests spoke the actual word of God when reading the Gospel during Mass. Father Couture taught that the Bible was not written by God. It is presented by men representing and interpreting the word of God. Whenever humans do things, there is opportunity for misinterpretation and corruption. The original scriptures were written in the ancient Hebrew language. Whenever concepts are presented in words, there is interpretation and opportunity for misunderstanding. Even the translations rely heavily on common metaphors of that time that may not presently apply. The biblical and other documents from these times had several authors. Each author was writing to a different audience. I could appreciate this variation from my research of modern science topics. There were great variations among these interpretations requiring me to evaluate them and make my own conclusion. Father Couture seemed especially tolerant in the different interpretations of the various cultures. He did not immediately dismiss conflicting interpretations like my family and the priests during my childhood. Father Couture gave them an opportunity to be considered. I was impressed with hearing this perspective from a scholarly priest.

Colleges often have unsolicited speakers who drift through the campus. Usually they have political, charitable, or social service agendas. Sometimes, they work with the college and get a place for their presentation and their presence is advertised in advance. Some wander onto campus and speak on the lawns. They manage to attract a few listeners. Once, a person described himself as the second Christ and dressed in robes like Jesus. He let his hair and beard grow long. I heard him preaching on the campus lawn to a few who seemed to be there for entertainment more than to be converted followers. Someone mentioned this to Father Couture during class. We all expected him to immediately dismiss this wandering preacher. Instead, Father surprised us with his calm tolerance. He listened as other students joined in the conversation rejecting this false prophet and wanting the school to repel him. We expected Father Couture to agree with us and report this person to security. Instead, Father Couture said, "Remember, Jesus was dismissed by most people during his lifetime." Father went on to explain that the closer we get to the millennium, the more we will see these prophets. Father Couture again impressed me with his wise acceptance of conflicting views.

I sometimes attended Mass at Saint Michael's Chapel. I was pleasantly surprised by the differences between the very conservative services at Saint Mary's and Saint Catherine's churches at home. The Masses at Saint Michael's were much more participatory with folk singers. It was more of a celebration than the formal rituals I knew. Mass was truly being celebrated while keeping the basic format of the religious service.

There were many well-planned performances in the student center. I remember the hype about a local band from Sunapee called the Steven Tyler Band. Since it was from near my home, I did not think that it was that great of an event. There were many local bands playing at bars and nightclubs. Nonetheless, I thought that I would stop by the student center where they were playing. I enjoyed their music but it was so loud that my ears began to hurt within a few minutes and I left. If I knew that they would eventually grow famous as Arrowsmith and be one of my favorites, I might have stuck around a little longer.

I very much appreciate Saint Michael's College pride at remaining a college of liberal arts. I gained a deep understanding of my science but also the history and culture behind it. Genetics was one of my favorite topics. Genetics explained our minor physical differences developed by isolating gene pools. Theology, humanities, philosophy, and psychology explained our cultural differences. These topics also developed differently among the isolated cultures. The science community widely accepts that humans began in Africa. Our ancestors all had skin darkened with the melanin pigment. We all have the same density of melanocytes, the cells that produce the melanin in our skin. The amount of melanocyte stimulating hormone emitted by the pituitary gland varies. As humans moved north, away from the bright sun, the group's gene pool favored lighter colored skin. It allowed better sun penetration to synthesize vitamin D to build strong bones. That is the only physical difference in our skin color. In theory, skin grafted from a person of different color would change to match the skin of the recipient. All groups share so many simple things such as blood types. Some of these simple characteristics may be present in greater frequency in some populations and even completely absent in others, but they are still in the greater human gene pool. As with any species, the more diversity in the gene pool, the stronger the species, and the more likely some will survive after a devastating environmental change. I wondered about a genetic predisposition to alcoholism. If it exists, it could be in all cultures or isolated in certain groups.

Though college was a difficult transition, I gained a refreshing outlook upon the world. I learned how to learn and to evaluate my learning. No educational program can teach everything. A good program teaches students how to research, discover, and evaluate knowledge. Our human differences are in our cultures. When I meet someone of a different culture, I try to sense their willingness to discuss our differences. When this happens, some very fascinating discussions ensue. One of my favorite conversations was with the Palestinian foreign exchange student. Most people would think that we are so different that we should be enemies. He and I discussed the many similarities between the Bible and the Quran and the value of all human life.

My science education helped me to develop skills from my experience in an alcoholic dominated home. Science is a way of making sense of our crazy world. It is systematic and based on observable and measurable facts. It can be verified by any other independent researcher. Science helped me escape much of the chaos during my childhood. Star Trek was timely during my adolescent development. I could identify with Spock's Vulcan commitment to logic and his need to find logic in everything. Daydreaming was my escape during the long, boring classes in high school. My daydreams often involved my mechanical pencil. The eraser extracted helium from the atmosphere so it could float like a zeppelin. The pocket clip was the landing gear. The cannon and LASER weapons were also mounted on the pocket clip. The pencil lead was the rocket engine. I flew the tiny zeppelin around my desk, books and papers rescuing tiny, imaginary people in destress. Perhaps it helped me rescue myself from my adverse childhood experiences. College was much too intense for daydreaming. Rescuing would be through knowledge and real events.

Science realizes that we can never understand everything and alcoholism is undoubtedly something that can never be fully understood. Spock would dismiss much of an alcoholic's behavior as illogical, then ignore it. I could not so easily escape it. My skills to make sense of nonsense were constantly tested. I could make sense out of some of my mother's world. That's how my sister, Cilla, and I developed the three-six-pack rating scale for our mother's state of intoxication and what behaviors to expect. During the first six-pack, we could relax and go about our normal activities. Mother was often generous during the last half of this first six-pack. Once into the second six-pack, Mother was looking for a fight and blaming our father for her demise. We did our best to avoid her but her need to fight was too great. If she did not find us, she would send our younger siblings, Gary or Debra, to find us. We would then be trapped in a no-win argument. Mother's frontal cortex for reasoning was shutting down. Her lower, animal brain wanted to fight. Like my grandfather, she was impossible to please and hurled insults at us. If she decided to use physical discipline, it would be extraordinarily brutal. During the third six-pack, she was completely unreasonable and her emotions quickly oscillated from volatile anger to intense self-pity and crying. She was less able to physically assault us. Her head often slumped onto her obese, shelf-like chest and supported by her fat-filled neck. It was a bit easier to sneak away from her, especially during one of her favorite TV shows. We knew that all we had to do was to outlast her. Soon, all the beer would be gone and she would go to bed. She was often in bed by six o'clock. We remained quiet so as not to wake her. If we did, she was most unreasonable and likely to respond with indiscriminate and brutal violence.

From various articles and books, I learned that alcoholics have a set of characteristics and the people near them have another set. As with anything about humans, no one can be described simply or completely. Much of the literature seemed as irrational as alcoholics. For instance, a child of an alcoholic may be irresponsible or highly responsible. Birth order also has a role, further complicating children's characteristics. There's little question that I am responsible to the point of compulsivity sometimes. My brother learned to be irresponsible because I got blamed and punished for his misbehavior. I could list many irresponsible things he has done but there are times he has been very responsible. He had a poor work ethic as a child but became a skilled machinist and dependable employee. Humans are too complex and adaptable to be so easily defined. All my siblings became disabled before retirement age. I continue to work multiple jobs and have an intense exercise routine well beyond retirement age.

Describing one's degree of intoxication seems very important to our culture. Sometimes it is comical. Other times it can describe a serious concern. I find its prevalence to be discouraging. Common speech, literature, media, comedians, etc. have popularized an immense vocabulary to discretely describe the level of intoxication. "Three sheets to the wind" described one's irrational behavior to a ship with its sails untethered. "Two sheets to the wind" could describe someone as having some rationality remaining but expected to soon have all three sheets untethered. Other terms to describe partial impairment included "bleary-eyed," "tipsy," "juiced," inebriated," "lit," "impaired," "under the weather," and "under the influence." There were many more to describe extreme intoxication: "feeling no pain," "drunk as a skunk," "blind drunk," "stinking drunk," "plastered," "blasted," "pickled," "stewed," "fried," "pie-eyed," "tanked," "smashed," "hammered," "wasted," "sloshed," "snockered," "wiped out," "fried," "under the table," "high," "loaded," "bombed," "blitzed," "gassed," "boozed," "staggering drunk," and many more. It seems sad that there are so many adjectives and even nonsense words to describe intoxication and people will understand them. All these terms seem to minimize or sensationalize irresponsible alcohol consumption. My mother often used "three sheets to the wind" and "feeling no pain" when describing others. She was proud of her reputation that she could drink any man "under the table" in a contest. "Under the table" confused me until my mother explained that that person was so drunk that she or he slid out of his or her chair and onto the floor "under the table." A drinking contestant won such a drinking contest when the opponent became incapacitated. Mother never accepted that she was impaired in any way by her drinking, regardless of the amount she consumed.

Alcohol is widely used as a social lubricant. Alcohol impairs the function of the temporal lobes that control rational thought. Our rational thought helped us avoid irrational behavior or taking unnecessary risks. The alert temporal lobes make us feel uncomfortable in new situations. We are less likely to take the chance of failure in making a new contact. Alcohol takes the edge off that feeling. We feel brave enough to risk the pain of rejection, hence lubricate our social interactions. Unfortunately, there is a dark side to this social lubrication. It can be used to take advantage of another's lower state of protection and seduce someone into an unintended sexual encounter or a criminal act. Human rationality can become so suppressed by alcohol that one responds more like an animal than a human. Moods change quickly and tempers erupt spontaneously. I have seen jovial people suddenly attack, punch, claw, growl, and bite a fellow partier.

I was confident in the many things I learned at Saint Michael's College. Beyond science, I learned much about religion, philosophy, and mythology. It helped me understand my immediate and extended family. I knew that there were many things I could not change. My grandmother is a good example. She had a complex and rigid sense of what was sinful and what was required to get into Heaven. Much of what my grandmother believed conflicted with what I was learning about our religion and others' religions. I knew that I could never convince her otherwise, so I never tried. A more concrete example is her plant identification, which was based on her learning from her Canadian family. For example, she called the trees shading her house rag leaf maples, which was correct. She called a tree across the street a silver maple, which was wrong. It was a quaking aspen, a popular tree, scientific name if *Populus tremuloides*. Silver maple and split-leaf maple are other common names for the rag leaf maple, scientific name *Acer saccharinum*. This is not to be confused with the sugar maple, *Acer saccharum*. The trivial nomenclature in these two maple species is an example of what frustrates me about botanists. I tried to explain to my grandmother that she was wrong. She said, "well," then looked down and said, "That's what we called them in Canada." Her tone and body language were my indicators that she disagreed, did not want to debate, and I could not change her mind. I accepted her rigidity and it was best to accept it. My grandmother deserved all my love and respect.

I accepted that even the most benign things in my family would never change. Grandma was a solid ethical foundation in our family. She had no experience with alcoholics but she had this inflexible characteristic found in alcoholics and their families. She couldn't understand the complexities of botanical nomenclature and certainly did not understand alcoholism. She cared very much about us and did all that she could. Our needs were far beyond her abilities but she remained our guiding light for what was right and wrong in the world. Grandma was the only one in the family who I could trust to always do the best she could for her family.

I became more involved with activities at college and joined the radio staff of the newly reactivated college radio station, WWPV. Boland took the lead. His goal was to be a professional disc jockey (DJ). We were all volunteers. Even though it was a low power, ten-Watt, radio station, we had to meet all the federal requirements. I helped with getting the station licensed and got my radio broadcaster's license. The country was in a police action most of us called the Vietnam War. The feds wanted to prevent propaganda against these efforts. When we met all their strict requirements, they warned us that they would be monitoring us.

I became more involved in campus life during my junior and senior years. There were bottle rocket battles and streaking between the dormitories. These were low-level protests against the authority represented by campus security. It was entertaining to watch security arrive and attempt to identify the culprits.

Football games on TV were followed by games in the snow on the lawn in "the quadrangle" formed by the four main dormitories. I attended many keg parties with limited participation. I observed a few pot parties. They were quite dull. I refrained from drinking until late in my senior year. I drank beer with my friends. I tried to keep up with them but, after a couple of beers, became too intoxicated for my comfort. I hated the clumsy fine motor functions. I was a control freak. It meant my safety in my mother's chaotic world. I felt uncomfortably vulnerable with any loss of body control. I needed to be constantly on guard. I could not imagine how my mother functioned at all with the amount of beer she consumed, even with her morbid obesity to dilute it. I remember my research on the possibility of a genetic predisposition for alcoholism. I learned how some genes need an environmental stimulus to activate them. There seemed to be some validity to alcoholism's genetic predisposition especially how sometimes it skipped generations. Skipping generations is characteristic of a recessive gene. I concluded that alcoholism resulted mostly from learned behavior. The few times that I could observe it skipping generations could be coincidental. However, if there was such a gene and if I had it, I was not going to risk stimulating it. I did not want to be like my mother.

I did not attend my college graduation ceremony. I was used to not celebrating rites of passage. My family was not interested any more than they were in other rites of passage during my childhood. Attending graduation would be a selfish act, which I have always avoided. Learning science exacerbated the perfectionism my mother and grandfather expected from me. The major difference was that my mother and grandfather's expectations varied widely, were often inconsistent, and sometimes irrational. I thrived with the consistent, logical, well-defined perfectionism in science. I gave up trying to please my mother and grandfather and learned to effectively reject their attempts to control me. It was easy to use my scientific logic with vocabulary they did not understand and to confuse them. I also drifted away from relationships with my siblings. We were all trying to find our paths in life. Theirs were much different than mine.

United States Army

During the fall of my junior year, two dating former high school classmates, Lenny and Steve, invited me to go on a blind date with them and Lenny's nursing school roommate. I turned down their first offer because it was just before the final exams and would distract from my studies. I was reluctant to enter a relationship given my family's experience. I was willing to consider it at some later time.

They invited me again during winter break. I tried to inform my friends that I was not in a position for a relationship. I gave the valid reason that I was trying to save money for school and find more work. Steve offered to pay for everything. He added that there was no expectation of a commitment. He and Lenny just wanted to enjoy the company of others. I accepted and met Kay. It was my best decision. Our relation developed during the period of double dating and eventually on our own. Her family was deeply religious and did not use alcohol. Becoming involved with someone who used alcohol to excess was my greatest fear. There was no reason to be concerned about it with Kay. It is not so much our shared interests that built our relationship. I tell people that I do not read romance novels and listen to country music. It is our shared values that became the foundation of our relationship.

I found no jobs for a biology major in my area. Returning to an environment where I was the only college educated person seemed strange. As college grew to a close, I looked back at how I would earn money. It seemed even stranger to need money for daily living instead of saving it for college. My mother could not be trusted and I was even more leery of her second husband, Frank. They had more money together so their drinking became even more out of control than when I was a teenager. I got an apartment as soon as I could instead of waiting until Kay and I were married.

I worked as a mechanic and gas station attendant at one of the jobs that I did through college. Gas stations were owned by the oil companies. In exchange for selling their gasoline, they provided space for mechanical work. An opportunity arose for me to have my own business in Laconia, New Hampshire. Kay and I had bought a mobile home that we moved from Charlestown to Tilton, New Hampshire. It amazed me how easily and professionally the mobile home contractors moved and set it up so well.

Operating the business went well. Kay worked at the local hospital. We bought a home but had little time to enjoy it or each other. The separation from my family was good. Only once did my mother stop unannounced by my business. I was too busy to visit her and she left. I developed a good customer base and enjoyed what I was doing.

During one busy day, there was an incident that flashed me back to my childhood. A mother came into my shop, dragging her ten-year-old daughter by her arm. This mother reminded me of my childhood. They arrived in an old, poorly maintained car like we had when I was a child. The mother was overweight and overbearing, like my mother. The little girl was as helplessly under her mother's bullish authority as I was at her age. She asked if I had a hack saw to cut a ring off the girl's finger. I looked at the ring that was crushed onto her finger. The mother explained that it came in a Cracker Jack box. She bit it, collapsing it onto her finger, and cannot get it off.

I told her that she should go to the hospital where they have a ring cutter that would cut it off without hurting her. I knew about cutting rings in this manner as I had done some as an orderly in the emergency room during one of my many jobs through college. Her mother dragged her daughter into the restroom from where I heard the water running, plunging of the soap dispenser, and the girl complaining about the pain. The mother came out and said, "Give me the hack saw and I will do it. I ain't got no money for a hospital." I looked closer at the collapsed ring, then brought them calmly into my shop. I took a wire cutter from my toolbox and snipped the ring.

I then pried it open and off the girl's finger. The girl expressed her surprised relief, "It didn't even hurt!"

I felt some satisfaction for having helped the little girl. It reminded me that I was not alone in a world with childhood poverty. Other children were not receiving proper care, like me as a child. Cutting that ring was simple for me but significant for her. I hope that my calm, confident actions that were completely different from what her mother demanded helped the little girl understand that her mother did not have all the answers. I knew that I would have no impact on the mother. She was never going to change. Perhaps I could be one unrelated adult whose care helped her set her own path in life as others did for me.

After several months, I realized how much this business consumed our lives, leaving little time for anything else. An army recruiter frequently stopped in to tempt my two helpers into joining the army. They were not interested. He turned his attention to me. The retirement benefit after twenty years of service was appealing. As I entertained the idea, I discussed it with my customers. One told me that my college degree made me eligible for a commission. I asked the recruiter about it. He sighed and said that he could arrange a guaranteed admission to Officer Candidate School (OCS). I later understood his sigh. It was a lot more work for him to schedule all the extra evaluations.

I traveled to Manchester, New Hampshire to take the written tests. They were intense and fast paced. One math test had fifty questions and only twenty minutes to take it. The answer sheet was oddly divided into two sections with a gap about two-thirds of the way down the page. I calculated the time allowed and the pace I would need to complete the questions. I monitored the time and realized that I would not be able to complete the test, which frustrated me greatly. I have always been able to complete all math tests easily in the time allowed. The first section was mostly basic arithmetic, so I got through it quickly. The second section had some algebra and trigonometry. These were all questions that I could easily do but took more time. I made it about halfway into that second section before the time was called. As I turned in my answer sheet, I mentioned my frustration to the army sergeant proctoring the test. He looked quickly at my answer sheet and gave a reassuring chuckle, saying, "No one makes it to the second part. You did well." My math skills got me into the college of my choice and they got me acceptance into the army officer candidate school. I would have to complete basic training before admission into the officer candidate school. There was also a specialty school for the army branch following it. I was scheduled for a physical, the last remaining hurdle to entry into the army. The medical examiner did not like my right eye's limited vision and intended to reject me. Fortunately, I still had Dr. Auten's assessment when I registered for the draft. Dr. Auten not only wrote that I was capable of military service, but he also recommended it. He was a retired air force colonel. The examiners were obligated to accept me.

My recruiter gave me the plane ticket, a piece of paper that was orders to report for duty at the Fort Dix eight-week basic training course. He gave me a list of what I could bring, which was very little. I easily carried it in a single suitcase. It was my first time on a plane. I flew from Hartford Connecticut to Philadelphia International Airport. There was a soldier waiting for me at the terminal. He told me to follow him. He stopped at another terminal where we waited. The soldier was not interested in engaging in any conversation. He seemed nervous as he paced back and forth in a small area. Another plane soon docked and we met two more recruits. He told us to follow him. There was an army bus in the bus loading zone. He walked quickly as we followed him onto the bus.

Our driver's nervousness seemed to continue as he drove us from the airport. He was obviously a very good driver in how he handled this large bus through tight traffic, constantly monitoring every vehicle around us. I finally saw the Fort Dix sign as we drove onto the army post. I heard loud bangs. The driver suddenly had a heightened sense of nervousness. He carefully and quickly stopped the bus. He set the brake, opened the door then stood up and turned to us. He said, "We have to get off the bus." I was puzzled and got up. He added, "Leave your things." We followed him off the bus. He stopped, stood at attention, and raised his arm in a salute. It was then that I noticed that the flag was being lowered. The bangs were from ceremonial cannons. There was a group of soldiers in dress uniforms collecting the huge flag, then folding it. He told us that we could get back on the bus. This was the army tradition of taps. I would soon become very familiar with the traditions of taps, reveille, and others. It is all part of the comradery among soldiers serving and having served in all branches of the military.

Our driver stopped in front of a gray, modular building on cement blocks. He opened the door then told us to get off and go into the building. Inside the building was a counter with three desks behind it. Two soldiers were busy typing. A third soldier stood next to one and was talking to him as he typed. We stood together, waiting to be greeted. Instead, the standing soldier suddenly, loudly, and very rudely told us to be quiet and sit down. There were benches against the outer wall of the room. We sat and waited. He seemed to overreact several more times when the other recruits tried to talk quietly to each other. He yelled loudly, "I told you to be quiet!" I was somewhat taken back from the rudeness of this soldier. I felt that he could gain compliance from these recruits in a much more respectful way.

It was quite dark outside now. Eventually, the standing soldier looked at us, then down at some papers, then verified our names. He directed us, one at a time, to the other soldiers at their desks. After these soldiers filled out the forms, we were sent back to our seats and reminded to remain quiet. When we were all checked in, the soldier made a telephone call. He then told us that someone would come to get us when they were ready.

I was becoming aware now that I was the only white person. Our bus driver, the other recruits, and the soldiers checking us in were all black. Soon the door opened and another black soldier entered. He moved quickly, stood straight, and spoke clearly despite what seemed like a slight speech impediment. He looked at the soldier who made the phone call and confirmed we were all going with him. He turned to us and said, "Come with me."

He walked briskly, making it hard to keep up with him. We walked past several buildings and finally arrived at the barracks. The soldier then stopped in front of the entrance and looked back at us. He took us inside, showed us our bunks and told us to leave our things. He then brought us to the mess hall. He explained that tomorrow, we would be issued our army gear and get haircuts. He looked at the other two recruits who had long, bushy hair. He said to them, "You will leave the hood behind you." Then to all of us, he said, "I will teach you to be soldiers. It will save your life and your buddy's life someday." He told us to call him Drill Sergeant Hump and Bump. I saw the name Massey on his uniform. He explained that we were recruits until we achieve the honor of being a soldier in the United States Army upon completion of basic training.

The next morning, Drill Sergeant woke us up early and brought us outside, in front of the barracks. He directed us to line up in a formation. He was very particular about where we stood and went to each of us. Sometimes he demonstrated how and where to stand. Sometimes he described what to do. Then there were those times when the recruit was so confused, he took them by their shoulders and pushed them into place. He then went to the front of our formation and introduced himself. "I am Drill Sergeant Hump and Bump. You will address me as Drill Sergeant Hump and Bump. That is my name because I move with a purpose. I hump and I bump. Nothing gets in my way or slows me down. You will move with a purpose, too." He motioned to another soldier standing to the side of our formation. "This is Drill Sergeant Long. We will work together to teach you how to be a soldier. Sometimes there will be both of us. Other times there will be only one of us. One of us will be with you at all times. We will teach you to be soldiers in the United State Army. What we teach you will save your life someday, and the life of your buddy." He seemed to have special pride in being a drill sergeant. The way he described the responsibilities of being a soldier helped me realize that he had been to Vietnam.

I noticed that our forty-man platoon was mostly black. There were three Hispanic recruits and five white recruits. Drill Sergeant Long was white. Drill Sergeant Hump and Bump taught us how to stand at attention, at ease, and parade rest. He then taught us how to right face, left face, and about face. He taught us how to "Fall in" and "Dress right, dress" to properly align ourselves. He then started to teach us how to march. "Forward, march." Every command was broken into two parts. The first one indicates the direction or motion. The second part is the command to execute the move. So, when he called us to attention, he first got our attention by calling, "Platoon!" When he was confident that we were aware, he gave the execution command, "Attention!"

Though I had seen military formations in person and on television, I was just now beginning to appreciate the details and coordination that it takes. When the Drill Sergeant called, "Fall in," we were expected to form in front and facing him. We all had to feel the rhythm of his commands. "Left," a slight pause, then, "Face," and we all turned in unison. "Forward," was the warning command. "March" directed us to start. Drill Sergeant Hump and Bump's greatest challenge was to get us to march in step. He was hard on the black soldiers who "bopped" or moved up and down as they walked and marched. "You are not on the block anymore. You will not diddle bop when you march." Drill Sergeant Hump and Bump then struggled to march us away from the front of our barracks. He called cadence, "Left, right..." then only "Left" as we moved along. We always started on the left foot. Our heel was supposed to hit the ground as he called the step. He and Drill Sergeant Long worked to keep our ranks straight and in step. Eventually, Drill Sergeant Hump and Bump called "Platoon," then "Halt." He moved to the side of the formation then called, "Right, face." We turned towards him. He said that the barbers were waiting for us inside. He explained that they were civilians and needed to be paid. He explained that two dollars would be deducted from our pay. He also added that the barbers often take some liberties as they cut the long hair. Drill Sergeant Hump and Bump said that this would help them leave the block behind and become soldiers.

There are four squads in the platoon. A squad comprised one of the four columns of our platoon, ten recruits. Drill Sergeant Hump and Bump explained. When he called squad four, it meant the back row. He then explained that when he told a squad to fall out, it was to go inside and take a seat. The remainder of the platoon awaited "at ease" outside. "At ease" meant we had to remain in our positions within the ranks but we could move a bit. Once inside, Drill Sergeant

Hump and Bump directed us around the outer wall of the barber shop and told us to sit down on the benches. He introduced us to the lead barber and asked him to help make us look like soldiers. He added that he could use any method he chose. He and the barbers began laughing together. Drill Sergeant Hump and Bump then took a position standing in the corner of the shop. The lead barber chose a Hispanic recruit, Rodrigues, who had long, wavey hair. He sat in the barber's chair while the other two barbers called soldiers with shorter hair to their chairs. The lead barber then asked Rodrigues what style of haircut he wanted. Rodrigues was confused, then asked for his choices. The barber and drill sergeant both laughed boisterously. The barber said, "You don't have a choice." He picked up the clippers and started cutting his hair on one side. Long clumps of hair fell to the floor. The barber then stopped and looked at the mirror in front of the chair. He asked Rodrigues "How do you like it." The hair was short on one side of his head while the remainder was still long and wavey. Rodrigues cringed at the sudden change in his appearance and only shrugged. The barber said, "Good. Now return to your seat." Rodrigues seemed confused and Drill Sergeant Hump and Bump told him to take his seat. Rodrigues returned to his seat with long hair on one side of his head was cut short while the remainder was long. He looked silly and seemed to feel ashamed. Drill Sergeant Hump and Bump stepped forward and told everyone not to laugh at him, warning, "Your turn is coming and everyone would share their experience." The barber called Jeffries, a man with a large afro, to his seat. The barber cut a path down the center of his head, leaving the bushy afro parted at the center. He told Jeffries to take a seat. For the next two other recruits, he cut just the front hair on one and patches on another. He called Rodrigues back and cut his hair leaving a tall mohawk before returning him to his seat. Eventually the barbers worked through all of us. Outside, the platoon was called to fall in and we took our places in the formation. Each squad made their way through the process. Those of us with a regular style haircut did not suffer this humiliation. Afterwards, Drill Sergeant Hump and Bump explained to us. He said that we are all the same. Hair does not identify us. Those hair styles belong back on the block, not in his army. I learned how much I relied upon hair styles to identify the person. With everyone's hair the same, it forced me to focus more on facial features to identify my fellow recruits. Now, we all have the same haircut and wore the same clothes. It forced us to evaluate each other on our merits defined by the army. I did not see any value in humiliating anyone to make this point.

Lining up for chow in the mess hall was the next lesson in humility. Drill Sergeant Hump and Bum brought us into the mess hall one squad behind the other. He then commanded us to face forward and "tighten the line." He was not satisfied until we were touching. "Make you buddy smile," he kept saying. I felt very uncomfortable having my groin against another man's buttocks and another man's groin against my buttocks. The recruit behind me was trying to satisfy the drill sergeant without having to press his groin into me. I felt his chest against my back as he held his groin away from me. None of us liked this position but we got used to it. It became easier the more we worked together on other things. It seemed to contribute to the trust building among us. I thought about Drill Sergeant Hump and Bump's purpose. If we learned to trust our comrades in our personal space and even with our most delicate parts, we could trust and protect each other.

There would be other times such as the race relationship classes. I remember one class with a Hispanic and a white presenter. The Hispanic presenter kept reminding the white presenter that he had a knife. The white soldier dismissed the warning. As the Hispanic soldier pressed him, questioning why he did not fear his knife, he replied that he had a BFH. After a few more exchanges, the Hispanic soldier asked, "What is a BFH?" The white soldier chuckled and said, "Big F-ing Hammer."

Perhaps doing something was better than nothing. Calling out stereotypes and making fun of them may help. I was not aware of the Hispanics having knives stereotype. I did not understand that there were any problems with racial identities in the army. It only put me on alert, wondering if I would find any problems. I knew about my Uncle Bernie's racial comments and how my grandfather would say, "Put them on a boat and send them all back to Africa" when he saw demonstrations on TV. I did not understand his reasoning. What if someone decided all the people heritage with his French heritage should go back to France? We have no more connection to France than the black demonstrators had to Africa. We are equal citizens of this country. I learned in college that we all had the same number of pigment-producing cells. A hormone from our brain explained the different skin tones. Pigmentation did not explain our cultural differences. Even these cultural differences were minor and learned from our heritage. Sharing and combining our experiences made us stronger individually and as a combat unit.

Drill Sergeant Hump and Bump developed nicknames for us. He had some general names for black recruits. Jigaboo was one of his most popular. Jigaboo was a derogatory name directed at blacks. I had never heard it before but I noticed the reaction from the black soldiers. They were confused when a black soldier called them by that name. He explained that it did not matter if someone called them a derogatory name. They are men who have the confidence to rise above those who used such names. He had individual nicknames for each of us. He started calling me "Professor." I assumed it was because he knew that I had a college degree. I did not like that he called me "Professor" because all I wanted was to blend in with others in the platoon. Sergeant Long always called us by our last names, which I thought was more respectful. Oddly, I developed a stronger sense of respect for Drill Sergeant Massey because I recognized his determination to make significant improvement in the lives of all young men in his care. Drill Sergeant Long just seemed to be doing his job, nothing more.

My mother taught us how to make excuses to avoid responsibility. Drill Sergeant Massey stunned me at first when he said that there were no excuses, only failures to plan effectively. This approach confused me but I learned as I listened to his explanation. If something is preventing you from fulfilling your responsibilities, it is your responsibility to overcome it. Even if you did not foresee the obstacle, your responsibility remains. You failed to properly plan for the obstacle you blame for your failure. Plan better. I liked this approach that was so dynamically opposite to the alcoholic's excuses that frustrated me all my life. "No excuses, Drill Sergeant," soon grew entrenched into my core values.

This no excuses planning skill I learned in the army remained with me. I make thorough plans and I plan for potential obstacles to an extreme. I find it difficult to begin a project until I have everything planned and readily available. My alcoholic mother made frequent promises that seldom became fulfilled due to some excuse beyond her control. I find it difficult to make promises until I am certain that I can fulfill them. I cannot disappoint anyone with an excuse or broken promise.

We were again processed through physicals. Most of us needed some dental work. It was no surprise that I should have glasses. The optometrist was inexperienced and had a great deal of trouble with my right eye. He did not understand that I did not have absolute control and interpreted it as me being noncompliant. His frustration grew and he eventually announced, "I'm going to prescribe plain glass for that eye." I agreed. Later, I found a civilian eye doctor who asked me about traumatic brain injury. When I denied it, he said that the only time he had seen a condition like mine was from a brain injury. I continued with the denial that I learned from my alcoholic mother and insisted that I was born this way.

As I increasingly lost control over that eye, I grew to accept the eye doctor's analysis. I thought about it for years and concluded that it had to be the time my mother knocked me unconscious with her broomstick. When I was seven years old, she was angry with my siblings and me for sliding down a forbidden bank in the backyard. It caused some sand to slide, which my father would have to shovel back into place. Her favorite punishment was kneeling around the wringer washer. She had a broom in her hands as she commanded us into the house. She hit us on the backside with the bristles of the broom as we passed her. We all cried and my siblings screamed in response to her yelling at us. Mother focused her anger on me, expecting me to know better and to have kept my siblings in line. Without warning, I heard the loud crack of the broom handle and strong downward pressure on my head, driving my head onto my shoulders. I began to fall to the floor but somehow was able to hold myself. My hands gripped the edge of the wringer washer. My vision blurred and narrowed into blackness. Sounds grew quieter and seemed to grow distant. My mother yelled at me to get up. I could barely hear anything. Her yelling and my siblings' screams were barely audible. I tried to pull myself up but my arms would not respond. I wondered why my hands could remain gripped on the edge of the washer when I could not move my arms. She repeated her command several times. Each time I tried harder. Finally, I was able to slowly pull myself up. My vision and hearing began to slowly return. I struggled getting my head up. Mother yelled at me to look at her. I struggled and finally looked in her direction. I couldn't bring her face into focus. I remember her sudden silence and loss of expression as I looked towards her blurred image. She suddenly stopped yelling and left the room. My siblings continued their crying while I tried to hold myself erect.

With this single burst of her violent temper likely fueled by her over consumption of beer, she made a profound impact on my life. I have a palpable dent across the top of my head that matches the broom handle. I cannot control my two eyes together. The vision in my right eye is legally blind. My left eyelid is partially closed and it is nearly impossible for me to open it fully. My right eye often drifts up and out. I believe that the eyelid and drifting eye are to block input from my right eye so that I can get a clearer view with my left eye. People wrongly judge others when their eyes do not match. Such judgements likely blocked many opportunities for me. It made getting into the army difficult. I have been rejected after many job interviews even when I was obviously the best qualified. I am often the target of ridicule. I felt fortunate to be in the army.

It took years for me to accept the diagnosis of a good ophthalmologist who told me that he had only seen my condition because of a traumatic brain injury. I always responded with my mother's denial, "I was born that way." It took a physician's observation during a routine physical that I was able to understand that my sinuses had collapsed. I recalled the event years later. It was my mother's backhand strike intended for my siblings. She missed and struck me.

It has been decades since I accepted that traumatic brain injury affects my eye. Still, my impulse to respond to questions about my eye is to say that I was born that way. My mother's effect on me demonstrates the power of an alcoholic's repeated lies. Though there are few pictures of me as a child, those before the injury show a slight ptosis of the right eyelid but both eyes focused forward. Later pictures show the right eye drifting away. The great effort to redirect that eye increased over the years. The contrast is undeniable yet the denial is the easiest response. I can now respond that the problem with my eye is the result of a traumatic brain injury caused by my mother when I was seven years old. It helps that the public is becoming more accepting of people with traumatic brain injuries.

On the third morning, Drill Sergeant Hump and Bump, called us to formation, "Fall in!" Walker, a black soldier, fell in on my left. We were in the second squad, the second row of the four-row platoon formation. I was developing an opinion that Walker was a bit of a jokester or maybe troublemaker. To get our spacing, Drill Sergeant Hump and Bump called "Dress right, dress." With this command, we looked to our right to be certain that we aligned with the person on our right. We raised our left hand to help the person to our left set the proper distance. If we touched the other person, he was expected to move but also remain aligned with the person in front of him. My left arm bumped firmly into Walker. I expected him to move but he did not. Sergeant Hump and Bump yelled to the platoon, "If your buddy doesn't move, move him!" I pushed Walker a little harder. He did not move. Drill Sergeant Hump and Bump moved past the first squad and stood directly in front of me. He was much shorter than me but had obvious combat experience in Vietnam and the determination to get what he wanted. We looked directly at each other and he said with greater emphasis, "If your buddy doesn't move, move him!" Thoughts of the racial relationship teachings and the composition of our unit being mostly black, I worried about the reactions of others if I pushed too hard. Certainly, Drill Sergeant Hump and Bump could handle himself, but could he stop the whole unit if it came at me. I pushed Walker harder. He still did not move, bent his knees, and defiantly leaned into me. Drill Sergeant Hump and Bump said with even greater emphasis, "If your buddy doesn't move, move him!" At this point, I was more worried about making the drill sergeant any angrier than I was about any retaliation from thirty or more black men. I pushed Walker harder. He pushed back. The drill sergeant's eyes and mine were fixed on each other. I bent my elbow and knees then rose with a powerful push that took Walker off his feet. Walker fell to the ground beyond the space that he should occupy. I braced myself for a potential attack by him and some others. Instead, Walker got up, brushed off his uniform, and took his proper place in the formation. A while later I wondered if there was a conspiracy between Walker and the drill sergeant. As I grew to know Walker better, I believed that he was being mischievous as usual and the drill sergeant used the opportunity to help teach Walker to become more compliant. There were no other significant problems throughout my basic training experience. Walker and I got along just as any others in our company. He remained the unit clown.

    I was suddenly and thoroughly plunged deep into learning about people of different skin life experiences but I wanted to know more about them. I was beginning to appreciate that we had many things in common, especially growing up in poverty. I listened intently to their conversations about family and parenting styles. They also seemed to have a strong sense of ethics that they learned from their mothers. We differed in our environments. Most of them were from the larger cities while I was from a rural farm environment. Their mothers had strong ethical standards while my mother compromised hers to hide and support her alcoholism. I got my ethical standards from my grandparents and college education. It is not the pigments in our skin that attribute to our diversity so much as it is our varied cultures. I learned from Darwin's concepts that a diverse gene pool strengthened the species, increasing its opportunity to survive. The expression of gene expression in a gene pool fluctuates according to how individuals are grouped. A strong group can have diversity and strength even if it does not match the larger gene pool. Our mostly black combat unit in training found strength with a minority of whites and Hispanics. Though I felt odd being in the minority, I learned to trust my fellow soldiers as we worked for mutual success and to serve our country. It was after my military service that I understood this comradery the best. Veterans feel a bond whenever we meet. It is like meeting a former classmate, but much stronger. Classmates may have some wonderful, shared experiences but veterans' bonds evolved from mutual support for survival against a lethal threat and a dedication to our families, communities, nation, and allies.

Drill Sergeant Hump and Bump worked intently with us at every opportunity to practice drills, moving, and marching in formation. I learned that there would be a competition and he wanted to win. My greatest challenge was staying in step while we marched. Uncle Bernie had taught me since I was very young that big, strong men took big steps. It was a huge adjustment for me to take the shorter, more rapid steps while marching. Frustrated one day, Drill Sergeant Hump and Bump asked Drill Sergeant Long to take me and two others to specifically work on getting into step. Walker the clown was one of the others. Drill Sergeant Long recognized that I was taking too long of a stride. Once I realized this, it was easier for me to adjust by striking harder and quicker with my heal. I do not understand why he assured me that rhythm came more naturally to the black soldiers. The racial remark made me uncomfortable. Walker had the unsteady diddle bop stepping and body movements that Drill Sergeant Hump and Bump said needed to stay on the block. Walker could not keep a rhythm, yet he was black. A component of rhythm is natural but specific rhythms such as marching are learned. I respected Drill Sergeant Long for using our proper names but that respect lessened with his blatant racial remark.

Training was physically demanding. I dreaded the command "Double time, march," which started the platoon to run. I was again challenged to stay in step at a new, more rapid pace. As I grew tired, I wanted to take longer strides. This would have caused me to get out of step. I felt that same dreadful feeling of my heart sinking in my chest when we began the two-mile individual run for the physical fitness test. We had to pass the minimum physical requirements. Running two miles in time was the most difficult. Fortunately, I met the maximum time and was strong in the other events. I met my grandfather's standards for strength on the farm, which helped in these other events. My grandfather had no concept of the endurance required in the army and that such endurance was the greatest strength. He believed that breathing hard was a sign of weakness. Breathing hard in the army showed that you were challenging yourself to improve your endurance. By the end of the day, I was exhausted.

Though we ran double time in basic training often, it was at a shorter stride. The stride lengthened as we became better conditioned. Long marches to training sites were in route step. I thought at first that it would be much easier because we did not have to march in step and I could use a longer stride. I was disappointed when the speed increased. These were even more physically demanding marches. I welcomed the command, "Quick time, march" that ended the forced march. The command was followed by cadence to bring us back into step. Some of these marches brought us around an airfield. We were so close that we felt the wind and heat from the jet engines taking off.

We had different cadences for marching and running. I still hear this cadence when I run.

> *Oh, Momma, have you heard,*
> *I'm going to jump from a big iron bird.*
> *Stand up, hook up, shuffle to the door...*

Drill Sergeant Hump and Bump was an airborne Vietnam veteran. He was a paratrooper who jumped from planes many times. I have a great fear of heights and no intention of becoming airborne certified. "Airborne" was often said as an expression of approval of something someone said or did. I could relate much better to different cadences.

> *Hi ho here we go,*
> *'Round the mountain we will go*
> *To kill the enemy just to show*
> *We are army soldiers on the go*
> *Up the mountain,*
> *Down the mountain,*
> *Around the mountain,*
> *Through the mountain!*

Once returning to quick time marching, the yellow bird was a favorite cadence.

> *A yellow bird*
> *With a yellow bill*
> *Landed upon my window sill.*
> *I coaxed him in*
> *With a piece of bread*
> *And then I smashed its little head!*

Morning came early and my whole body hurt. Drill Sergeant Hump and Bump yelled "Reveille!" as he rapidly entered our rooms, turning on the lights. Each room had eight bunks, four on each side. Drill Sergeant Hump and Bump strode quickly to the far end then started turning over bunks of those still in them. I can still hear his heavy footsteps, calling "Reveille," and demanding we get out of bed. From that moment, we had to rush to make the bunk to army standards, so having one's bunk overturned made it more work. I found a mindset to help me get out of bed quick enough. I always slept on my stomach. I realized that it was hard to push my tired body away from the mattress. I began to imagine pushing the earth away from me using my understanding of Newton's third law of equal and opposite forces and points of reference. I imagined the inertia of my tired body having greater resistance to a change in motion than the earth. It seemed to make it a little easier to push the earth away rather than to lift my sore, tired body. I also reminded myself of what helped motivate me in college. If anyone can do it, I can, too. I remember my grandfather's demands that I was never good enough. I found satisfaction in knowing that, even as strong as he was, he did not have the endurance to do much of the physical activity required in the army. My grandfather could never do the running, not even in his prime, which also helped motivate me. I needed to break the psychological hold he still had over me. He dominated my life as a child, trying to convince me of my inferiority to him. I gained a great deal of satisfaction to overcome the many hours he berated me on how stupid, incompetent, and weak I was compared to him.

My education and physical fitness far exceeded that of the man who called me stupid and weak. I also believed that, with imagination and determination, I can meet my goals. I must only have motivation.

We settled into a routine after a couple of weeks and had more time in the evening to care for our things, especially perfecting the shine on our boots. The drill sergeants developed a more personal relationship with us. It helped us to understand army methods and expectations. The purpose of the Kiwi wax was to protect the boot from water, thereby keeping our feet dry. The shine was proof that there were enough Kiwi on the boot. Like everything in the army, it was taken to excess. A dull shine would protect the boot but it had to be spit shined. Drill Sergeant Hump and Bump said, "I am not training heel and toe soldiers." He insisted we shine the whole boot and not the easier heel and toe that only give the perception of a good shine. I accepted this difficult goal because it was consistent with my own perfectionism from my family and science education. I later understood the greater implication of not being a heel and toe soldier. Some just try to look good, thus shining only the heel and toe. The army calls this "eye wash." Heal and toe soldiers took shortcuts in other areas, ultimately being less prepared for combat.

Drill Sergeant Massey expected us to excel in all areas, not just enough to make it look good. It made as better soldiers and better men. "I keep my shit tight," was Drill Sergeant Hump and Bump's phrase to imply he always had everything under control. That control extended over everyone he led. "Slackers" were ones who did not meet his standards. They had excuses for their substandard performance. Using an excuse was an indication that you failed to foresee and correct an obstacle. "No slack due, Drill Sergeant," was the response he demanded from us when he expected better planning.

Drill Sergeants praised us with "outstanding" comments. They explained that such praise meant that we stood above our fellow soldiers. I wondered about how being outstanding was inconsistent with working as a unit. Drill Sergeant Hump and Bump especially stressed working together and helping the weaker fellow soldiers to contribute to the unit's mission. It was a difficult transition for me but one I eventually welcomed. My mother had excuses for her drinking. None of them seemed valid to me, now.

We learned how to thoroughly service our M16 rifles. I was a bit intimidated by its complexity at first. I quickly adapted and found its simplicity. My uncle's friend, George Goodwin, had taught me about hunting, fishing, and marksmanship when I was a teenager. He taught me how to disassemble and clean rifles. The M16 was much more complicated but well designed for easy disassembly and reassembly. The drill sergeants challenged us to do it in less than a minute, then with blindfolds. They explained that we may have to do it in the dark during combat.

There were times that we felt ridiculed. We must call our M16 a weapon. Calling it a rifle was acceptable. If someone called their rifle a gun, they were required to run a certain number of laps around our unit. While running the laps, the violator must yell "This is my weapon and this is my gun. This is for fighting and this is for fun." When chanting this is my weapon, they raised it with both hands. When chanting "This is my gun," the violator released one hand from the rifle and grabbed his groin. "This is for fighting" raised the weapon. "This is for fun" grabbed the groin.

The evenings were times we could shower without being as rushed. I still had to shave in the morning to pass either drill sergeant's inspection. I felt a little disadvantage when many recruits' beards were still developing. One of these evenings was interrupted with loud, incoherent screaming from the showers. We ran in to find one of the Hispanic recruits hanging from the shower stall with his belt around his neck. Another Hispanic recruit was lifting him by his knees and yelling in Spanish. With our additional help, we were able to take him down. He appeared to be fine but the drill sergeant called the medics. They took him and the other two Hispanics. Later, Drill Sergeant Long told us that they would not be returning to our platoon. If any of them remained in the army, they would have to restart their training in another unit. These recruits didn't speak much English but seemed to be doing fine with the training. I wondered what drove one to attempt suicide and why all three had to leave our platoon. I was impressed on how everyone immediately came to his assistance and how calmly and passionately Drill Sergeant Long spoke about it.

The army leaders took everything to excess, often finding trivial and insignificant things upon which to establish their dominance. Human nature compels many to find fault in others to establish who is better than the other. I suppose this helps them feel secure. We had morning inspections when drill sergeants found "gigs." Sometimes it was advised to do better next time. Some gigs had to be corrected immediately. Aligning the shirt and trouser front seems was called the gig line, because so many times it was the source of a gig. Tiny threads on our uniforms, trousers had to be properly bloused with the boots, the cap was worn only outdoors, subdued brass had to be completely black, dress brass had to be shined to perfection, and haircuts had to meet strict standards. It made sense that we had to be clean shaven so that gas masks can seal tightly with our face, but the extreme was not necessary. A little stubble left on one's chin would not interfere with the seal. A short piece of thread did not diminish the purpose of the uniform.

We practiced putting on the gas masks in less than nine seconds, which had to be done before warning our colleagues. If you took the deep breath needed to yell a warning, you would likely inhale a fatal dose of the gas. The gas mask significantly muffled our vocal warnings. We also gave a visual signal with arms raised. The upper arms were held parallel to the ground. Our forearms extended upwards and our fists were clenched. We moved our forearms back and forth, towards then away from our heads while repeatedly yelling "Gas!" We practiced this like other things so often that we could do it without thinking.

They brought us into a hut filled with tear gas and made us remove our masks. We had to recite our names and service number before we could leave. The purpose was to instill confidence in our masks. The recitations after removing the mask emptied our lungs and gave time for the gas to affect us. I was one of few who felt little effects from the irritating gas, just some minor tearing and running nose. Others were almost completely incapacitated, vomiting, and collapsing outside.

The hard work with long hours on my feet on the farm helped prepare me for the physical demands, except running. Fortunately, I had strong legs from being on my feet all day. I only needed to improve my breathing. The army dispelled my grandfather's misconception that breathing hard was a sign of weakness. During the physical testing times, I learned to judge my pace by how hard I was breathing. If I was not breathing hard, I needed to pick up the pace. Running in formation was the most difficult because I had to remain in step and repeat cadence from the drill sergeant. Returning cadence was to encourage breathing, but it slowed mine. I was becoming well-conditioned physically. Qualification with the M16 was easy once I got accustomed to the round rifle sight. I was comfortable with a rifle from shooting racoons and birds on the farm and with my friends. Many of the recruits from the cities had never handled a rifle and had a difficult time. Shooting the M16 rifle presented another challenge from my past. My mother's brutal discipline caused the brain injury that affected vision in my right eye, making my left eye dominant. The hot brass ejected from the right side of the rifle. Because I had to hold the rifle on my left shoulder, the brass would hit my right cheek. Though there was a brass deflector, many times the hot brass shell casing still struck my right cheek, causing some minor but painful burns. My childhood helped in the most important part of marksmanship while leaving a cruel reminder.

Army academics were never challenging. My study skills provided no advantage with such simple topics. The boring classes gave ample time for my mind to wander. I wondered about human nature and the perfection to extremes in the army. Why did boots have to be "spit shined" when a simple brush shine protected them just as well? My most common "gig" during inspections was for imperfect shaving that was only noticeable up close. The purpose of shaving is to allow the gas mask to seal tightly against one's face. Minor razor stubble would also not interfere with the seal. Mustaches are allowed after basic training because they do not interfere with the seal. Criticism was always accompanied by how good the inspector was and how we should be like him. Such one-up-man-ship ratchets standards beyond reason.

Intense army inspections revived my childhood feelings when my mother and grandfather always told me that I was not good enough. Their criticism initially motivated me to meet their standards. When I did, they found something else to criticize. I set higher goals that were far greater than anything they could do to escape their hurtful criticism. I tried to set goals that would outperform my army criticizer, like I did as a child. I did not realize that I was immersed in the human struggle to prove one's personal worth by being better than everyone else. I only wanted to avoid the painful criticism and did not intend to belittle others. Unreasonable army standards revived my childhood pain. My mother and grandfather separately and repeatedly told me that I would never be good enough, like my father. Now I hear drill sergeants telling me to raise my standards to be like them. At first, when my grandfather and mother criticized me, I tried to change. I could never avoid their criticism and eventually I stopped trying. I mentally tuned out their hurtful criticism to protect my psyche. I became resentful when they compared me to my father. Half of me was from my father's genes. I could not change my genes so I silently revolted against their attacks. I refused to let anything hold me back. I coached myself repeatedly, "If anyone can do it, I can," to overcome their destructive mindset. Ironically, I inherited my father's math skills, which got me into college and the army. It opened doors for me that my mother and grandfather could not understand. I only had to prove to the drill sergeant that I was good enough. At least his standards did not change. I could do it.

Completing basic training was a celebrated rite of passage in the army. We were no longer civilians. We were soldiers. Our obligation was greater than any ordinary citizen. We swore an oath to protect the citizens with our skills and our lives. Drill Sergeant Hump and Bump was proud. It was the only time that I felt everyone in the army personally cared for the success of others. Everywhere else, it was too competitive. The army identified enemies, foreign and domestic. In the competitive civilian world, the enemy is each other. I will always respect Henry Massey the man and Drill Sergeant Hump and Bump the drill sergeant who did his job with personal passion. In perspective, this was a very minor rite of passage for me. Because rites of passage were never recognized and certainly not celebrated in my family. I enjoyed this honor and welcomed its responsibility. We are soldiers for life and share a common love-hate relationship with their drill sergeant. We would willingly risk our own lives for our fellow soldiers and the people we swore to protect. I was a member of a group with a strong sense of camaraderie that would last a lifetime.

Graduating basic training is a significant milestone, a rite of passage in the army and in the life of many young adults. We earned the title of soldier. It welcomed us into a select group that is a small portion of our society whose very existence is to protect that society. Our induction stressed honor and responsibility. Even though this was a major accomplishment, it was just my first step in serving our country. I was the first person in my family to graduate college and did it despite my family's efforts to sabotage it. Now, I was the first soldier to join the army full time. My Uncle Bernie joined the Vermont National Guard to avoid being drafted into the Vietnam War. He boasted about doing as little as possible. My father's flat feet kept him out of the Korean Conflict. My grandfather's essential farming occupation kept him out of both world wars. I was adding steps to my recovery from my mother's alcoholic psychological damage she caused to me. The physical harm done to my eyesight and sinuses caused by her blows to my head remain significant permanent reminders.

I had a few days leave after graduating basic training with orders to report to Officer Candidate School at Fort Benning, Georgia. The army paid for the travel but I had to find my own way there. Kay was able to join me, now. The army provided housing but not on the post. It would be later that I learned to appreciate what I learned from Drill Sergeant Hump and Bump. He reinforced my concept that I could do anything anyone else could do if I was properly motivated. He brought racial injustices into focus, though I did not agree with all his methods. His intentions were pure. He had a good heart, was a genuinely good person for whom I have utmost respect. I learned how to pace my running that would benefit me throughout my life. I learned to keep that pace and lengthen or shorten my stride to maximize my conditioning. I could feel my heart and lungs working. If they were not working hard, I lengthened my stride. If I was breathing at a point where I started to fade or stumble, I shortened my stride. Keeping my legs moving at a constant pace kept me moving. Once I stopped, it was very hard to get moving again. Physical perseverance transferred into mental perseverance.

Because I had a college degree, I entered the army as a private first class (E3). Once I started Officer Candidate School, I was paid as a specialist five (E5). If I did not complete Officer Candidate School, I would be returned to the rank of private first class and assigned a military occupation based on the army's needs and my abilities, usually infantry. As we started Officer Candidate School, we had to select our top four choices of the sixteen officer occupations. One of these four had to be one of the combat arms. One could put combat arms in all of one's top four if one wanted. My first choice was the chemical corps. I felt that my science degree would make it likely. The combat arms I chose as my fourth choice was cavalry, tanks. We would be assigned a specialty upon completion of the program but there was no guarantee that it would be one of our choices.

Officer Candidate School was much more demanding than basic training. We had tactical officers instead of drill sergeants. The program was designed to put us under stress to evaluate our stamina in combat. We learned about a recent legal requirement to provide seven hours of sleep every day. It soon became obvious that this was unattainable. We had to meet exceptionally high standards for our quarters and personal appearance. The only way to meet these standards was to get up in the middle of the night. The tactical officers purposefully avoided enforcing the sleep time requirement. It was like they had been through it and understood.

Many of my fellow officer candidates had been in the army for several years. They had earned a bachelor's degree while in the army, making them eligible for this fourteen-week program. Only three of us in the class of one hundred forty had no prior army experience. I greatly improved my physical conditioning in basic training but this program brought it to a much higher level. We began and ended our day with physical conditioning exercises that included running two miles. We ran everywhere we went. We ran five miles every Saturday morning and tested every Sunday afternoon. The physical test consisted of pushups, sit ups, horizontal bars, inverted crawl, run dodge and jump, and two-mile run. We were expected to exceed the maximum score in every event. We had to complete thirty-six pushups, fifty-two sit ups, and fifty-four horizontal bars each within one minute. The standards for pushups and sit ups were strictly enforced. For a pushup to be counted, it had to form a straight line from elbow to elbow across one's back and arms at the start and arms fully extended at the top. For a sit up to count, both shoulder blades had to meet the ground and the back on one's neck had to go beyond one's hips. I learned that I had to slam my body back on the ground to be fast enough to achieve the maximum score. Lowering my body took too much time. My hands behind my head protected my head from striking the ground. The inverted crawl had to be completed within twenty-eight seconds and the run dodge and jump with twenty-two seconds. The two-mile run had to be completed within fourteen minutes. It seemed impossible when I started officer candidate school but I managed to exceed all these standards. Just when I thought that I was going to meet these high standards, I learned that we had to complete a five-mile run in less than thirty-six minutes. Even though it was extreme, it was more attainable than the demands of my mother and grandfather. I was soon running seven-minute miles consistently, whether it was for two miles or five miles. I found satisfaction in running faster than my tactical officer the one time he joined us on the five-mile run. He was among the elite West Point graduates.

  I attended officer candidate school during the summer months in Georgia. It was so hot that the sun melted the shoe polish on my boots while standing in ranks. My feet felt like they were in an oven inside my black boots absorbing the sun's energy. When the temperature reached ninety-five degrees, all unnecessary physical activity stopped. Our commander seemed to purposely neglect to check the official temperature or purposefully ignored this requirement. Again, I benefitted from the hard work on the farm. The heat and humidity were like working on the farm. We did our physical training regardless of the weather. The heavy rains were a welcome cooling relief during our long runs.

  There were four platoons in Officer Candidate School. They were half the size of the regular sized platoons in basic training. The tactical officers, who we called "tac officers," were lieutenants with a year or two experience. My tac officer was a West Point graduate and had spent two years in an infantry unit as a platoon commander. He was very quiet. He seemed unhappy with this assignment. He rarely provided any advice like Drill Sergeant Hump and Bump. He just did his inspections and directed us to make the corrections. We were "gigged" for every flaw. Gigs could be the condition of our uniform, improper shaving, haircut, or our barracks. We were not allowed to have a static display but most of us did. Inside our laundry bag was not inspected. That is where I organized my clean laundry above my dirty laundry. My uniform displays were to the exact dimensions required in our manual. Being gig free would be important later to earn time off post. We were committed for the first eight weeks to remain on campus and with our platoon. We could take half an hour to go to the barber on Saturdays.

We attended classes during the day in a large building about a half mile from our barracks. We ran to class, to lunch, back to class or training site, then to the barracks. We stood at parade rest in the line for chow. Before moving in line, we came to attention, took a step, then returned to parade rest. To enter the mess hall, we had to complete six pull ups on the bar across the entrance. If you failed to make all six satisfactorily, you were sent to the end of the line. Besides the shame of failing the pullups, the last person would have only five minutes to eat. Fortunately, I had arm strength from farming. Though there were times when we were exhausted, but it was rare that anyone failed to do all the pull ups.

High ethical standards were stressed throughout the program. An officer always conducts himself or herself to the highest standards. The officer's words were always the truth, even greater than sworn testimony in court. All records and reports were accurate with special effort to avoid any bias. Everything we did was thorough, never superficial, and to the highest standards possible. Army standards were clear. I welcomed these expectations coming from a family with varying standards that were often unachievable or elusive. Army ethical standards were consistent with my grandmother's Catholic guidance and scientific methods I learned in college.

Some bad publicity about atrocities to Vietnamese civilians influenced our trainings. Officers were obligated to refuse illegal orders from their superiors or suffer criminal penalties. We were taught to say, "Sir, I cannot follow that order" or "Sir, I must respectfully refuse to follow that order," then state the reason. We learned that keeping records of the events leading up to the order, the order itself, and the events following were crucial to our justification against any repercussions to refusing the order. No one wanted to be in such a position and we hoped that it would never happen.

After eight weeks, we were able to attend religious services for up to two hours on Sunday mornings. Our wives were allowed to pick up and return us. Kay and I chose to pray by ourselves in the bedroom of her quarters. We had decided that we were stable enough now to begin having children and we "prayed" for our first child together at our army quarters. We agreed that if our first two children were the same sex that we would go for a third. This agreement was modified after our first child. Taking care of a small baby was a lot of work. We did not want an only child and decided two were enough.

We earned a few privileges after our first eight weeks. We wore blue ascots to show our status over the other classes. This was another rite of passage to be enjoyed. Privileges involved more freedom within the barracks in the evening, which made it more relaxed. We were allowed eight hours on Sundays to spend with family. During our final two weeks, we wore white ascots. Privileges included much less supervision during the evenings and weekends. We were able to spend overnight on Saturday. We did not always have physical exercise in the evening, but the Sunday afternoon physical tests remained. They were moved to four o'clock instead of two o'clock to allow more time with our families. Part of the one-mile track was shaded, making the run a little more tolerable. We were all in great shape by now. Most of us met the goal of achieving the maximum score in all criteria. I proved to myself that I can do anything humanly possible when sufficiently motivated.

It was during one of these final tests that I overheard a discussion among my peers. We had completed our two-mile run and were waiting for the others to finish. The conversation caught my interest as I listened to our fastest runner evaluating another runner still on the track. He spoke about keeping his head up, looking straight forward. There should be an arch in the back that lifted the chest forward. This posture took weight off the chest and allowed for freer breathing. He also advised using the back leg for the greatest thrust and especially taking advantage of the powerful calf muscle. The lead leg should be held high for maximum distance in stride. Lowering one's profile kept the knees bent for better effect and lessening the impact. I remember and use this advice in all my running.

 I have continued running throughout my life and reap the benefits of good health from the intense, daily exercise. There was a period of a few months when I did not run due to the demands of a job that I hated. Ironically, it was driving a truck that my mother had chosen for my career. I hated dealing with the inconsiderate traffic. The long, odd hours made it difficult to find regular time to run. When I found a better job with the police, I got back to running as a necessity. My knee that I injured in the army hurt so badly that I did not think that I could do it. The persistence that I learned in college and the army kept me from giving up. I started by running a half mile for a few days. I then ran it twice a day. After a week, I extended it to three quarters of a mile. I was getting back into my army pace when I extended to a mile. After three weeks, I was running a mile and a half. My conditioning improved over the next month and my knee no longer hurts. I worked it up to two miles and eventually three miles. I remained determined and set limits for myself. I never stopped during one of my runs. I kept the same pace. I varied my stride to meet my condition. If I did not breath hard enough, I lengthened my stride. If I was becoming exhausted or running up a hill, I shortened my stride. Once I took that first step in my run, I did not quit until I completed my goal. I still run three miles every day, weather permitting. Never do I slow to a walk and never run less than the three miles. With modern technology to monitor my exercise, I am amazed that I still run at the pace I learned in the army, decades ago.

 While I continued listening to their conversation, my peers spoke about another officer candidate. They were joking that he had drank too much the night before and was hurting. He hid by some bleachers at the far end on the first lap on the one-mile track. He rejoined the group on their second lap. He ran only one mile but submitted the time for two. I was deeply concerned. Such an ethics violation would get him expelled from Officer Candidate School and subject to the Army Judicial System. It would be a terrible outcome after so much effort. I accepted the officers' ethical standards and their consequences. They were clear, consistent, and reasonable. I thrived with such certainty having grown up in a chaotic alcoholic home where rules changed to meet the alcoholic's needs. It bothered me to be aware of such a violation. I wish that I had not heard it. I was learning that even the most admirable profession is practiced by humans. Humans are imperfect and often corruption finds a way.

My tactical officer was speaking to us in the auditorium during one of these final days. He spoke generally about ethics and high standards of performance. He seemed awkward and to be just killing time. Suddenly, he called us to attention. It confused me at first, then I heard him report to a superior officer. The army division is commanded by a major general with two stars and he was walking down the aisle. He returned the lieutenant's salute and asked us to sit down. He wanted to speak to us very briefly before we graduated. He seemed very relaxed and informal.

His words that I have called forth many times were, "You all are going to make mistakes. I expect you to make mistakes. You will learn from them. I want to emphasize that I want your mistakes to be acts of commission, not omission." It puzzled me that he did not expect perfection on the first try. All my previous leaders expected perfection every time. He wanted us to do something and not ignore what needed to be done. The general spoke in very calm tones that were very reassuring. My tactical officer called us back to attention as the general walked away. The general quickly replied, "Sit down. Relax while you can." I will always be impressed by his genuine concern for us and his calm, confident assurances.

During these last days, we received our assignments among the sixteen different military occupational specialties (MOS) for army officers. We had ranked our top four choices in order. A combat branch had to be in the top four. We were reminded the proper course name is the Basic Infantry Officer Candidate Course (BIOCC) and that any of us at any time could be transferred to the infantry. We were also reminded that once we accepted our commissions, it was for life. We could be called back to duty at any time our country needed us. The ones that chose infantry as their first choice got their choice. The valedictorian also got his first choice. He was a very successful infantry staff sergeant and we thought that he would choose infantry. He surprised us by choosing administration. He explained that it was to save his marriage, which eventually failed regardless of this effort. Like many other soldiers, they blamed the profession instead of their conduct. He had boasted about his many affairs during our few times for social conversation. I never worried about my marriage. Kay and I built our relationship on shared values, not necessarily shared interests.

No one else selected my Chemical Corps as a first choice. I thought that my biology degree was most applicable and would ensure my acceptance. We assembled into formation to get our orders assigning us to the specialties. Each one would require yet another several months of specialized training and education. As members of my platoon got their orders from our tactical officer, most were joyful for getting their choice, raising my positive expectations. When the lieutenant gave me my orders, he waited for my reaction. I was assigned to field artillery, which was not even in my top four. Armor was my fourth choice. He chuckled and said what I heard from others during my entry into the army, "That's because your math scores were too high." Another officer candidate was jealous because he selected artillery but got infantry. Of course, I studied ballistics but I thought it was simple enough for anyone to do. Even the tac officer agreed that I should have been assigned to the chemical corps. He thought that I would do better in small group leadership than leading larger groups of combat soldiers. Apparently, the army thought differently and I had no choice but to accept my fate. Field Artillery School was at Fort Sill, Oklahoma.

Graduating Officer Candidate School was a significant rite of passage. It seemed like I was making up for the lost celebrations of the rites of passage during my youth. My mother dismissed many rites of passage that mean so much to a child's sense of self and accomplishment. As children grow, each rite recognizes its significance and rewards it with new privileges and responsibilities. I already had the responsibilities of caring for the house, yard, and siblings much too early. She neglected all the school promotions and graduations. She even neglected our birthdays, taking the money that my paternal grandparents sent in a card. I did not even get a birthday cake. If we wanted a cake, we had to bake it ourselves. The only thing I got was punishment or harsh criticism for not meeting the premature, impossible, and elusive expectations of my mother and grandfather.

The army has clear standards and assessments to confirm that each milestone has been met. Achieving the milestone meant recognition in the form of rank, pay, or assignment. I now had power and recognition that I never had in my family. I have achieved a second significant rite of passage recognized by promotion and pay. In exchange, I gave the army my lifetime commitment when needed. I learned much about army leadership and I now must gain the skills as an artillery officer. There will be many more rites of passage in my future. I swore a meaningful oath, second only to my marriage vows. The pledge of allegiance seems grossly inadequate in comparison to the oath of office. We swore an allegiance to the Constitution of the United States, the most fundamental beliefs of the people of this county. My oath was far greater than any pledge to a flag and what it represents.

> *"I, George Michael Sanborn, do solemnly swear that I will support and defend the Constitution of the United States against all enemies, foreign and domestic; that I will bear true faith and allegiance to the same; that I take this obligation freely, without any mental reservation or purpose of evasion; and that I will well and faithfully discharge the duties of the office on which I am about to enter. So help me God."*

The army was always generous with travel time, extra pay, and additional expenses. I was left to travel by my own means unless I requested special assistance. I could stay in barracks at Fort Sill but, if I wanted to bring Kay, the housing was on our own. It added stress to the transfer, not knowing if we could find a place to stay.

Fortunately, there are landlords around military installations that seek army officers as tenants because we were more reliable. We found a small house the same day we arrived and a few days before I needed to report to duty. Kay and I made another successful trip into uncertainty.

Field artillery school was a lot more than I expected. I was surprised that it was six months long. We learned much more than cannon ballistics that I expected. I joined the culture and pride among artillerymen. They emphasized a gentlemen's stature and confidence of a demanding and potent force in war. We never called our cannons guns just like rifles are not called guns. The Navy has smooth bored, high velocity but less accurate guns. Ours are rifled. Grooves in the barrel caused the projectile to spin, stabilizing its flight, making it more accurate. We call them cannons or howitzers, but never guns. Red is our celebratory color and Saint Barbara was our patron saint. She was brutally murdered by her father when she converted to Christianity in the third century. He was then struck down by lightning. Field artillery is compared to this lethal lightning from the sky in defense of our patron saint. We celebrate this heavenly artillery event every December 4. Interestingly, Saint Valentine lived during the same period as Saint Barbara. Emperor Claudius executed Saint Valentine when he tried to convert the emperor to Christianity.

Artillery officers are also trained as fire support officers. In the past, each branch had its own forward observers and fire support coordinators. We were instructed in how to acquire, accurately locate, and properly attack targets. I was once again haunted by my mother's brutality. My training officers expressed great concern over my one-eyed dominated vision. They said that I would have a great deal of difficulty directing fire onto a target due to poor depth perception. I was confident that they were wrong. I learned about depth perception in college biology and psychology. For objects more than a few feet away, binocular vision no longer played a role. Determining distance afar required other visual clues such as other objects in front or behind, their relative positions and size. It also required good map reading skills where I excelled. As it turned out, I was one of the best at directing fire onto a target. Perhaps it was because my peers struggled with their binocular depth perception while I was used to functioning without it.

There was a lot to learn. Besides forward observation for our own unit, there were positions beginning at battalion level to coordinate fire from all other branches, including army mortars, helicopters, naval gunfire, air force, and marine artillery and air support. Army intelligence coordinated with us so that we knew which were potentially available and to prioritize targets. Those already shooting at us received the highest priority, immediate suppression. We often did not see these targets directly. We relied upon reports from members of the unit to which we were assigned.

My instructors warned us that fire support officers assigned to a tank battalion would be kept close to the commanding lieutenant colonel. They move so fast that he often lost track of his location and would rely upon us. This worried many of my peers who got their training from ROTC (Reserve Officer Training Corps) in college. I was competent in my map reading skills and not worried. We were all reserve officers. Regular commissioned officers graduated from West Point. They were referred to as "ring knockers" because they wore the West Point ring. They tapped it on the table to draw attention to their superior status. I saw a comparison to my first college roommate who tried to impress me because he was from Scarsdale, New York. I was growing very competent in my artillery skills and unimpressed with any irrelevant status. There were very few West Point graduates in my artillery assignments. Most West Point graduates were infantry officers.

We learned how to operate and maintain all the howitzers presently in use. Though the actual operation was by enlisted soldiers, knowing how to operate them was essential for a good artillery officer. Each artillery battery was the equivalent of an infantry company in command structure. Each cannon battery had two sergeants first class and one sergeant major. The sergeant major was called "First Sergeant" or "Top" for brevity. The title "Top" recognized his top enlisted position in the unit. He answered only the battery commander. The two sergeants first class were called "Smoke" and "Chief of Smoke." The nickname smoke comes from the amount of smoke the cannons made. It compared them to all the power and smoke that arose from an active cannon battery. They were under the immediate command of the executive officer called the "XO," who was typically a first lieutenant. A firing battery's executive officer was a command position due to its importance, complexity, and supervision of junior officers. Additionally, during active war times, the battery commander would be spending most of his time with an advance party preparing for the next movement. The executive officer was in command during his absence. A staff sergeant filled the role of "Chief" for each cannon section. Unlike an infantry company, an artillery battery has a fire direction center (FDC). It is led by a second lieutenant called the assistant executive office who had a staff of enlisted soldiers. He could be called by several titles. He could be called assistance executive officer, "AXO," or more commonly fire direction office, "FDO." He was directly supervised by the executive officer.

An artillery battery was set up on a central axis, called an azimuth, pointing towards a battle area assigned from headquarters. The cannons were "laid" on this axis by the chief of smoke. Direction and elevation for the cannons were calculated in the fire direction center. Each artillery round has four components. For the common projectile, there was a high explosive in a steel casing. A fuse needed to be placed on the front of the casing. The fuse most often was set to a timer that was activated by the spin of the rifling when launched. An air burst immediately above the target was preferred for maximum effect. The timer could be set super quick for it to detonate on impact. This might be preferred for hard or fortified targets. Each round was rammed into the cannon and bags of gunpowder placed behind it. The amount of powder, called the charge, could be varied depending on the distance to the target. Lastly, the cannon's breach was closed and a primer inserted. The primer looked like a rifle round without the bullet. It also had a primer like the rifle round. The lanyard was connected to the breach mechanism that struck the primer like the firing pin of a rifle.

The assistant executive officer decided what ordinance to use when attacking a target, depending on the request, target description, and our inventory. We often carried specialty rounds. The forward observer may wish to add smoke to the battlefield to hide the movement of the unit to which he was assigned. We could also shoot flares that burst high in the air then parachuted to light the battlefield at night. The forward observer may wish to obscure the vision of enemy shooting at him. It took time for smoke canisters to burn long enough to produce the needed smoke. If the forward observer called for "immediate smoke," we could include a few rounds of white phosphorus that burst into clouds of white smoke. If the forward observer was calling for "immediate suppression" of enemy shooting at his unit, the fire direction officer would likely mix high explosive rounds with white phosphorus to both disrupt and blind the enemy. It was forbidden to shoot white phosphorus directly at enemy soldiers. Phosphorus violently reacts with the water. It would melt flesh off bones. It would be cruel and painful. We could, however, attack vehicles and munitions with white phosphorus. It would ignite the fuel and munitions, causing them to burn or explode. This seemed to contradict ethical standards because soldiers would be around this equipment. My cannons were the army's largest cannons and were nuclear capable. It could shoot a tactile nuclear weapon. This required much advanced planning, authorization, and the highest ethical standards. If the president came into my firing point and ordered me to shoot the nuclear weapon, I would have to refuse his order. I must have supported tactical information before using that weapon.

Communication is essential in artillery. We had intense capabilities to remain informed of the battlefield needs. The communications were operated from the fire direction center. Calls for fire included specific jargon. "Adjust fire" calls meant that the base piece would shoot one round. The forward observed would adjust the next round from the last one, ideally bracketing the target and closing in for an accurate kill. Once the target was accurately located, the command "fire for effect" would bring the entire battery onto the target. The call could be a "time on target." These often came from headquarters when multiple cannon batteries were going to hit the target all at the same time, devasting it within two seconds. If the rounds were going to be within six hundred meters of friendly forces, we included "Danger close" in our request. The cannon battery would take extra effort to assure the accuracy of their calculations and cannon settings. A call could include a "Splash" request. For these, the fire direction center would transmit "splash" five seconds before the round was going to explode on target. This is useful for forward observers who needed to stay protected or were adjusting fire from a helicopter. With that notice, the forward observer knew when to stick his head up or tell the helicopter pilot to increase altitude and exposure from their safe location. "At my command" meant that they would not fire the round until I gave them the command. Such a restriction was done with great consideration. It would require a cannon to be dedicated for a longer period of time and not available to fulfill other missions.

Some messages were transmitted in code. The coded message was in groups of three letters separated by a pause. The radio operator would record the letters to be translated from the rotation in the code book. Coordinated attacks might be transmitted in code to not alert the enemy. Any communication regarding the nuclear weapon would be in code.

Artillery officers were required to have and maintain a secret clearance. We were entrusted with vital information about our unit's abilities, those of other military branches, and our allies. We were being trained in nuclear weapons, both cannon and missiles. We saw many demonstrations of these capacities during these six months.

I was selected to call the air strike by two air force A7 fighter bombers. I made the radio request for air support by contacting our operations command. It was quickly approved and I was given a time on target, 10:12:20 hours, the initial contact time 10:11:45 hours, and the radio frequency. They required a marking round to assure the success of their attack. This was transmitted in code that had to be decoded.

I contacted the artillery unit providing support to our area and requested smoke. Smoke canisters would be easily visible and would mark the target for a longer period. The firing battery replied that they had only high explosive and WP (white phosphorus). Since the timing was critical, I chose the white phosphorus "at my command" and requested time of flight and splash. They replied "time of flight two minutes twelve seconds. I needed the round to land five seconds before the aircraft arrived, which meant that I would have the bullet in the air before my initial contact. I contacted the artillery unit and advised that that I intended to command one round of white phosphorus (WP) at 10:10:03 hours followed by "splash." They accepted the fire mission. At 10:09:00 I contacted the firing battery to assure communications were ready. At 10:10:03 I radioed "Fire, Splash." The battery responded "Fire, Splash" acknowledging that I now had a bullet in the air but no contact with the air force jet, yet. I switched to the air force frequency. I was nervous beyond any scale. At 10:11:45 I heard "Alpha Five One at the CP" spoken very quickly. The jet was at the contact point. I acknowledged "Roger, Alpha Five One at the CP." I nervously waited for my artillery marker. The cannon battery announced "Splash" then my bullet hit the ground and a white cloud immediately formed. I felt some relief. Then I heard "Alpha Five One in the POP" (pull up point). I saw the jet flying straight up and could see the pilot looking over his right shoulder. I replied "Roger, Alpha Five One, target is a tank four hundred meters northwest of my white smoke. The pilot replied, "Tallyho on the target" to acknowledge he was ready to engage the target. I watched as the jet gently but quickly rolled and dove towards the target. I saw the smoke from the thirty-millimeter, rapid-fire tank killing cannons in front of his aircraft. The jet accelerated away as the bullets tore a path over the tank. Then I heard the blur noise of the rapidly firing Gatling gun followed by the exploding ordinance that completely obliterated the entire area of the target. Suddenly I heard on the radio, "Alpha Five Two in the POP." I replied, "Roger Alpha Five Two, target is last ordinance." He also replied "Tallyho on the target" as we watched his jet roll and attack like his predecessor. He dropped a five-hundred-pound bomb. The old tank hull went flying and flipping through the air. Since the first aircraft hit the target, the second attack would assure the kill. Had the first aircraft missed the target particularly if it was moving, I would direct the second aircraft from the last ordinance. For instance, I could say, "Target is five hundred meters east of last ordinance." I could also direct the second pilot if there were multiple targets. As was expected, I transmitted to the pilots that the target was destroyed. The mission was successful and I was immensely proud. I had controlled the most awesome power beyond any expectations I ever imagined. The fire power was awesome but the planning and coordination was impressive. These pilots were from the Air Force National Guard and most certainly outranked me. They could have been from the regular air force, navy or marines. All these different commands came together with split-second precision and accuracy.

During another training activity, the instructors took us to a bunker on the edge of an impact zone. It was an embankment obviously built by the army engineers. It had two entrances into a tunnel-like safe space. As we entered this dark tunnel, we saw small, thick glass windows towards the impact zone. The back wall was lined with old mattresses to help stop any shrapnel that might find its way into the bunker. I was not afraid but became aware of how much trust I was giving up in my guides. Once we were all inside, two large noncommissioned officers closed the steel doors at each end of the tunnel. Our instructor guide explained that we would now see how a danger close mission looked and get a sense of what it was like for an enemy under our attack. One of the noncommissioned officers at the door radioed the mission to the battery. Within a few minutes, the first round landed. It made a bang and thumping sound that we felt inside the shelter. Through the windows we saw the black smoke of the explosives and the dirt and dust blasted from the ground. Other rounds followed and increased in frequency. Soon, it was a relentless barrage. The banging, thumping and vibrations were continuous. The entire area outside the bunker was filled with black smoke, dust, and flying dirt. I felt "enough already, I get the point" but the artillery continued. It was very demoralizing. I was trapped in this bunker and at the mercy of whoever was firing the artillery. Eventually it stopped. The sergeant confirmed by radio that there would be no more rounds before he opened the door.

This experience was intended to show us how devasting physically and psychologically our actions can be. It also showed us how important it is to be extra careful when the request for fire support was danger close. In civilian life, danger close is a metaphor often used in conversations. Topics or people can get dangerously close to us or our families. To me, it is not the same as dangerously close to explosive ordinance. The only thing more frightening to me was riding in a speeding car operated by my intoxicated mother. I felt the same helplessness and a strong desire for it to end. The difference was that I was safer in the artillery barrage. Death or serious injury could happen any second with my mother.

Our instructor took us outside and stood by the many craters. He explained that these were one-zero-five (one hundred five millimeter) howitzers, the army's smallest active cannons. He wanted us to understand that even the smallest howitzer is deadly and demoralizing to the enemy. He then taught us to do crater analysis. We inserted a stick into the channel made by the fuse and measured the angle and direction from which it came. This is valuable information for a counterattack. We searched the crater for shrapnel until we found some with markings or band marks. From these, we could determine the exact type of round.

On another training mission, we observed other aircraft attacking the battle zone. We heard the distinctive thump, thump of the Cobra helicopters as they flew along the river below tree level. They began firing their thirty-millimeter tank killing Gatling guns like the A7s had. It was different in that the helicopters flew much slower so more smoke rose from their front. The gunner on the aircraft needed no direction from a forward observer to locate their target. The weight of the ordinance caused a fully armed helicopter to be lower in front. The recoil from these Gatling guns had a noticeable effect on the aircraft. They still tore up the battle zone very effectively. Next, we heard the low growl of an air force A10 "Wart Hog" with its distinctive large jet engines. We saw only one that flew around the impact zone rather nimbly and selectively firing his tank killing Gatling gun. It had the advantage of being on site for up to two hours. The pilot was protected by thick tungsten armor and all the control systems were backed up.

Our class time covered methods and means to attack various targets. Ethical conflicts were stressed intensely. We were coming out of the Vietnam Era and there were many accusations of injustices against Vietnamese citizens. Whole villages were destroyed when there were no combatants in them. The picture of the naked little girl running down the road after her village was attacked with napalm went worldwide, embarrassing the United States government. She stripped off her clothes that were on fire with the napalm. Other children were running with her. It was a horrible awakening for many military personnel. Our instructors stressed many times that commissioned officers not only could refuse an illegal order, but it was also their responsibility to do so. Directly refusing an order was likely to lead to intense repercussions that the individual officer must weigh against evidence that the order was illegal.

Artillery did not shoot napalm but we shot white phosphorus. There are only two reasons to use white phosphorus. One is for immediate smoke to obscure the battlefield. The other was to set on fire the enemy's mobile equipment. When white phosphorus contacts diesel fuel, it immediately ignites it. The dilemma remains that this equipment is being operated by soldiers. We were not allowed to fire white phosphorus onto soldiers separated from any machinery but against those operating or riding in it was acceptable. I hoped that any target that I was attacking would be parked equipment or stored ammunition.

White phosphorus on the clothes or skin cannot be rubbed off. It would almost instantly burn through clothing then the skin and muscles to the bone. I understood how this worked having learned about similar properties of pure sodium and potassium in college. These were so reactive with water that they had to be stored in oil to prevent atmospheric water from reacting with them. To get them to react, we removed a small piece from the oil. We scraped the oil off a small portion to expose the bare element. It reacted so violently with water that it was like a small out of control rocket. It emitted light as it reacted. The pure element was replacing the hydrogen in the water molecule. Such a tiny piece would burn a hole right through one's hand. I cringed to imagine what a person would suffer from a large amount of phosphorus over a large part of the body or inhaled. If I had to fire it at occupied equipment, I would want it to be the absolute last resort.

Later, while assigned to the 24th Infantry Division at Fort Stewart, Georgia, I was sent to the Air Transportability School at Fort Eustis, New Jersey. I learned how to load cargo aircraft. It began with the proper weight and distribution on all military cargo planes. We also learned about rail and marine transportation of army units. When I returned to my unit, I was expected to draw up plans to mobilize the entire division in the event of war. I had to develop many scenarios with the varied cargo planes that might be used. It was a tedious task that filled any free time I had. Once completed, I brought it to division headquarters where they kept it on file. Ten years after my full-time commitment, the 24th Infantry Division was deployed to Desert Storm. I maintain a certain quiet pride that they must have used my plans. I was called back into service, then sent home because I was not needed.

I enjoyed the six months of field artillery school. It was mostly regular business hours with a few times in the field for long days or several days at a time. Kay did not want to stay home alone all the time, so she found a job as the school nurse at job corps. She did not like it. Most of what she did was to deny students who were trying to get out of going to school. Sometimes, she treated youngsters who were injured in a fight. She described how some having teeth marks.

There were times she worked and I was off duty. I spent this time exploring the game reserve. I was trying to take photographs of the wildlife with an ordinary camera. I got too close to a large buffalo and he let me know. I respected his low growling and foot stomp and immediately retreated. I bought a thirty-five-millimeter camera with a telephoto lens. I was able to safely get much better photographs of buffalo, elk, longhorns, and prairie dogs.

Kay and I had most evenings together. We frequently called Kay's mother in northern Vermont to keep in touch with her family. I had little opportunity during basic training and officer candidate school. When I had the opportunity in field artillery school, I either connected with my intoxicated mother or got no relevant information about the family. My family would have no understanding of what I was doing and did not seem to care. I stopped calling my family.

I listened to discussions about careers in the army. I entered the army because the twenty-year retirement was attractive. It would provide a reliable income while freeing me to pursue other interests or careers. I learned that early promotions were mostly automatic at first. The critical promotion would be from lieutenant colonel to colonel. This would happen in the eighteenth year. Those who did not make the promotion would get the RIF (Reduction in Force). They would not receive any pension. Because I had enlisted time, I would be allowed to take the lower rank to complete the last two years. I asked if I would be reduced to private first class. The reply was that I would likely be reduced to staff sergeant. I was not interested in such a reduction. I investigated other twenty-year retirement careers and felt police work was my best alternative.

Being in the army gave us the opportunity to see what it was like in other areas of the country. Kay and I discussed these places as possible places to raise our family. We found that each place has its advantages and its problems. The older members of Kay's family were growing ill. We felt that we would have to deal with the disadvantages at any place so it would be better to be nearer to her family. Our hometowns did not have the great services, especially the emergency services. We felt Claremont would be the best place for us when my army active-duty obligation ended.

Graduating Field Artillery Officer's School was another rite of passage. It did not receive the fanfare like basic training and officer candidate school. It was much less physically challenging and I did not find the academics difficult even though two in my class were reassigned to infantry for their academic performance.

Unlike basic training, I had no choice of assignment coming from field artillery school. I was ordered to the Twenty-fourth Infantry Division at Fort Stewart, Georgia. The division was decommissioned and was now reactivating. It was being rebuilt from nothing. Like my previous transport orders, I was given time to report for duty at my new unit. Once again, we set off into the unknown. We were lucky to find a small house nearby. It was in worse condition than our Fort Sill home. The humid Georgia environment was taking its toll on it. Also, a new experience for us was the number and size of the cockroaches. One ran across my bare foot in the bathroom one night and I mistook it for a mouse. We were eligible for government quarters when they became available in four months. These quarters were nice but the army demands were high. They had to be kept in perfect condition and the lawns and shrubs had to be trimmed regularly. This was a challenge when I was gone on extended assignments for training or in the field. We got a deficiency notice a few times.

My first assignment was typical for new artillery officers. I was a fire support officer with a crew of five in the Second Battalion of the Thirty-fifth Field Artillery (2/35thFA). Its howitzers were the presently smallest, one hundred five millimeters (M102 howitzer, 105mm). I respected their capacity since these were the type that bombarded our position in field artillery school. In the second world war, these were the primary cannons supporting the front line. I had a staff sergeant and four privates. The privates comprised two teams of forward observers. There was very little for us to do daily. Sergeant Rawlings managed to keep the soldiers busy practicing several skills such as map reading, target location, and radio transmission jargon.

Sergeant Rawlings was an experienced noncommissioned officer (NCO) with more than his share of commendations and reprimands. He has been in the army for eight years and has served in Vietnam. His rank was sergeant (E5). He should have been a staff sergeant (E6) by now if he had stayed out of trouble. He spoke his mind, which often got him into trouble. He and I got along very well. A good sergeant can make or break a new lieutenant. Sergeant Rawlings taught me about the informal army procedures and some of the enlisted jargon not taught in officer candidate school.

I heard the term "redneck" several times. I asked Sergeant Rawlings what it meant. He explained that a redneck was a white person who did not approve of integrating black people into previously exclusive white establishments. When a black person sat beside a racist white person at one of these bars, the white person would get so angry his neck would turn red. I learned another explanation later. Rednecks could be what we used to called hillbillies in high school. Their necks were red from farming in the hot sun. They typically lived simply, were less educated, and unsophisticated.

Sergeant Rawlings was a good resource in helping me understand the information I received during the race relations classes. The army's standards of behavior were clear. The underlying racism was not so clear. Sergeant Rawlings believed that racism was innate. Genetics was one of my strongest and favorite college classes. I could not accept that racism was inherited. I feel strongly that it is learned. Anything learned can be relearned, if the person is willing. We did agree that racism could not be eliminated in the most hateful racists. We could only demand soldiers to follow the army's expectation for behavior.

I thought about my own family. My grandfather said many derogatory things about Jews. Uncle Bernie believed "Darkies" were inferior. During the 1960s riots, he often said, "Put them on a boat and send them back to Africa." I wondered if he thought that some people might say something similar about his French heritage and send us back to France. My grandmother saw everyone as equal under God. I had learned the genetics and how some diseases can develop in isolated populations but there was no meaningful difference among us. Humans began in Africa. As some migrated north, away from the brighter sun at the equator, our skin lightened. Lighter skin was necessary for the reduced sunlight to manufacture vitamin D in our skin. Some populations grew fatty eyelids to protect their eyes from extreme cold. It affected the shape of their eyes. The Japanese were one of these groups. None of these differences made any population any less or greater than another. My grandfather and uncle would never change their views. White supremists are always going to be white supremists. We must realize that we are likely only going to suppress their thoughts. I fear that racism will thrive whenever and wherever it has permission. We cannot give up hoping that they will someday correct their ignorance.

The Twenty-Fourth Infantry Division was being reactivated and new equipment was arriving all the time. The smaller cannons provided direct support to a battalion of front-line soldiers. Each battery had six cannons. The towed cannons were being replaced with the lightly armored self-propelled M109. It fired a much larger projectile that averaged one hundred pounds. It was six inches or one hundred fifty-five millimeters in diameter. The larger one hundred seventy-five-millimeter towed cannons were being replaced with self-propelled M110A1. They provided general support for the entire division. These were the largest cannons, weighing twenty-nine tons with an inside barrel diameter of eight inches. It shot projectiles greater than two hundred pounds. The projectile had one hundred pounds of high explosive in a one-hundred-pound casing. The casing fragmented into shrapnel when the round exploded. A single round had an eighty-meter kill radius with a casualty radius of three hundred meters. Instead of six cannons, we had four. The cannon placement was eighty meters apart, consistent with their kill radius. It was also nuclear capable, though it never shot one.

After two months, I was reassigned as the fire direction officer in Bravo Battery in the First Battalion of the Thirteenth Field Artillery. Another significant rite of passage for a junior artillery officer. The position was empty for several months as the division was being reactivated. The obvious shortage of artillery officers explained why I was assigned to artillery when it was not my choice.

I enjoyed the fire direction officer's position. There was plenty to do and we practiced all we could. The ARTEP (Army Training and Evaluation Program) standards were to have a bullet in the air within two minutes of the call. We had one minute to get the information down to the cannons and they had another minute to fire it. I had a good crew that consistently exceeded these standards.

The smaller cannons provided direct support to a battalion of front-line soldiers. We provided general support to the entire division. We could provide support directly to the front line but we also attacked targets deeper into enemy territory. My crew consisted of a staff sergeant, a corporal, and seven privates. The radio operator received and announced the fire mission. We had two teams of four soldiers to provide fire direction control for twenty-four-hour operations. One soldier plotted the location and gave the direction and distance to the target. Another calculated to elevation (angle) for the cannons and the time of flight. The fire direction officer decided the type of round while supervising the calculations. A radio operator communicated with the forward observers and the cannons. A private drove our armored personnel carrier, the M577 command post carrier. We had an auxiliary fire direction center in the event the primary one was damaged. The crew would be split between the two centers on opposite sides of the firing point. We were always busy.

We were still waiting for our equipment while the division was being activated. We moved with jeeps and trucks and set up tents. One day, we were going through some "dry fire" (no live rounds) exercises in the field. We did not yet have the armored personnel carrier and were operating from a tent. One day, a strange person walked into the tent. He immediately started asking questions without introducing himself. That is when I noticed the two stars on his lapel. I called "Attention!" and he said to relax. He was the division's commanding general, Major General James Vaught. He had never seen a fire direction center operate and wanted to watch us. The general went to each soldier as he worked and asked him to explain what he was doing as though he was teaching the general who knew nothing. The general then asked questions of each soldier about what they thought about their jobs. He seemed very pleased and calmly left. He was so kind to the soldiers. His manner was much like the general at the officer candidate school. I began to wonder why the generals were so kind while the captains, majors and lieutenant colonels were such jerks.

We were always busy but had time to get to know each other in these tight quarters. The radio operator was from Maine. The driver was white soldier from Georgia. His family truck farmed. I had to ask him because I understood that my grandfather used his truck to go to market. They used the truck in the field to harvest vegetables in addition to going to the market. My grandfather used his tractor with a trailer in the field.

Albright was the highlight of the group. He was black soldier from nearby Alabama and also lived on a farm, only they did not even have a truck. They sold their vegetables at a roadside stand. He spoke slowly, softly, and pronounced his words with extraordinary effort. At first, one might think that he was like the poorly educated hillbillies that I knew. I quickly learned differently. It seemed like he turned into a different soldier when a fire mission came into the center. He was the critical direction and distance calculator. He was good, loud, clear, fast, and always accurate. Albright had excellent math skills and was well spoken. We all enjoyed his keen sense of humor.

I was fortunate to be promoted to executive office when the present one was transferred early. This was a major rite of passage. Not all artillery lieutenants received the good fortune of this assignment and it was rare for a second lieutenant. Lieutenants typically spend a year in each job before moving to the next, more demanding position. A second lieutenant would almost automatically be promoted to first lieutenant after two years. Since the first half year was in field artillery school, we were promoted within a year and a half of work in an active unit. Lieutenants may be moved earlier than a year when one does not do the job well. It was rare for second lieutenants to hold such a position. I soon learned how it happened.

A cannon battery is mostly the responsibility of the executive officer. The eight-inch battery has four cannons with thirteen soldiers in each section. The cannon section was led by a staff sergeant who has two sergeants and two corporals. Helping the executive officer were two sergeants first class called "Smoke" and "Chief of Smoke." Smoke was their informal title because the cannons emitted large amounts of smoke and these noncommissioned officers could "bring smoke" under the backside of any soldier who needed it. Accompanying the cannons were M548 Ammo Carriers. These were equipped with fifty caliber machine guns to protect against enemy aircraft and armored vehicles. The fire direction center is technically under the executive officer (XO) but is almost entirely entrusted to his assistance executive officer (AXO) also called fire direction officer (FDO). The maintenance section was also mostly under the control of the executive officer. There were many other responsibilities, the most significant was training schedules.

Excited about my new position, I set out to observe the soldiers. I checked the training calendar prepared by my predecessor and it indicated that the cannons were in the main division motor pool being painted. I found the cannons lined up on the edge of the parking area but no one was around. I went to the office and found the warrant officer managing the facility. He explained that they will not work on anything unless the unit has people present to move the equipment and help with the work. He was very helpful when he took me to my cannons and explained that all the hydraulic hoses must first be coated with grease to keep the paint from damaging the hose.

I went to the sergeant in charge of my five-person maintenance section. He said that providing people to prepare the cannons for the general support maintenance was the responsibility of the cannon crews. I returned to our garrison office and met the first sergeant. He was a tall, strong, and confident soldier. Though I outranked him, he answered only to the battery commander. Wise lieutenants knew better than to try to intervene. I asked him what was going on with my soldiers and he was abrupt but correct. He said that I need to take it up with Sergeant First Class Short, my senior noncommissioned officer holding the title of "Chief of Smoke."

I finally found Sergeant First Class Short walking across the garrison. I intercepted him and asked him what was going on. He told me that the cannons were in the general support motor pool being painted. I told him that I knew that and the painters were waiting for soldiers to man the cannons. He told me that he was handling it and started to walk away. I stopped him and told him that both our maintenance and the division motor pool schedules required the cannons to be painted now. Our cannons were out of service and needed to get back online as soon as possible. I remember his reply, "I told you that I would handle it. Now you just go back to your office and leave me alone." I replied, "Sergeant, I am responsible for this unit and I need to know what is going on." I was keenly aware that addressing him as sergeant and not by the other titles such as chief, chief of smoke or sergeant first class was demeaning but I needed to establish my authority. It was also significant that he never saluted me. I do not seek such salutations but he was showing disrespect. He refused to tell me, walked away while repeating that he was taking care of it. I asked him "Where are the soldiers?" He again replied that he was taking care of it.

I now knew why my predecessor was suddenly transferred. No one would say why but I was beginning to understand. This sergeant had sabotaged him by being unproductive. I went to the battery commander, Captain Pierce, with this problem. I sought his advice and authority to deal with Sergeant First Class Short. He wanted one more chance for the sergeant first class who had seventeen years in the service. I agreed and found Sergeant First Class Short in the battery's motor pool. I took him aside and asked directly, "Where are my soldiers?" He replied defiantly, "They are my soldiers and you don't need to know. Go back to your office and do what you do there." I explained to him that he was violating an order and he still refused to tell me and walked away. I understood why my predecessor was prematurely removed. He could not control this subordinate.

The army has a dual system of justice. There is the Article 15 route of nonjudicial punishment and court martial. The battery commander can punish soldiers with the rank of staff sergeant and below. He can reduce them by one grade and take up to three months of their pay. Sergeants first class and sergeants major could only be disciplined under Article 15 by a battalion commander or higher. We went to Lieutenant Colonel Ellison who commanded our battalion. He asked us to prepare the Article 15 nonjudicial punishment and bring it to him. He then called for Sergeant First Short. In the formal meeting, Sergeant First Class Short remained defiant of my authority and insisted that I was intruding. The battalion commander reduced him by one grade and transferred him temporarily to the service battery. Either party could appeal the Article 15 results and go to a court martial. The service battery in an artillery battalion performs many supply and support functions such as ammunition transport, high level maintenance, and survey. Staff Sergeant Short was soon transferred to administrative duties at the division level where he would be given another chance.

I finally met with my soldiers. They immediately expressed relief that "Chief" was gone. That is all they knew because they would not have known about the nonjudicial punishment. They all realized that I had something to do with removing Sergeant First Class (SFC) Short. Rapidly identifying SFC Short as a problem and having the confidence and knowledge to address it boosted my self-esteem and immediately established a good relationship with the soldiers. SFC Short was a bully. It is unfortunate that he had seventeen years in the service, nearing retirement, and this second lieutenant with barely over a year and mostly just training experience took him down. I did not dwell on this then. I was too busy. My predecessor failed to address the issues with SFC Short and make this newly activated battery combat ready. He and his assistant paid a price for it.

I was powerless during my childhood to make even the simplest decisions. I was under the constant control of my mother who had all the physical and emotional power over me. The summers on my grandparents' farm put me under the similar control of my grandfather. He was a demanding perfectionist with constantly changing expectations. Mother was equally demanding and became very unreasonable when she was drunk. They controlled me by belittling me. Mother also used physical violence. As a commissioned combat officer, I now had power far greater than theirs. There were tremendous differences between members of my family and me. They wielded their power to serve themselves. I used my power to protect my soldiers and country. I followed clear guidelines on how to use that power. I developed a perfectionist compulsion from my family and brought it to an even higher level in college and now the army.

The army recognized that much or our strength was in the education of our soldiers. It reminded me of my funding for Saint Michael's College. My loan started with the title National Defense Student Loan (NDSL). At the end of the Vietnam Era and harsh public opinion, it was changed to National Direct Student Loan with the same abbreviation. Saint Michael's College matched this loan with a grant that enabled me to attend college.

Information was distributed with recommendations to enroll in a Pepperdine University extension program on the post. Courses were on Thursday and Friday evenings and all-day Saturday. They flew in adjunct instructors from all over the country. Since Friday was almost always a maintenance day in my unit requiring us to be in garrison, I knew that I would be able to attend most of these classes. They recommended a master's in business administration, human resources management. The Army paid for two-thirds. I enrolled.

I learned a lot during this master's program. Studies in leadership were the most relevant for me. We all recognized the absolute authority of military command. However, that is during combat when there is little time for participation in decisions. Leaders are most successful when they guide others to develop common goals and a plan to achieve them. Most decisions in the army could solicit input from the soldiers involved. I learned that people are more likely to succeed if they had a part in the planning. Even if there is a better way, it may be best to let them do it their way.

This master's program caused me to reflect on leaders throughout my childhood, education, part-time jobs, and sports. Our schools especially encourage competition. They teach that our success depends on scoring higher than the average on tests. In sports, we must be the fastest, strongest, or most skillful. Though sports have some expectations of teamwork, the underlying expectation is individual performance. They may speak about leadership and social skills, but little is done to develop these skills. Evidence lies in how the team captains are selected. The best player gets to be captain. Team captains are more likely to get sports scholarships. How can a team function effectively when there is so much competition within?

Certainly, there is a lot of competition within the army for the best positions and to earn rank, but the real challenge is in working together. As an artillery officer, I enjoyed leading a team with varied skills. We had forward observers to locate, identify, and target the enemy. This requires a lieutenant, a sergeant, privates as drivers and to maintain the position, and a radio operator. The fire direction center receives the fire mission, decides how best to engage the target, performs the necessary calculations, and issues commands to the cannon sections. This starts with the radio operator, targeting decisions from the lieutenant, two privates to calculate direction and elevation, and a driver. The cannon section receives the commands, prepares the weapon, sets the cannon sights. This requires the telephone operator, a sergeant, a corporal to set the deflection, another to set the cannon elevation, several privates to prepare the weapon by setting the fuse and the amount of powder. There are two privates who drive and maintain the cannon and ammunition carrier. All these actions are coordinated with the battalion operations center as they monitor the greater aspect of the battlefield. All these actions are required to be done in less than two minutes. We typically had a round in the air in less than a minute. We competed against the enemy, not each other. We get to live by winning as a team. As a cannon battery executive officer, I lead all these actions, the training, and maintenance that made it all work efficiently. No one can do it alone. Therefore, no one can take credit for it all.

When I compare my adult life to the expectations of my family, I realize how fortunate I was that there were other people to guide me. My grandfather was the alpha male who ruled his family with absolute authority. He commanded every detail of our lives from how to hoe vegetables to very limited recreation around his farm. My mother used the same dominating tactics, driving my father away. She used the controlling leadership she learned from my grandfather to dominate our lives and support her alcoholism. I am forever grateful for my algebra teacher, Daisy Hronek, for encouraging me to go to college and helping me take the first steps. My mother boasted that they were classmates in school, which may have helped me to initiate a trusting relationship with her. Such a relationship was necessary to break free from my mother and grandfather who convinced me that I was not qualified for college and it was out of reach financially. It was my math skills and success that drew regular praise and encouragement from Mrs. Hronek. At just twelve years old and in the eighth grade, my education already surpassed my mother and grandfather. They needed paper and pencil to do the simple arithmetic that I could do almost instantly in my head. They would never understand the algebra that I could do at twelve years old that eventually took me to calculus in high school.

The army offered to pay two-thirds of a master's degree program on post. Pepperdine University flew in instructors to teach the courses. There was a considerable amount of psychology in this program, both individually and organizationally. I learned about motivation and the classic studies on workers. Many of these studies involved workers in large factories and assembly line productivity. Though most of this did not involve the army, the underlying concepts could be applied in any situation. We are the same people but just performing different tasks in another environment. I completed the eighteen-month program in thirteen months.

"Smoke" was now "Chief of Smoke" but enjoyed the shorter title of "Smoke." We were not at full strength and did not get a second sergeant first class. Sergeant First Class Miller spent several months in Vietnam. He progressed through the ranks in a very active cannon battery. Back then, you were considered weak if you wore earplugs. They are required now and punishable by the military code of conduct if you did not wear them. Sergeant First Class Miller suffered from substantial hearing loss. I had to be standing next to him and speak unusually loudly for him to hear me. The military was no longer giving early discharge for hearing loss disability because it was preventable. Ear plugs in our unit were mandatory and we were required to demonstrate that we had them by dangling the holder from our shirt pocket button. Earplugs tend to get dirty and appear disgusting. So, this was yet another unused static display. I carried the earplugs that I used in my pocket.

Sergeant First Class Miller was well respected by the soldiers who worked hard to please him. He was dynamically the opposite of Sergeant Short who led with threats, intimidation, and favoring his chosen soldiers. Soldiers trusted Sergeant First Class Miller. He had high standards that were consistent and fair. His leadership style was calm and patient with the expectation that others performed their best according to their training. When someone did not perform to his standards, he provided additional training and assistance so that they could. I liked his leadership style and its effectiveness. I enjoyed working with him and learned a lot.

Our mission was to supply general artillery support to the Twenty-Fourth Infantry Division. It was a mechanized division and moved fast. We were B (Bravo) Battery. One of the three cannon batteries in the First of the Thirteenth Field Artillery (1/13FA) assigned to the Twenty-four (24th) Infantry Division. When in the field, we were challenged to keep up with the constantly moving division. During our quiet times in garrison, we maintained our equipment and honed our skills. We did a lot of cross training. We needed to stay combat ready with the relatively high turnover in the army. Two days a week were spent maintaining our equipment. It included the howitzers, ammo carriers, fire direction vehicles, command vehicles, rifles, machine guns, tools, and personal gear. During the other days, we practiced and cross trained our skills. The constant training was necessary because most soldiers were transferred about every year. There were few assignments that lasted three years.

Time spent in garrison required guard duty that was rotated among all units about every six months. I was the soldier manning a post during basic training. Now, I was the officer of the guard. I had to inspect and monitor the operation. I let my driver sleep and used my personal vehicle to do inspections. I often found soldiers sleeping at their post. Such a violation was subject to nonjudicial punishment. I woke them and told them to report to their sergeant and left it with him.

Officer of the guard duties included inspecting the division mess hall. This was a large facility feeding the entire division, twenty thousand soldiers. One night when I left the mess hall, a military police vehicle followed me. I took several turns as I went to the motor pool and the vehicle continued to follow me. Since I wanted to sneak up on the guards, his presence would alert them. I decided to stop and flash my rank, then demand he leave. Much to my surprise, a major stepped out of the passenger side. Both the driver and the major looked into the back of my truck as I saluted. I still asked for an explanation. The major said that they had had a problem with people stealing from the mess hall. Their suspicion was aroused by a privately owned truck leaving the mess hall. He was satisfied and left.

In addition to guard duty, we lieutenants had battalion staff duty about once a month. Its purpose was to have leadership available twenty-four hours, seven days per week. It was staffed with a lieutenant, a sergeant, and a private. The lieutenant was required to check the battalion premises every two hours. This included the barracks. We moved into modern set barracks that were three floors high. Each floor had four rooms in which eight soldiers were housed. We were expected to inspect one room on each floor. We had a master key to assure entrance should the rooms be empty at the time or intentionally locking us out.

I walked into a room that had the door ajar. In there were a dozen soldiers in a circle. One soldier was rolling a joint. The paper was on his right thigh as he sprinkled marijuana onto it. As I always did, I demanded the identification cards of all the soldiers. They were always immediately compliant, as it is very serious if they refused an officer. Private Second Class Osborne was the one rolling the joint. I demanded that he give it to me. He crumpled it in his hand and looked towards the ceiling. I repeated my command and started reaching for it in his hand. Private Osborne ran out the door. I commanded him to stop but he kept going. I recorded the names of every soldier present and returned their identification cards. I retained Private Osborne's identification card. I told them that I would be advising their battery commander who would decide their fate. The battalion commander decided to take Private Osborne's case. He reduced him to private and took six months' pay. His battery commander could have reduced his rank but could only take three months' pay.

Lieutenant Colonel Ellison wanted us to rid his battalion of marijuana. I seemed to find more than all the officers combined. He spoke to me one day to make certain that my searches were random as required. I told him that mine were random in that I entered each floor and simply picked the noisiest room. He explained that this did not seem to be entirely random and said that I should do something differently. He said, "Don't get me wrong, I like what you are doing to get that crap out of my command. Just be certain that you are being random." I interpreted it as, "You're doing a good job. Keep it up." I did not think that he wanted me to do anything different. He was just doing what he needed in case any actions he took under Article Fifteen would survive a court martial appeal.

About every six months, we had division staff duty. I was the officer in charge of the entire army post with more than twenty thousand soldiers and commanded by a major (two stars) general. It may seem like an awesome responsibility but I felt very much out of place. I knew the artillery well and could manage infantry, but I knew little about the calvary (tanks and helicopters) and division administration. I was also in charge of retiring the flag. This is what was happening as I rode the bus into Fort Dix. Now I oversaw the ceremony. A squad of infantry soldiers came to lower and fold the flag on a shared schedule like mine. They performed with all the precision and respect of all military units. I was also responsible for pressing the button to fire the automated cannons and playing taps at exactly five o'clock. I was happy to have a sergeant from another unit who knew as little as I did, so we struggled together. Once the flag was retired, most of what we did was answer the phone, follow the administration's calendar of duties, and relay messages. There were no inspections like battalion duty. The sergeant and I remained in a small room all night. It may have been an awesome responsibility for a lieutenant to be responsible for an entire army post with twenty thousand soldiers but I found it to be a most unpleasant duty. It might have been much more pleasant if I knew what I was doing.

Because my battalion had the army's largest cannons, we were nuclear capable, though no artillery unit ever fired a nuclear weapon. The ethics of using a nuclear weapon were placed upon us. We were expected to reject an unanticipated call to fire the nuclear weapon. Nuclear surety involved battlefield awareness. Battlefield awareness involved a series of coded informative messages. We had two teams that decoded the message to assure twenty-four-hour availability and in case of a casualty of one team member. A team consisted of one officer and one senior enlisted, noncommissioned officer who was on the nuclear team. The decoding materials were locked in a safe with two locking mechanisms. Each team member had to dial his combination to open the safe. Once open and the message decoded, it was logged and returned to the locked safe. If any action was needed, we would consult with whomever it required. Messages typically described battlefield conditions and the nuclear alert status. The alert would be terminated using the same communications.

If we had a nuclear mission, the nuclear weapon would arrive by helicopter in a prescribed manner. The executive officer was the primary person to receive it. The battery commander was the alternate. We occasionally received practice rounds in our readiness exercises. We had a crew to assemble the weapon in a tent that we usually located next to the fire direction center. The round would be assembled by the crew simultaneously with the fire direction crew calculating the settings on the cannon and the nuclear weapon. The executive officer oversaw both these operations. It would be the battery commander in his absence.

The nuclear weapon would be fired from a separate, remote location. This required a much higher level of competence. The fire direction center needed to set up a separate chart to plot the remote location and the target to make the calculations. The assistant executive officer then the executive officer separately verified the calculations. The cannon with a skeleton crew and the nuclear weapon would go to the remote location. Setting the cannon required the same effort as setting up an entire battery. Once set, the executive officer verified all the settings. While this was being done, the drivers of the cannon and the executive officer's vehicle would hastily dig a protective trench behind the howitzer. Such protection was necessary. Even at maximum range, we would still feel the effects of the massive amount of radiation that would be released. There was always a time on target so that friendly soldiers could also take cover. The nuclear weapon would be an air burst. The awesome blast of a nuclear bomb is only a part of the destructive force. The radiation would also be lethal over a much greater range.

Nuclear surety was by far the most difficult and significant thing I ever did. A team of evaluators made rounds to all units like ours. They had a thousand points to check from the original message to the weapon on target. Everyone feared their evaluation because they were strict. We were the first unit to achieve a perfect score. It contributed to my earning the Army Commendation Medal along with bringing my cannon battery into combat readiness. I did not do this myself, of course, and realized that it involved four separate teams: decoding, assembling the weapon, calculating the settings, and the cannon crew. However, it is the executive officer that puts it all together and makes it work. All artillery officers have performed all these functions during training. We had great pride in our collective technological abilities.

This Army Training and Evaluation Program (ARTEP) sent another team of evaluators to watch my entire battery as we occupied a new firing position. Before we move to a new location, the battery commander takes a team and prepares the new firing position. He brings the Chief of Smoke and someone from each of the sections and decides where their section will be located. The crew makes the initial preparations to the site and strings communication wire so we can communicate over the large distance and noise of the arriving diesel engines. The executive officer oversees the breakdown of the position and leads the entire battery to the new location. The cooks seemed to always need special attention. Each section member meets the cannon or other vehicle at the entrance to the new firing point and guides them into position. Often, a survey crew sets up the aiming circle, the device that sets the cannons on the correct azimuth. The Chief of Smoke, my senior enlisted assistant, typically calls the directional data to the cannon sections over these telephone lines. Once the data matches, the cannon is ready to fire and said to be "laid.". As the executive officer, I monitor the whole operation and step in if needed. We were good at what we did and rarely had any difficulties. We easily met the seventeen-minute standard to lay the entire battery, usually within half the time.

As we occupied a position during one of these evaluations, I noticed the battalion commander, Lieutenant Colonel Ellison, standing on the edge of the firing point with his driver. It is impressive to watch soldiers running in front of twenty-nine-ton howitzers and guiding them into position. As one cannon section rolled in after the other. The section chief jumps off and takes the hydraulic controls to lower the recoil absorbing spade. The massive cannon sets its spade deep with great force into the earth at the point determined by the battery commander. One can hear the powerful diesel engine set the spade, first lowering then lifting the front of the army's biggest cannon. Chief of Smoke's would be waiting at the aiming circle and give the initial command, "Battery, aiming point this instrument." The communications soldier announces his section number followed by "aiming point identified." Chief of Smoke communicates the data to accurately place the cannons in their assigned direction. Each section chief takes charge and sets the giant spade in the ground to absorb the recoil of the blast and keep the cannon stable. As I watched, I thought that the cannons were pointing in the wrong direction. I calmly walked over to the aiming circle to check Smoke's data.

When I got to him, I asked him, "What's your azimuth?" This is the direction that is given to us by operations headquarters. He told me and pointed to a grading stake with the azimuth written on it and said, "Survey gave it to me." I asked Smoke to let me check. He had set the aiming circle correctly according to the survey but I still felt something was wrong. I "floated the needle" which is how we get the magnetic direction like a compass when we do not have the survey data. We prefer using survey data because it is more accurate and aligns best with the other two batteries in the battalion for missions that concentrate our fire on large targets. I saw right away that the survey data was sixteen hundred mils, ninety degrees, off. I told Smoke that I would take over because the survey was wrong. I called over the landline, "Battery!" with a pause, then "Aiming point this instrument!" This is the command that originates the battery-laying operation. By using this command in the middle of the process, it signaled to the battery that we were starting over. Such a command could confuse the crews but my section chiefs knew and trusted me. They could see that I was now operating the aiming circle. Each section responded, "aiming point identified." Once each section received the new direction, they had to "pull up the spade," turn and reset the cannon.

It is impressive to watch four of the army's largest cannons occupy a firing point. It is even more impressive to watch all four simultaneous lift their spades and shift sixteen hundred mils in place. The typical track vehicle locks one track to turn. These howitzers had amazing engineering allowing the spinning tracks in opposite directions to pivot in place. From this point, it was like our usual clockwork synchrony to lay the battery. After I declared each cannon laid, the battalion commander came over to me. He asked, "What happened?" The lieutenant colonel was a former survey officer and always favored them. I tried to suppress my anger and frustration with the survey crew. I pointed to the stake that Smoke showed to me and said, "Sir, your survey was wrong. I laid the battery by floating the needle." I showed him with the aiming circle so that he could see for himself. I was proud to point out that we still had the battery ready two minutes sooner than military standards. He said nothing more and walked off.

If I had not noticed this error and allowed the battery to continue, we would have certainly been shooting outside the intended impact area. It could have killed fellow soldiers and maybe civilians. My fellow lieutenants would likely not notice this error. I felt proud to notice it so soon and take effective, corrective action.

The next day, the battery commander informed me that the colonel had a meeting and now requires the executive officers to always lay the cannons. This meant that I had to run out of the armored personnel carrier as soon as it could drop the tailgate. I was the furthest from the door because I would be in the top hatch, directing the personnel carrier driver. I had to take off the communications helmet that I used to guide the driver, strap on my steel helmet, grab my M16 rifle, and struggle through the vehicle. I could quickly locate the position of the aiming circle as we entered the firing point. The armored vehicle was often still moving when I broke out in full sprint with my M16 rifle in my arms. One nighttime exercise, I ran straight into a tree and fell to the ground. As I laid on my back and looked up though the branches at the stars, I was thankful for the protection of my helmet. I also realized no one would know what happened to me. I needed to get the battery laid, so I got up and ran to the aiming circle marked by a dim green light.

No one likes such drastic changes in procedures. There was no discussion. We had no explanation for the reasoning. We were expected to comply without question. I did not like it. It triggered my feelings about my grandfather's irrational expectations. It also triggered the feelings that I had for being responsible for my brother's behavior. Instead of my brother, it was the battalion commander's favorite child, the survey unit. Perhaps my mother and grandfather helped prepare me for obedience without reason. If anyone could do it, I could. I was determined to do it better than anyone else.

Back in garrison after these field evaluations, Battalion Commander Lieutenant Colonel Ellison decided that he wanted his whole battalion to do physical training together on the last Friday of the month. The battery commanders convinced him that they were too busy to conduct the drills so it fell on the eight lieutenants. Because I was now the senior lieutenant, I was selected to do the first one. I stood on the raised platform on the athletic field and waited as each battery commander marched his unit into place at sunrise.

Everything about the army is very detailed. The uniform for physical training was fatigue trousers, OD (olive drab) T-shirt, and combat boots. It was one of the few times that we did not display our rank. It was not necessary because we knew each other and our respective authorities. The platform I stood upon was also of perfect dimensions, eight feet by eight feet and four feet high. Each battery moved to their specified locations in sequential order. The largest units were the three cannon batteries, followed by the service battery and then the administrative battery. The cannon batteries took positions in the center and in alphabetical order. The command battery was on the right of the formation. The service battery was on the left. I had all five battery commanders facing me with their units behind them. I returned the salute of each commander as they formally turned control of their commands to me. The commanders then marched to the rear of their respective commands. This simple tradition gave me an awesome feeling. I gained command of a battalion of combat ready soldiers. This was the largest unit over which I took control. It was awesomely frightening. The battalion commander and sergeant major arrived separately and stood behind the administrative battery. The relinquishing of commands done properly would have been to the battalion commander, then me. The battalion commander seemed to like showing up and watching from the sidelines.

 I looked over the five formations of soldiers. I had to space them to safely do the conditioning drills. It was something that I had done but with much smaller forces. I was looking over nearly five hundred men with the battalion commander and five captains looking on. I had never been so nervous but I knew all the commands well, almost robotically.

 "Battalion!" I yelled. Five hundred faces focused on me. "Attention!" prepared them for the first move. "Extend to the left, march!" They automatically raised their arms to measure adequate spacing. The column on the right remained in place. All the others moved to the left until their fingertips were clear. We always growled to show our motivation when we did this. I had never heard five hundred men growl together. I am certain that we could be heard over most of the army post. When I was satisfied, I commanded "Ready, Front." They dropped their arms and lined up directly behind the front person. I then commanded, "Left, face!" Everyone was facing to my right. I repeated "Extend to the left, march!" and the movement was repeated. When they completed the extension, I commanded, "Right, face." The synchronous movement of the entire battalion was impressive. I felt so small standing on my platform. Next, I needed to offset them. "From front to back, count, off." The front row yelled "One" followed by "Two" until the last person counted. I then commanded, "Even numbers, one step to the left, move." Now they were ready to safely do our conditioning drills.

The required script for people leading conditioning drills had become second nature to me. We all took our turns in Officer Candidate School and I often did it with my own Bravo Battery. I could recite it like a robot, without having to think about it. I just had to be loud enough. I could select a soldier to join me on the platform to demonstrate the exercises, but I decided to do it myself. I instructed, "The first exercise of conditioning drill one is the side straddle hop. The side straddle hop is a four-count exercise done at moderate cadence. The starting position is the position of attention. I will demonstrate one repetition." I then demonstrated the exercise while counting "One, two, three – one." The first three numbers were the cadence and the last "One" was having completed one repetition. I then asked, "Does anyone have any questions pertaining to this exercise." I learned from Drill Sergeant Hump and Bump the necessary format of this last question. If I did not restrict questions to the exercise, they could ask anything about what is for breakfast or the weather. No one ever had any questions so I said, "I will count the cadence and together we will count the repetitions. We will do ten repetitions of this exercise. Ready, begin." I counted "One, two, three" then heard a resounding "One" from the battalion. It was an awesome feeling to lead such a powerful, combat unit. We continued through all ten repetitions. After each exercise I commanded "Battalion, at ease." This was to give a few seconds to catch their breath and make any necessary adjustments to their uniform. To bring them back, I commanded "Battalion, attention!" Each conditioning drill had six exercises, including a two-mile run. I was expected to lead the exercises then return them to their battery commanders for the run. It would be impossible to control an entire battalion running around the post. I brought them through the other conditioning drill one exercises: the turn and bend, the eight-count pushup, the lunge and bend, and the leg circular. After the final exercise, I commanded "Battalion, fall in." This brought them back to their original positions, again with the growl in unison. I yelled, "Commanders, post." The battery commanders moved to the front. I raised my salute and waited for theirs. When the battery commanders were ready, I returned it, they were back in control of their units. It felt a little odd that superior captains were saluting me. The proper sequence should have been for me to turn my back to the unit, raise my salute, and wait for the battalion commander to present himself in front of me. He, in turn, would relinquish to the battery commanders. Lieutenant Colonel (LTC) Ellison wanted me to relinquish directly to the battery commanders. The deviation from tradition and standard protocol did not bother me. The less I had to do with LTC Ellison, the better I felt. He was an arrogant West Point ring knocker.

When I finished, I felt like a huge load was taken of me. I was left with an awesome feeling of power to be able to direct such a large-scale exercise flawlessly. I jumped off the platform and ran to my Bravo Battery for our two-mile run. As I ran with a heightened sense of vigor, I felt an immense sense of pride for myself and my fellow artillery men. We are a well-trained unit that functions with the precision to fulfill our mission to protect our great country. Captain Pierce led the way. Sergeant Sharpe called the cadence to keep us in step. I always set the pace from the front right position next to the formation. These flawless, complex procedures were a huge contrast to the chaos in my family.

There was a minor dissention among the lieutenants. The others lacked the confidence to conduct physical training activities to even small groups. There are several paths to obtaining a commission. West Point was considered elite. The Reserve Officers Training Corps (ROTC) was the most popular. These are offered during college. Saint Michael's College had an Air Force ROTC. I was not interested in it then. I knew that there was a two-week summer commitment when they did most of their intense military training. I needed to earn money for college expenses. If they did any physical training leadership it would be to a very small group. They would have never had large assembly experience that I had in basic training and the Basic Infantry Officer Candidate Course (BIOCC). Though I was willing to do it every month, the battalion commander decided not to do it again. I was disappointed because this was the one time that we were all together and doing the same thing.

The officers' wives approached Kay about joining their group. They did many worthy things from community service to organizing social events but did not seem well organized. Kay and I are both willing to give our time and share our resources but we do not care to waste a lot of time or feed the rumor mill in their gossip sessions. Kay was the only wife with her own career as a nurse in the local hospital and did not have much time to deal with the constant posturing. She also did not like the pseudo-ranking within the organization based on their husband's rank. Kay earned her nursing status on her own merits. She participated only when it was necessary, worth her while, and she had time.

I was enjoying my success in the army. I knew the technical aspects of it well and performed the skills equally well. I was confident that I would be successfully promoted but knew that I would never make the higher grades necessary to achieve twenty years for retirement. Except in very rare situations, only West Point graduates got these promotions. We called them "ring knockers" because they all wore the West Point ring. If we did not respect their status, they drew our attention to the ring, often by knocking it on a table. Lieutenant Colonel Ellison was a ring knocker. He personified the role of an angry lieutenant colonel who must make the promotion to full colonel or face the RIF, reduction in force. Lieutenant colonels wore a silver oak leaf. Colonels wore an eagle insignia, hence the phrase, "full bird colonel." LTC Ellison seemed desperately in pursuit of his bird.

If I remained in the army, my next tour would be either three years in Germany or eighteen months in Korea. Kay would not be able to accompany me to Korea, which was my most likely next assignment. We decided that we had seen life in other parts of the country and could decide where we wanted to raise our family. It seemed like every place we lived in had its good points and its bad points. We felt that we might as well go home. Her grandparents were growing frail and we could best support them and the other family at home. I remained committed to serving my obligation well. Unlike my mother, I fulfilled my commitments. My grandmother's commitment to her family was the best example in my family. My mother always broke her promises and failed to keep any commitments she made. My grandfather's expectations were inconsistent. I was determined to complete mine well, like I did with my college commitment. I was the first in the family to complete college and I remain the only one to complete a military commitment. My daughters completed college and my grandchildren will soon. My daughters now have their master's degrees. One could conclude that I have successfully escaped the confines of my birth family and given new direction to mine.

I learned a lot in the army. The obvious responsibilities were readiness training, maintenance, and supervision and evaluation of the soldiers assigned to me. Junior officers have many extra duties assigned to them. There were administrative responsibilities such as assigning newly arriving soldiers to balance the sections. I was the armor officer responsible for all the small arms, their maintenance and assignment to soldiers. I was the security officer that included safety of all equipment and personnel. It included securing firearms and munitions. Cannon battery executive officers averaged about seventeen extra duties that we not part of his training. It gave me confidence that I could be assigned an unfamiliar task, study it, and quickly master it. This was my greatest transferable skill when leaving the army. I will struggle with a new job for a while as I gain the mastery, but I will master it. It was like learning a topic in college. Once I have it mastered, I am fully confident in my abilities. I only must find motivation to overcome my weaknesses and apprehensions.

As I approached our driveway to our government quarters at the end of a workday, I was surprised to recognize my mother's car in the driveway. I saw a lawn chair on the front lawn and my mother's second husband, Frank, lying face down beside it. I knew that he was drunk because this is how I would find him at his home. I was livid. Much of an officer's professional image is what he does after hours. Those who partied hard or did anything that could embarrass the army did not get promoted and dropped out of the service. Having a drunk stepfather displayed on the front lawn for the entire neighborhood to see would not go well with the battalion commander. He would expect us to control our family and not let it interfere with our ability to provide dignified service to our unit. It falls under that broad net of conduct becoming of an officer of the United States Army.

As I walked past Frank, I felt certain that I would find my mother inside and she would also be intoxicated. She expected that I would be happily surprised by her unannounced visit from so far away and give her a warm welcome. It had been more than a year since I last saw her. They were on their way to a vacation in Florida and wanted to stop in for a visit. She got no positive reception from me when I immediately verified her intoxication. I yelled at her to get Frank off the front lawn right away. I told her that, if they were going to drink, they were not welcome and must leave first thing in the morning. Mother started crying and gathering her things. I rarely saw her cry except when she was severely intoxicated and blamed my father for her demise. I asked her what she was doing and she replied, "You said that we had to leave." The last thing I needed was for them to leave my house drunk and get in an accident or get stopped by the military police at the front gate. I told her not to leave, get Frank off the front lawn, go into the guest room, and stay there until morning. She must leave in the morning. I did not want anything to do with them.

I left at five o'clock the next morning while they were still sleeping off the alcohol and did not see them again. I felt guilty leaving them with Kay but I had little choice. I had to report for duty. This was the first time that I rejected my mother so definitively. I had the power and confidence of an army combat commissioned officer and years of frustrated anger. The army expectation that commissioned officers must control their family was the reason I needed to expel my mother from my home. I made the separation from her alcoholism when I joined the army, but it still followed me from twelve hundred miles away. My mother had the potential to destroy my hard work in a whole new way. I was glad that they were gone when I returned home at the end of the day. I loved my mother but I could not and would not allow her alcoholism to continue to adversely affect my life. I needed to completely escape. I was in control of my life, now. If alcohol was that important to her, let it be her choice to stay away from me. I was glad to escape the chaos of my childhood and live in a well-structured military environment.

My mother would never accept that she was an alcoholic. Since she was not an alcoholic, she denied that her drinking could not possibly affect her life or anyone else. It was so pervasive that she began drinking at her job collecting tolls for the Cheshire Toll Bridge between Charlestown, New Hampshire and Springfield, Vermont. It was a perfect job for her, directly across the street from where she lived. She started with a mixed drink before work. Because once she started, she could not stop and it quickly increased to bringing a strong mixed drink to work. She was very devious about having alcohol at her work. It would be too obvious to bring it when she relieved the toll collector on duty. She had it delivered by my younger sister or Frank. Sometimes Frank covered taking tolls while she went and got it. She let her friends drive through without paying a toll. The drunker she got, the more friends she had. The company noticed when her receipts were far below expectations. I saw her once, quite drunk and dancing to the music on the radio in the toll booth. The only time I saw her happy was when she was drunk. My older sister, Cilla, heard that someone complained about her being drunk on the job. Mother never admitted to why she lost her job, but we are confident she got fired.

During one of my breaks from college, my employer, Bob Frizzell, came to me once to complain about my mother. He had ventured into raising veal calves. They are raised in stalls to limit their motion. Restricting their motion assured that more of their feed would go into growth and not be burned during activity. It also produced meat that was more tender. Mother and Frank would feed them twice daily and clean their pens. Bob came to me to convince Mother that she was overfeeding the calves to the extent that it was unprofitable for him. Bob said that he tried speaking with her but she did not change. He added, "She was a little under the weather" when he spoke with her. Obviously, he was referring to her being drunk.

I recognized that he was in a difficult situation because he valued our relationship and my quality work. Though he did not say it, I knew that Bob was also concerned about safety on his farm. I greatly resented that Bob was trying to make me responsible to control my mother. It was an impossible task. I had tried to control my mother's drinking all my life and knew that it was hopeless. I hated the way he placed me in this position. I respected Bob and would help him with anything possible, but this was impossible. I wished that he had just fired her. I appreciated that he valued my relationship with him and came to me with the problem. Because I respected him, I approached my mother and got the response that I expected. She replied, "He doesn't know how to care for animals." My alcoholic mother was an expert on everything and no one else knew anything. She never raised cattle. Bob had studied agriculture at New Hampshire University and grew up farming livestock. Mother barely graduated high school and grew up on a vegetable farm with two working horses and raising pigs and chickens. Bob was far more qualified than she. I refused to engage in a hopeless argument with her and just walked away. Bob eventually fired her from that job, too.

My mother never admitted being fired from these positions. She undoubtedly would deny that her drinking had anything to do with it. Whenever the topic came up, her reply was, "I don't do it anymore." "It" was working at the toll booth or veal barn. She eventually gained employment as a nurse's aide at the Springfield Convalescent Center. She did fine there, working the day shift. I imagine that there were days she was anxious to get off work and have her beer. She was well practiced at getting blithering drunk and getting up the next morning completely sober. It seemed a bit odd to me that she chose to work at a nursing home. Only when she was drunk, Mother spoke about working in a nursing home when she was a child. She cried while she described herself as a victim of having to work with elderly, helpless people. She cried most about one that died and she had to give her a bath. She was employed there when she died.

The battery commander and first sergeant had left for the day one Friday afternoon, so I was alone in the battery headquarters. I was finishing up a few things, then I would turn responsibility over to the "CQ," Charge of Quarters. This was usually a sergeant and a private who remained awake all night as "fire watch" and general safety within the unit. Since I lived closest, they could call me if there were any problems that the battalion duty officer could not handle. My battery commander and I preferred that they contact me with any problems. If they contacted the battalion staff duty officer, it would go into the report for the battalion commander. It was always best to keep everything within our unit as much as possible ourselves.

An unfamiliar staff sergeant dressed in class A uniform (dress uniform) with administrative insignia formally reported to me in my office with a salute. He introduced himself as Private Albright's recruiter. He wanted to check in with him. I assumed that Albright expected him and that they would celebrate reconnecting. I brought him to the barracks and found Albright. I then left them to whatever their plans were.

A few minutes later, the staff sergeant reappeared at the door to my office with Albright behind him. He asked permission to approach me. A salute was not necessary because he had already reported to me in this building. The sergeant had a document in his hand. He explained, "Albright made some statements on a routine survey. He said that I helped him on his entrance exam by giving him some of the words. He now agrees that this was not true." The sergeant then started to hand a piece of paper over to me. A commissioned officer could fill the role of a notary public on military legal documents. I did not take the document and let him stand with it as he continued to hold it out to me. I asked Private Albright if it was true. I could see that he was feeling very uncomfortable as he struggled to speak, not actually saying anything. I looked at each of them reading their body language. I knew Albright well and felt that he very likely reported the truth on the survey and did not want to retract his statements. I also understood the pressure recruiters were under to increase their number of recruits. It frustrates them when a recruit fails the entrance exam, which was common in Albright's home state, Alabama. I looked at the staff sergeant and recommended that they both go to JAG, the Judge Advocate General, where they could find a lawyer. I explained, "Either Albright was lying on the survey or he will be lying if he signs your form. In either case, you both need a lawyer." I expected Albright would suffer some discipline if he admitted to falsely accusing his recruiter. They left my office. I heard nothing more until a few weeks before I expected to leave the army. I was ordered to appear at a court martial at Fort Rucker, Alabama for three days. Such an order is the equivalent of a civilian subpoena. The army doesn't subpoena witnesses. They order them to appear. Further complicating things is that it was very close to the date that my first child was due to be born.

I have served on several court martials. Like civilian responsibilities, we were expected to perform jury duty. Only unit commanders were exempt. Juries convened for a two-week period. We decided all cases that came before the court martial during this period. Like civilian courts, accused people have a right to a jury of their peers. If a soldier appeals the commander's nonjudicial punishment under Article Fifteen, he or she has a trial. The offense could be sent directly to the court martial should the commander decide that it was too serious for his or her limits under Article Fifteen. As I looked at the composition of the jury, I noticed that we were all commissioned officers. Defendants were all enlisted soldiers. I wondered about the validity of the statement, trial by one's peers. I also wonder about swearing to "tell the truth, the whole truth" while being restricted to only answering the question. Such a process often overlooks the whole truth.

I served on a court martial for two weeks just two months earlier. Courts martial are composed of five officers, which assures that they are all college educated and can understand army discipline and the law. The judge was a JAG officer. Since he was covered in a black robe like a civilian judge, we couldn't see his rank. Attorneys, like doctors, begin in the army as captains. Judging by the age of this judge, I expected that he held the rank of lieutenant colonel. The highest-ranking officer on the jury becomes the jury foreman. On our jury was a major, a captain, and three lieutenants varying in experience. Unlike civilian juries, we could ask questions of each witness. Questions had to be handwritten and presented to the judge. We listened as the judge read each question. The judge then solicited responses from the lawyers. Sometimes, the judge disallowed questions without seeking input. When the case concluded and our judge turned it over to the jury. He read the jury instructions just like a civilian judge.

Jury deliberations begin with each member writing the verdict they believed to be just on a piece of paper and handing it to the foreman. It was supposed to be anonymous but it was soon obvious who made each submission. If the decision was not unanimous, we discussed the reasons for our decisions. Anonymity was lost at this point. Fortunately, we were always in agreement. Once a guilty verdict was established, we each wrote down our recommendation for sentencing. The foreman then arranged them from least to greatest in severity. He read the recommendation and we voted. Only a simple majority was needed for the sentencing recommendation. Simple logic favors the middle level sentence. We might modify it in the reduction in rank, money forfeited, or time in jail with some additional discussion.

Two courts martial stand out to me. The first one involved a survey crew led by specialist four. The rank is equivalent to a corporal but lacked the command authority. Nonetheless, he was in charge as the senior member of the crew. A private second class in this crew was charged with assault. We learned that this was an appeal of the company commander's Article Fifteen, nonjudicial punishment. As we listened to the prosecution, we had some sympathy for the defendant. We could see that the specialist was highly competent and took great pride in completing assignments to his high standards. It sounded as though the specialist four was being overbearing and the private pushed him out of his personal space. The defending lawyer might have won or at least achieved a minor sentence had he not placed his client on the stand. The private's testimony showed a long-standing and perhaps racist relationship with his Hispanic supervisor. The defendant was white, over six feet tall, while his supervisor was quite short. The defendant said that he was angry about being corrected in his techniques. The specialist was trying to show him how to do it when he shoved his supervisor hard enough to cause the specialist to collide with a tree and fall to the ground. Deliberations were brief. The foreman major did not even ask for our written verdict. We easily came to an agreement of guilt. We also decided to reduce the private second class to the lowest grade, private, and take six months of his pay. This was more than the company commander could do under Article Fifteen. It was not wise to have appealed.

The second case involved two artillery soldiers, a sergeant and a corporal. The battery commander was seeking court martial because he felt Article Fifteen would be insufficient. He charged them with stealing another battery commander's jeep. Army Willys jeeps did not require a key. Like most military vehicles, you turned on a switch then pressed the starter. It was secured by a chain bolted to the floor, looped over the steering wheel, and padlocked. This left some mobility of the steering wheel. These two soldiers were returning from a night on the town and were quite intoxicated. They thought how funny it would be to swap the battery commanders' vehicles between two batteries. The jeeps were parked in front of the offices only a short distance from each other. The parking lots were large enough so that this would be easy to do if they were sober. Instead, they went out onto the road and into a ditch just a few feet away. The jeep was stuck in the ditch, spoiling their plans.

The judge explained the elements of the crime of automobile theft. A car thief must intend to take the stolen property with the intention of denying the owner its possession. Their prank never intended to steal the jeep, so we easily found them not guilty. We felt that the battery commander should have charged them with unauthorized use of the equipment under Article Fifteen.

The time for me to appear as a witness in the court martial was rapidly approaching. So was the birth of my first child. We had waited until the army hospital reached its prenatal quota so that we could have a better hospital and a civilian doctor. The civilian doctor would give some continuity of care. In the army, you get whoever is one duty at the time. I had access to this information as a privilege of my rank. Ultrasound was new and lacked much detail. It could accurately measure skull diameter to determine the age of the fetus and predict due dates. It was the beginning of our always seeking the best option for our family. Kay and I were relaxing the evening before I was to leave for Alabama. The orders required me to be there three days, as needed. We hoped that she would not have the baby while I was away. Just as we settled in for the evening, Kay's water broke. We went to our local obstetrician at Hindsville Memorial Hospital.

At the hospital, the doctor decided to induce labor. We anxiously awaited to learn whether we were having a son or a daughter. The ultrasound suggested the possibility that the baby's hand might have moved outside the amnionic sac. This would stop the development of the hand. The baby could be born with a deformed or no right hand. Mary was born at two thirty in the morning. It was a terrifying time for me. I was so worried during the violence of childbirth that Kay seemed to be suffering. I began to worry that she could die during childbirth and what my future would be without her, leaving me alone with a newborn baby. We delayed having a child for many years because I did not feel adequate to fulfill such a huge responsibility. I started rethinking my decision to leave the army because I knew that they would help me care for the child if I lost Kay.

Mary was born just fine. The nurses announced that it was a girl. Kay looked up and said, "No, it's a boy." I assured her that it was a girl and that her private parts were a little swollen due to the hormones during delivery. She then realized that she did not see well without her glasses. After our time with our newborn and the nurses took her for evaluation, they asked Kay if she wanted anything. She asked for a popsicle. I chuckled but she said that it would help sooth her. By the time the nurse returned with a popsicle, Kay was asleep. As I chatted with the nurses, I learned that ours was a typical delivery. It only seemed extraordinarily violent because I was inexperienced. I left to go to the court martial.

I picked up Private Second Class Albright and we traveled in my car. The army pays mileage regardless of how you get there. This way, PVT Albright would get some extra money without the expense. I already knew PVT Albright better than most soldiers. I learned a lot more about him on the trip. We discussed family, school, and reasons to join the army. He grew up fatherless and in poverty, like me. Also like me, he was the first in his family to serve in the army. PVT Albright intended to go to college after his service in the army. He had not decided what he was going to study but was thinking about law enforcement. We talked about our favorite teachers and growing up without our fathers.

PVT Albright testified first. He was a great witness. He remembered many of the words that the recruiter gave him and their definitions. He was not able to tell the jury that he already knew these words because the questions were never asked. I suppose that it was irrelevant to the recruiter's crime. The prosecutor asked me much broader, open-ended questions. I was able to recount conversations with the recruiter and PVT Albright and explained that PVT Albright knew these words. I wanted very much to say that this was not surprising to me but the question was never asked. The jury asked me several questions. The judge read each one. Two were to clarify statements made by the recruiter. One asked me what kind of soldier Albright was. The judge read the question then said that he was not going to allow it. The jury must make their own decision on PVT Albright's credibility based on his testimony. I looked at the jury as they looked at me. One first lieutenant leaned particularly far forward as he looked at me. I could see the cross rifles indicating that he was an infantry officer. I was glad that he was a combat officer and would understand my expectations of PVT Albright's performance. Our eyes met. I smiled and nodded my head. He got the answer he wanted. I had told the prosecutor about my newborn and he asked that I be dismissed. The judge, attorneys, and jury agreed. I left PVT Albright behind. He took the bus back to the post. I will never know for sure but I expected a guilty finding for the recruiter. I am only curious about the sentencing.

When I returned, I chose to take some extra time with my new family. Kay and Mary were both doing well. We began preparing for my final days in the army. The most challenging part is to leave the quarters spotless. The inspectors were brutal. I had been through many army inspections and conducted some myself. They take perfection to the extreme.

When I returned to my battery, Captain Pierce said that he had been waiting for me. He said that the colonel wanted to see me. We walked briskly to Lieutenant Colonel Ellison's office. He presented me with the Army Commendation Medal in large part for the perfect nuclear surety inspection but also for the success of bringing Bravo Battery from its reactivation to being fully combat ready.

There were only a few more days left before I began my terminal leave from the army. I prepared my assistant executive officer to move into my position. It was not certain, but likely. Quinton Martin was a West Point graduate. He had a five-year commitment. Most West Point graduates considered an army career to be a given. Quin, however, wanted out as soon as his commitment was fulfilled. Like many West Point graduates, he had a degree in engineering. He could do well in a civilian career.

I rented the largest U-Haul trailer and pulled it with my truck. The Army had some temporary cottages for this transition. Kay and Mary stayed in one of these cottages as I drove the truck and trailer to Frank and my mother's house. I hated that I had no other place to go. Transitioning out of a very secure and predictable environment to one with so many uncertainties is difficult. I drove nonstop, unloaded our belongings into Frank and Mother's garage, returned the trailer, then flew back down to Georgia. I made one last check with my unit, then drove my new family back to New Hampshire.

Seeking work was difficult and quite demoralizing. I came from having been in command of ninety soldiers and able to control a whole battalion of more than five hundred. I had the awesome power of an artillery battery with nuclear capabilities and I was trusted with national security secrets. I had planned and executed an airstrike. I could develop plans to load an entire division onto aircraft to transport them to the battlefield. Now, I was struggling to find even menial labor. I understood how soldiers return from serving honorably in positions of great respect, responsibility, and trust and fall into deep depression. I was driven with the responsibility of a new life who depended upon me. Our future finances were not as bad as most. Kay would easily find a nursing position but wanted to spend three months with our new daughter.

I hated being at my mother's house. I worked quickly to find property and build a house. We bought the land with the money we saved while in the army. The bank would not approve a loan because Kay was not yet working. We bought an old apartment building at

47 Walnut Street in Claremont. It needed major repairs, which we set out to do. During this time, Frank, an avid yard sale enthusiast, was selling my things. He sold my college notebooks for fifty cents. My tools were all lost. He was telling people that I was a lazy bum and sponging off him. When I heard him tell someone, I reminded him who paid to bail his drunken self out of jail. We cleaned the main apartment and moved in as soon as we could.

I started working as a supervisor at Holson Company, a photograph album manufacturer. I did well for about a year, then I came into ethical conflicts with a new production manager. I left and drove a delivery truck for a few months before getting a position with the Claremont Police department. At last, I had a respected job with a twenty-year retirement. I thought about teaching high school after these twenty years. Kay had returned to nursing at Valley Regional Hospital. We worked opposite shifts as much as possible to care for baby Mary. My older sister Priscilla, "Cilla," helped when our shifts overlapped.

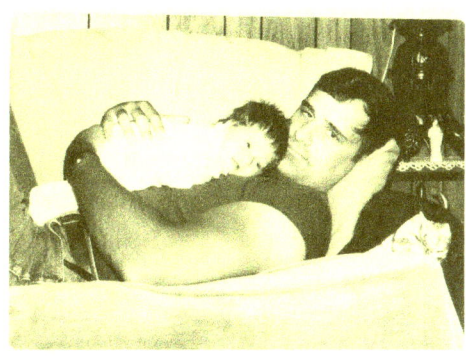
Bonding with my newborn daughter, Mary.

I was intensely worried about properly raising my daughter. I recalled all that I had learned in college and wanted to do everything right. For the first few days of her life, I felt that it was an awful lot of work with no immediate rewards. Mary was only a few days old when I was relaxing on the couch, while lying on my back. Mary was face down on my chest, sleeping. Feeling a little trapped at first, I began thinking about our bodies' close connections. Half of her genes were mine. Her little heart, half from my genes, was beating next to mine. Our hearts were closer together than she could have been to Kay's, even before birth. She was so dependent on us. Our hearts beating so closely together was a powerful bonding experience for me.

To raise my daughter properly, I relied upon what I learned in college, especially Piaget and Erickson. What I feared most, I also learned in college. We tend to parent the way we were parented. I was determined to break my family's curse of brutal domination and alcoholism. I spent much of my time interacting with Mary, knowing the stimulation would encourage her development. I marveled at her tiny little hands and proudly watched as she learned to control them. I had my second powerful bonding experience in the first months as she laid on her back on a blanket on the floor. I lightly tickled her stomach. She responded by laughing with her tongue between her lips, half laughing, half raspberrying. She laughed with every action, whether I touched her toes or poked her belly. She and I absolutely enjoyed each other. Nothing else mattered to us.

I took Mary on many walks around Claremont for exercise and natural stimulation. Kay and I had bought a stroller but I very quickly rejected it, preferring to carry her. I knew about the importance of touch and enjoyed the safety and close contact over the distant, impersonal stroller. She walked more as she grew older but we were always in contact, by hand or carried. We always greeted each other with a hug. Those little arms around my neck are the greatest feeling in the world. Keeping her safe was my greatest responsibility.

I escaped the pattern of parenting the way we were parented. My mother strictly controlled us with strict limits, often with a single or no toy and a small space on the floor. There were no affectionate interactions with my mother. She never played or participated in anything with us. I cannot remember my mother or any member of my family ever hugging us. Her control over us was to make things easier for her. She did little to enhance our development. She often said, "My kids come first" but we did not. Beer came first. Her favorite TV programs came second.

I learned that children learn best with varied stimuli. I also wanted to avoid having unreasonable expectations by providing the opportunity to succeed without strict demands or limitations. It was an awesome responsibility. My daughter deserved nothing less than my best. Watching her develop confidently through many milestones was a great reward. We celebrated each of her achievements. There were no such celebrations when I was a child. The family resources were insufficient and the alcoholic's needs superseded the needs of the child.

I finally got a job with the Claremont Police Department. I went through all the simple academic, polygraph, and psychological tests. I did not have a lot of respect for some, especially the polygraph, otherwise known as the lie detector. I knew that it only indicated a reaction and not the truth. I remember a question, "When did you last beat your wife?" It stunned me so much that I am certain that it showed a reaction. I could not imagine that anyone seeking to join the police would ever be involved in beating anyone. I struggled through my shock and confusion to answer "Never!"

The psychological exam started out fine. It involved a two-hour set of questions intended to describe one's personality. I had studied these enough to know that I would test high in areas of control and detail orientation. I told Kay that I hoped he would not use the very subjective Rorschach Test, called the ink blot test. When he brought them out, I sighed and said, "The Rorschach." He said, "Yes." I decided that I was going to make him pay for it. I knew that I had far greater experience with microscopes than he had. As I described amoebas, paramecia, and algae, he wrote rapidly on his pad. He then leaned over to me and asked me to point out what I was seeing. I described amoebas and paramecia feeling on clumps of algae. The narrative of his report described me as being very intelligent and confident.

I was proud to be part of what I expected to be an ethical and admiral profession. I soon learned that it was not the case. I wrote about this in another book, *A Cop in a Small City: Examining Mission and Integrity*. As I contemplated the reasons, I began to see some commonalities through my experiences. My ethical standards developed over many years. It began with my grandmother who was a devoted Catholic and very detailed. When I was young, my mother's ethics were strong. I learned to disregard her transgressions as her alcoholism advanced. My math and science classes in high school taught me to follow precise procedures and report accurately. Saint Michael's College helped me to further develop these values to a very high level. My commissioned army experience also demanded high ethical standards. Pepperdine University Graduate School helped me apply these standards to individuals and organizations.

I was deeply disappointed as I watched my police colleagues break speed limits, use vulgar language directed at citizens, distort facts, conduct personal business while on duty, accept discounts at restaurants and rentals, stalk women, inflate timecards, exaggerate testimony, use excessive force, and even outright lie on reports and in court. Many times, I heard them say, "I don't get paid enough for that." At first, I tried to ignore these things and stay focused on what I did. I started to get dragged into this by defense attorneys and citizen complaints. I always responded truthfully. My peers began to resent me. The chief even called me aside onetime to tell me that I was "no better than anyone else." He referred to my education and said that it was not applicable to the work I did. The chief could not have been more wrong about my education. I reflected on his education. He had a bachelor's degree but from a school known to abuse the GI Bill, a money mill. I taught a course there. The students immediately balked at my high expectations. His college went defunct when the GI Bill money stopped. His degree was worthless. My degrees are from thriving, credible colleges. They are complete degrees, having completed all the degree requirements in the program at that school. I learned to value less what I call composite degrees. These are the ones that transfer credits from numerous schools and even give credit for life experience. I find that these degrees are much less robust than mine.

I began to make sense of the differences in what I expected to what I observed in the ethical standards within the police department. When I heard "I don't get paid enough," I thought that they get paid very well compared to other professions. I thought how that person lacked education or skills to earn even half of what he was making in another position. They talked about professionalism and doing things scientifically but they had no idea about what they were saying. Few had any post-secondary science education. Most could not define professionalism. They hated challenges from attorneys. Some attorneys compared prostitution was a profession to police officers with questionable testimony. My police colleagues lacked the education to be truly competent in their jobs. Police training was intended to meet minimal levels, just enough for appearances. No one around me could survive the rigors of a higher education.

The few with military experience were all enlisted and were never promoted to sergeant. They would not have been held to the high standards as commissioned officers.

Most of my police colleagues were divorced or in tumultuous relationships. I heard about strained relationships in the army and now with the police. They all blamed the profession and accepted it as a price for their dedication. At first, I worried that it may affect my marriage. I listened carefully as they spoke about their failing relationships with what I learned about their personalities. Many cheated on their spouses. I realized that they needed something to blame other than themselves. It is not shared interests that bind a marriage. They are shared values. Kay shares my high ethical standards and strong commitment to our family. Our marriage remained strong.

Police officers' education can be seen in their reports. The Claremont Police Department's second highest ranking officer rarely wrote anything. When he did, at least every third word was misspelled, the wrong word, wrong tense, or improper grammar. My field training officer (FTO) shared some advice when writing a driving while intoxicated (DWI) report. His was only a small paragraph long. He said, "Don't write too much. The more you write, the more attorneys pick it apart." Both spoke about struggling through high school and belittled anyone with more education. My DWI reports were three to five pages long, sometimes more. I described everything and included some quotes. My detailed accident reports were accepted without any challenge. I included the physical evidence, quotes, photographs, diagrams, calculations, and the references from which I got the formulas for my calculations. I spent no more time writing my reports than the others spent. Most of my arrests pled guilty while most of his went to trial and acquittal. My FTO had a very poor conviction rate. My conviction rate was perfect.

I made observations about the people I arrested. Most were drunk at the time I arrested them or drunk when they committed the crime. Drugs and alcohol seemed to be the primary driving force towards criminal behavior. Even the most respected members of the community committed crimes, especially driving while intoxicated.

Social and economic status played a secondary role in trapping people in property crimes, such as theft and burglary. I grew up with an alcoholic that regularly drove intoxicated. Mother did not steal things but would quickly and without remorse take advantage of anything misplaced or when a store clerk gave her too much change. Mother also felt entitled to take any of my money or belongings as it suited her. It taught me to be empathetic for others.

The least educated person in the Claremont Police Department held the third highest rank. He had a graduate equivalency diploma (GED), the minimum required by police most departments. Even the army required at least a high school diploma. He became the department's juvenile officer. He had a poster in his office that said, "Move out now while you still know everything." He brought a false accusation against me that led to my suspension, then termination. I insisted on my right to a public hearing and won. He, the chief, and his second in command prosecuted me. They all looked like fools. Many more details are included in a chapter of "*A Cop in a Small City: Examining Mission and Integrity.*"

Our courts contribute to distorted ethical standards. Witnesses are sworn to "tell the truth, the whole truth and nothing but the truth." However, the witness can only answer the questions from prosecutors and defense attorneys. For instance, I was testifying in a case regarding the assault of a prisoner upon a police officer. The officer charged the detainee with unprivileged physical contact. He was not present during the trial because he was testifying in another court at the same time. Police officers who bring weak cases spend a lot of time in courts. It was my arrest. I charged him with disorderly conduct for inciting violence and resisting arrest. His resistance involved a brief foot chase. He was too drunk and out of shape to be much of a challenge, however, it was his intent that counted against him.

The prosecutor guided me through the elements of the crime. The detainee raised his hand against my fellow officer while I was fingerprinting him. He placed his hand on the officer's chest. The defense attorney rightfully tried to establish that it was justified use of force. He focused on the exchange of insults between that officer and my prisoner. He asked repeatedly, in many ways, the insults that could justify the action. My answers did not tell the whole truth that I swore to do. I knew and respected the defense attorney. Finally, I answered, "It wasn't the insults that led to the personal contact." My emphatic response seemed to help him formulate a more open question. He replied, "Oh, what was it?" Now the door was open. I described how my fellow officer rapidly intruded into my prisoner's personal space, stood within inches of him and stepping on his toes. The officer was yelling threats of violence. The prisoner only raised his hand in the small space between them and his hand rested on the officer's chest. The judge ruled it as justified, nonviolent use of force. He found my arrestee guilty of my charges. If it had not been for my ability to prompt the defense attorney to ask a different question, this person would have been wrongfully convicted of assault on a police officer. This would have a profound effect on any future sentencing or jail status. There are many times that witnesses are not able to tell the whole truth in our system of justice.

I have spent a lot of time reflecting on why the ethics among many police officers are often so compromised. It is one of the professions where I found that having high ethical standards or doing the job well hurt peer relationships. I believe that fellow police officers felt it made them look bad when someone functions at a higher standard than they are willing to achieve. Some common characteristics in these professions seem to include less education required for great power over others. I remember the words of a police colleague who was an army military police private. I mentioned an encounter I had with military police when they were encroaching on my authority over my unit. He said that his standard response was, "Sir, I believe that you are confusing your rank over my authority." It was how the military police were trying to impose inapplicable infantry standards on my artillery firing point. We do not store munitions in one place. I ordered the military police soldier to leave my firing point because he was causing a safety risk around my canons and did not comply with our requirements for a helmet and hearing protection. He returned with a major in his command who outranked me as a lieutenant. Most notable is that he arrived with a helmet and hearing protection. I would have reported him to my chain of command if he did not comply with our regulations. I explained it to the major who agreed with me. I explained to him how the artillery operates, which he understood. I am solely responsible for the safety of my soldiers and equipment. They never bothered me again.

I was troubled by the free and reduced prices offered to police officers and how these privileges were accepted as though it was owed to them. Places like convenience stores offered free coffee. Fast food restaurants might offer half price. Landlords my reduce the rent. These establishments justified these favors because they wanted to attract police. They believed that it made them and their customers feel safe. They did not say that it was a marketing ploy. People think that cops know the best places to eat, so they will go there. I felt that these places expected special treatment when they called the police. I purposefully avoided these places, on and off duty.

Perhaps the worst police ethics is how many police officers violate the law and expect to be let off by any police officer who catches them. They "flash the badge" and the cop who stopped them lets them go. There is a "no rat" expectation that is identical to that of the criminals. One does not report fellow officers' misbehavior. If asked, the expectation is to lie on behalf of one's fellow officer.

These undesirable qualities persist in police organizations because there is no effective education in ethics and personal values. Communication is strictly controlled through the chain of command. There is little direct supervision and the supervisors are often no better or worse. The experienced police officers are the gate keepers to new hires selected based on who will think like them. The best police officers view themselves as an equal member of the community. Good, ethical police officers leave the profession. A culture of superiority perpetuates among those who remain.

Kay and I had discussed the number of children that we wanted. We agreed that if we had two of the same sex, we would have a third child. A few weeks after Mary was born, we returned to this discussion. I said, "I don't know about you but I don't care about having a third child. It's a lot of work and responsibility. I will be happy regardless of the gender." Susan was born while I was a police officer. We were confident parents, now. I absolutely enjoyed having two daughters. I took Mary on walks about town and the trails before Susan was born. At first, I carried Susan when she accompanied us. There were times I carried both in various combinations, in my arms, on my shoulders, and on my back. These were special times for us.

Sometimes, when I arrived home from working the day shift, I found my mother's car in the driveway. She was always drunk when she visited. She chose her visiting times when I was not there. Kay was too naïve and did not want to offend my mother. As I walked in the door, Mother did her ever so recognizable throat clearing while pulling at the top of her blouse and said she had to leave. Every time, I told her not to come when she had been drinking. I was giving some serious thought into not allowing her to come at all. We were about to build the home we originally wanted. I was planning not to allow her there. I needed to escape her alcoholism. I did not want my daughters to be exposed to it. I worried that she might get into a serious accident or be arrested for driving while impaired leaving my house. Like the army, it would reflect poorly upon me. I also worried that my mother was at high risk of taking my daughters when she was intoxicated. Unlike my siblings, I would never trust my mother to be alone with my children.

I was on police patrol one night when the neighboring town, Charlestown, police dispatcher called me directly over the county radio frequency. I thought that they might be asking for my assistance in a traffic accident, which I did sometimes because I had the specialized accident investigation credentials. Calling me directly was not the proper channel. The dispatcher should contact my supervisor, not me. When I answered her call, the Charlestown dispatcher said that there was a "ten twenty-six." This is the code for a fatal accident. It was consistent with my expectations of a call for assistance. She then added that it involved my parents. I recognized that she was trying to tell me that one of my parents was dead, but I was confused about my parents not living together. I thought that she was making a mistake. As it unfolded, I learned that my parents were trying to get back together again. I went to the hospital and waited for the ambulance to arrive. It backed up to the emergency entrance, the doors opened. I saw my father struggling to get out, obviously intoxicated but apparently unharmed. My ten-year-old half-brother, Scotty, was also in the ambulance. He had a noticeable scratch on the top of his head.

I was ready to return to patrol but my supervisor, Sergeant Don Fontaine, said, "No." He had already called in someone from the next shift, who brought me home. My sister, Cilla, and I decided that we needed to tell our grandparents. It was past one o'clock in the morning when we knocked on their door. We all sat in the kitchen as Cilla and I struggled for the words. How do I tell my grandparents that their daughter is dead? To break the silence, Pop started talking about planting his garden. It bothered me how he did not ask what was so wrong that brought us out at this time. Instead, he resorted to routine things about himself. Finally, I said, "Mom died in an accident." I told them where and that dad was driving. Pop and Grandma looked down in sorrow. Grandma said that she would notify the priest to dedicate the Mass to her. Only Cilla cried.

I returned Cilla to her home. When I got home, I found that the Charlestown police had left a message on my phone. They wanted me to identify the body. I knew that it was temporarily at the fire station. I called the Charlestown Police Department to arrange to meet them. They said that it was no longer necessary for me to identify the body. My Uncle Bernie did the identification. I was a bit puzzled about how they knew to contact him but felt relieved. Strangely, I felt a little cheated out of what I believed was my duty as the family patriarch.

After calling the Charlestown Police, I got my camera and went to the accident scene. I was very surprised to find the car still there. It had crashed through the wooden guardrail of the Old Claremont Road bridge over Clay Brook. The front of the car was in the brook as it rested on the steep bank. Night photography is slow and the results are uncertain. It would be daylight soon, so I decided to wait to take more pictures with better lighting.

The wrecker arrived. I photographed the car as it was pulled up the bank. It was now very clear how the accident happened. Dad took the corner too wide and hit the wooden guardrail. The end of the rail detached from its post and penetrated the grill of the car. Dad no longer had control as the car was impaled on the wooden beam. The beam then completely detached because it was held only by nails. The wooden beam penetrated the engine compartment, going between the engine and the right fender. It penetrated the dash by the glove compartment, passed through the passenger compartment like a huge lance, and punctured the roof above the back window. The beam remained impaled in the car from the grill through the back window. It struck Mom in the face. She might have noticed the sudden explosion of the dash in front of her before the violent blow to her head that killed her almost instantly. My little brother was riding in the center of the back seat. The scratch on his head was from this beam as it passed through the passenger compartment across the top of his head. Scotty came very close to dying that night.

Later, when I saw Uncle Bernie, I asked him about the injuries. He grew silent and faced partially away from me. I could tell that this was hard for him. Without words, he brought his left hand with the fingers slightly spread apart to the front of the lower left part of his face. He then made a quick motion across the lower left side of his face towards the back of his head. I knew from the fatal accidents that I had investigated that much of Mother's face was missing and what remained would be gruesome. Uncle Bernie looked down and walked away from me, seemingly fighting tears. He probably did a huge favor for me by identifying her body instead of leaving the responsibility to me.

I was entitled to three days bereavement time but took only one. I struggled with many mixed emotions and felt the best therapy was to return to work. Over the years, I have wondered about the irony. Mother dispensed her form of discipline by striking us in the head. In public, she pulled our hair or pinched us wherever she could reach discretely. She twice caused severe damage to my head. The first one was when I was seven years old. She blamed me for leading my siblings while sliding down a forbidden bank when we were bored within the confines of our small yard. She hit me with a broom handle across the top of my head and knocked me unconscious. It left a dent in my skull and loss of control over my right eye. The second one was a few months later while she was driving the car. She often swung her backhand wildly into the back seat to punish us for arguing. She boasted about being able to hit all four of us with one stroke of her back swing. Since I was being quiet, I did not expect it as I sat sideways behind her playing with my string. The backswing missed the others and landed directly on the left side of my face, collapsing my left sinus, pushing it into my right sinus, and forever restricting airflow through both sides of my nose. The injury also took away most of my sense of smell. Though I felt the intense pain deep into my face, I did not cry. Mother's only power over me was pain. I suppressed the pain she caused to counter her unfair, brutal power. If she could not hurt me, she would have no power over me. I had already learned to permanently turn off the pain of her hair pulling. I felt only the strain on my neck when she pulled my hair. Even with the intense pain deep in my face and blood running from my nose, I was more concerned about the way she rubbed the pain away from her hand as she drove the car. As she rubbed her right hand with her left, the car swerved back and forth. Every time that we rode with her while she was drinking, I always worried about her ability to control the car. These were the scariest times of my life, more than any time in the army or any police with lethal weapons. Anything that further impaired her driving added to my fear. I quietly dealt with my bleeding nose and did not cry for fear that she would give me "something to cry about." By hiding my pain, I successfully denied her the power over me.

Ironically, after years of striking us in the head and causing permanent injury to my head, Mother died from a blow to her head. Was it karma or divine justice? It did not feel that way to me. I struggled with the confusing conflict of infantile devoted love for one's mother against the intense hatred of her drunken brutality. I wanted to insulate my daughters from my mother's influence, especially when she was drinking. We were about to build a new home. Because she was always drinking when she came to my current home, I was considering not allowing my mother into my new home. Somehow, I thought that I should feel guilty thinking about denying her access to her grandchildren. That decision was now moot. I refuse to allow myself to feel guilty for being relieved of the very difficult task of confronting my mother with an absolute decision. She certainly would label me as being mean and unreasonable and cry, claiming that she was the victim. My greatest loss was Mother as the family historian. I would have to rely on my grandmother, now. Grandma knew about the family genealogy but very little about our lives with my mother. That task is now limited by what my older sister and I remembered. Cilla died several years later, leaving me feeling very alone with my childhood experiences.

My mother's premature death also contributed to the ever-increasing deterioration of my sibling relationships. I was the only one with a college education and my wife, Kay, was a nurse. Our professional lives were vastly different from the more menial jobs my siblings performed. Also strikingly different is that Kay and I had a strong, unbreakable relationship. My siblings had multiple failed relationships. Kay and I never smoked or consumed alcohol. The smoking was already affecting my siblings' health and contributed to their eventual premature disability and Cilla's early death. They all "spanked" their children while Kay and I never did. Our new house had an open kitchen and living room that was ideal for large family gatherings at Thanksgiving. We built a pool that enriched family gatherings during the summer. We managed to have a few years of celebrations but eventually drifted further apart, mostly due to my siblings' failing health.

Our parenting style focused on the relationship with our daughters. I read a very good book called, *"The Shelter of Each Other,"* by Mary Pipher, PhD. The fundamental concept in Dr. Pipher's book is that families protect each other from the outside, cruel world. The family is most successful when it focuses on the relationship more than the behavior. Family rituals play a large part in these relationships.

Kay and I bargained for privileges and never had any serious discipline problems with our daughters. Rituals and routines from our daughters' perspective were central to our relationships. Predictability builds security and trust. One of my favorite routines was at bedtime. I carried each daughter to bed and tucked them in. We talked about their day, discussed future events, and discussed any other concerns. Once, Mary expressed some concern about her friend who was grounded. Since we never needed any significant discipline, I suspected that she probably did not understand what being grounded meant, so I asked her. She explained that it required a shovel in the back yard. I suppressed my chuckle and explained it to her. Another time, she expressed concern about a friend's parent being fired. She thought that it involved a lighter being placed under that person's butt. These seem silly but it shows the very literal thinking of a child trying to make sense of this crazy world. It also shows the value of just listening to one's child and helping her understand.

I vowed to never parent like my mother. As children, we were not allowed to interrupt our mother's television programs. We had to wait for a commercial to speak with her. Our concerns had to be stated and resolved before her program returned. She was expeditiously dismissive of our concerns. She rejected most as unattainable. Other people can do those things but not us. There were times she promised to do as we requested. The promise acknowledged our concern and made us happy for the moment. Unfortunately, her promises were almost never fulfilled. She sent us off happy with an empty promise. Sadly, we could never break this cycle. In my mother's world, the parent's needs came first. Any statement about her children coming first was lies from an alcoholic's distorted world. Sadly, my mother felt that she was the best possible mother as she often criticized other mothers.

I approached things very differently with my children. Their concerns or any need to talk with me were far more important than anything that I was doing. No matter how hard it was for me to stop what I was doing, I always valued their concerns more. Nothing was more important to me than my children. I demonstrated what my mother only claimed to do.

I learned how alcoholism often skipped generations. The stories my grandfather told about his father indicated that he was an alcoholic. My great grandfather could "down a pint without swallowing." My grandparents rarely drank alcohol. My mother was a hardened alcoholic and unwilling to even admit a problem. I refused to let alcohol affect my life but I worried intensely that it could skip a generation and land on my daughters. When opportunities presented themselves in real life or in movies, I tried to explain to my daughters how alcohol negatively impacted that person and those around her or him.

Kay worked every weekend. My weekends were filled with time with my daughters that we mixed with chores and projects around home. I was trying to rush Mary through her bath once when she was a toddler. I opened the drain while Mary was sitting in the water. She immediately stood up screaming "No" then grabbed me firmly around my neck. At first, I suspected an act of defiance but her reaction was too intense. It was fear. I closed the drain and stopped the water. I asked her what was wrong. She said that the water was swirling and going down and she was afraid that she was going with it. I realized that this is what happens in some cartoons. I took her out of the tub, dried her off and wrapped her in the towel. We knelt beside the tub. From this safe perspective, I held her close and showed her the drain and the tiny holes in the drain cover. I rubbed my fingers across the drain cover and explained that she could not fit through them. We placed her bath toys over the drain to show that they could not possibly pass through it. I opened the drain and we watched as her smallest toys stopped at the drain cover. I had to wonder why authors of cartoons for children did not consider how their actions might seem real to very young children. For several weeks, I was cautious to take Mary out of the tub before draining the water. My greatest responsibility is to keep her safe and free from fear. I also made it a priority to watch more of my children's shows with them. Together we critiqued the unrealistic parts of their shows.

I was gaining confidence in my abilities to parent. My mother would have dismissed my concerns and even ridiculed me and called me stupid. I was successfully separating my parenting skills from my mother's.

My daughter and I sometimes discussed her dreams. They were also connected to what she saw on television. It made sense. We process daily experiences as we lie awake and in our dreams. I remembered my own childhood dreams. Most shows were westerns. I dreamed about being captured and raised by Indians. Somehow, I felt safer when I dreamed of living in an Indian village. Perhaps these "wild savages" in the movies were my rescuers. Their civilization was more orderly than the chaotic life with my alcoholic mother.

To help them feel safe from her nightmares, I carefully tucked them into bed each night. We discussed the day's events and what was planned for tomorrow. I strived to provide predictability and security that I never had as a child. If they were sick, I stayed by their side while they slept. If they called out at any time, I came immediately.

My sister, Cilla, often helped watch our daughters when Kay and my work shifts overlapped. I could trust her to care for them in our home. I knew that she spanked her own daughter but I was confident that she would not have to discipline our daughters, who were always compliant. Cilla played with them and they very much enjoyed her except for one thing. Cilla did the traditional birthday spankings that we never did. Once, her spankings were more energetic than Mary could tolerate and she cried. Cilla felt bad and stopped doing them.

Parents learn how to parent from their parents. My mother and grandfather would have laughed at me and called me stupid if I feared the drain like my young daughter. Instead, I felt a tremendous sense of guilt for failing to protect her against something she feared. My parenting style developed from the various courses I studied at Saint Michael's College. All that psychology, religion, philosophy, biology, and so much more gave me the insight and freedom to be a very different parent than my parents and even my grandparents. My siblings' parenting style was much like my mother's. They idolized her. I remained hesitant about my abilities until I became a grandfather. I got to enjoy the young children again on the weekends with confidence. Very strong bonds developed during these times that will last throughout our lives.

My education was essential in breaking my cycle of abuse. My mother's and grandfather's discipline styles were brutal and demeaning. They were also so controlling that they continued it well into adulthood. I am extremely protective but I also realize that I cannot always be available for them. Quality parenting styles teach children to evaluate situations and develop their own strategies to protect themselves. We could provide guidance and security with our trusting relationship with our daughters. There was never any need for punishment. There were many opportunities to celebrate their accomplishments.

We also provided safety and built relationships with our rituals and rites of passage. Morning routines, mealtimes, bath times, and bedtimes were consistent. Each had its own established ritual. We celebrated any rite of passage. Birthdays and promotions into the next grade at school were celebrated with food, presents and increased privileges and responsibilities. School work was always done before dinner. We ate dinner together as a family while we discussed the day's events. We relaxed in the living room during the evening, often cuddling on the couch. Many times, a daughter's feet were thrust into my lap followed by the command, "Rub my feet!" The soles of one's feet are excellent stress relievers when rubbed. Rubbing also increases the circulation, making their feet feel better.

All good parents encourage their children to eat a balanced diet. We started telling our daughters how important it was to build strong muscles. I managed to get a few extra bites by checking their muscles. I would gently squeeze her biceps, then say two more bites of the green beans and one of the potatoes. It was such a routine that they demanded, "Check my muscles" when they wanted to stop eating. She would then eat the one or two more bites I deemed necessary. Years later, they realized it was a trick. I smiled and said, "It got you to eat more vegetables." Even though they now realized that it was a silly trick, they understood that it was genuinely in their best interest.

We did other silly things, too. Our pickup had a four-speed transmission lever on the floor. Susan always sat in the center because she was the smallest. I sometimes pretended to accidentally grab her knee to shift the truck. I did everything with my daughters that I would have done if they were boys. We wrestled, which descended into tickling. I remembered the painful ticking from my Uncle Bernie and his refusal to stop. I always gave the power of control to my daughters. I tickled them when they asked and immediately stopped when they requested it.

My ritual of carrying my daughters to bed continued into their early teens. Our bedtime discussion became varied and more intellectual. Some questions were about sex. When Susan was born, I expressed my relief to Kay that she would have to have the birds and bees discussions. I still got the questions and felt it was my duty to answer them. I answered them directly in a language they would understand as any biologist would answer his daughter. It seemed to me that I was getting more questions about sex than Kay was getting. I asked Mary why. She said it was because I answered directly while their mother seemed to talk around the topic without providing a direct, simple answer. I met my limit when the question was about the best feminine hygiene product. "You are going to have to ask your mother that question."

The close relationship I had with my children along with the excellent education I received at Saint Michael's College helped me understand my childhood feelings and to heal. Kay and I built a close relationship with our children from infancy. They learned to trust us for their basic needs. Later, they trusted us to protect them from dangers in this world. As they grew older, we could not and should not have isolated them from undesirable influences. We cannot always be there to protect them. We had to teach them to protect themselves and eventually their own families. I tried to help my children without making them dependent upon me. My grandfather tried to keep his family dependent upon him to maintain control over them. I carefully relaxed protection to prepare them to control over their lives independent from me.

City Administration

I LEFT THE Claremont Police Department after six years. A new position within public works better fits my education and ethical standards. The change meant that I would no longer be in the twenty-year retirement group but I would still be in the New Hampshire retirement system. The position was titled Industrial Pretreatment Coordinator. It was a position mandated by the United States Environmental Protection Agency (USEPA). Because Claremont had some large, regulated industrial sewer users, it was required to have a program to regulate and monitor their use of the sewer. Claremont had a history of violating its discharge limits to the Sugar River. The reasons pointed towards heavy discharges from one or more industries that overloaded the sewer plant's capability. The City of Claremont was about to be fined hundreds of thousands of dollars for these violations and neglecting to implement this mandated program. This position appealed to me because I would finally use both my degree in biology and master's degree in business administration. The substantial increase in pay made up for leaving the twenty-year retirement group.

I studied the federal and state regulations and the USEPA notices of violations. My army experience in unfamiliar, diverse positions gave me confidence that I could fulfill this novel position. I learned that I first had to establish a local authority to regulate the businesses. Claremont's sewer use ordinance needed significant changes, which I wrote. I worked with the City Solicitor Jack Yazinski, then submitted it to the state environmental agency for approval. While approval was pending, I worked on a rate schedule so that the program would be self-funded. Once this was all accomplished, I met with the larger businesses to explain the program and how I would monitor them.

It required inspections of their facilities to assure proper control of materials that could impact the sewer system. It also involved routine sampling of their industrial discharges to the sewer to verify compliance with the contaminant limits. Putting together this novel program was in line with the responsibilities I had in the army. I had experience taking great responsibility and learning it well.

Soon after everything was in place, there was a sewer plant upset and we violated our discharge limits. It was an amazing coincidence that I had the automatic sampler set up outside Claremont Paper Mill. I caught them red-handed. My police experience was very useful. I made the affidavit, filled out a complaint, got a warrant, and brought it to the police department to be served. I had proposed the maximum fine, five hundred dollars. City Manager Robert Jackson related to me his conversation with the mill's owner. Harvey Hill came to his office with my complaint and summons to court. He said, "Who is this f...ing Sanborn and who does he think he is?" He then threw a check for five hundred dollars on the manager's desk. He pleaded guilty to the charge. The EPA was watching us. They knew about it from the required report we submitted for the sewer discharge violation. The EPA investigators were pleased with our efforts, then brought forth their own fine of one hundred twenty-five thousand dollars. Soon after, the paper mill was sold. The new owner was very respectful and always operated the factory within limits.

I became aware that our composted sewer waste had increasing levels of metals. The elevated lead level was most concerning because they were approaching the limit for its beneficial use in horticultural applications. Sewer compost would change from an income resource to a burden of hazardous disposal. It sent me back to the books and research articles. I learned that these were all plumbing metals. The greatest cause of plumbing metals in wastewater is a corrosive water supply. Claremont's water supply is entirely surface water, influenced by acid rain. Our water was slowly dissolving our pipes in the street and in homes. It hastened the corrosion in the distribution system, restricting the flow of water. This impacted water pressure and fire protection. With a little more research, I learned about treating water to reduce the corrosive effects of acidic surface water. I visited the water treatment plant and learned that the plant was designed to treat for corrosion prevention. I discussed this with the chief water treatment operator, Bill Mates. He also had a master's degree, so I thought that I could speak with him as a peer. Unexpectedly, he refused to consider using the corrosion prevention ability designed into this plant. It would add two thousand dollars to his annual budget. I tried reasoning with him that just one of our pipe replacement costs far exceeded it. He felt that was not his problem. The water was fine when it left his plant. It was true that the water met regulatory standards but not industrial standards. The water was too acid.

I went to see the city manager, Bob Jackson. He had mentioned several times that he got his education in Ohio and was once a chemistry teacher. I thought that it would be easy to explain why we needed to add corrosion prevention to the water treatment plant budget. I soon realized that he did not understand this simple water chemistry. Even when I tried explaining it to him, he was not understanding. I began to doubt that he had any education in chemistry. What he did understand was the costs. He didn't seem concerned about the slow deterioration of the plumbing. What really got his attention was the inevitable extreme cost of sewer compost disposal if we didn't do something. I won a leap of faith from him to insist that we begin corrosion prevention at the water treatment plant. The chief operator resisted. He steadfastly maintained that the water met all requirements when it left the plant. He insisted that the problem remained with the operators of the distribution system. I prevailed. Bill Mates resigned his position. The senior operator, Bob Metcalf, replaced him. The treatment included corrosion prevention and we soon saw a remarkable drop in the heavy metals in our sewer compost analyses. I was guardedly proud but knew I was alone in my understanding of the true scope of this success.

The present public works director asked me if I knew anything about the new cross-connection requirements. I did not but was willing to research it. I learned that it was also called back flow prevention. It is possible, especially in our hilly community, for water to flow backwards with pressure fluctuations or a water line break. It could siphon water from someone's home or business. For instance, if a garden house was left in a pool and the supply line broke, it could siphon water out of the pool and into the public water system. As I researched it, I learned about the many devices that would prevent this from happening. Some were simple air gap devices. Others were quite complex, expensive, and required routine testing. These devices were used on pressurized systems such as a fire protection system.

Unlike the outdated sewer use ordinance, Claremont had no cross-connection ordinance from which to start. I researched other communities and found that few had anything. From the federal regulations, I wrote the cross-connection ordinance. Like the industrial pretreatment program, I wrote a fee schedule to fund the program. The skills to test these devices were typical for a water distribution worker. I found the training requirements and opportunities, then arranged for two water department employees and me to attend the training for certification.

I reflected on how my combination of education and experience served me well. Understanding the complex science underlying the regulations and my military experience helped immensely. I was accustomed to taking on an unfamiliar responsibility. This was just another time that I reminded myself, "If anyone can do it, I can." Industrial pretreatment was new for everyone in the country. I also had the command experience to stand up to powerful opposition when I knew that I was right. Maybe I acquired some of my grandfather's strong personality to maintain an unwavering position of authority.

I was undeniably the opposite of what my family had conditioned me while I was a child. So many times, I was told that I was too stupid and how other people can do things that our family cannot do. My education and successful experiences improved my sense of self-worth and confidence. I gained satisfaction by proving my grandfather and mother wrong. They could never understand what I was doing now. I broke my family's barriers with self-reassurance and determination. I was promoted to captain in the army reserves, which further boosted my esteem. That determination got me through college, the army, and gave me the confidence to deal with one of the toughest federal agencies, the United States Environmental Protection Agency.

The publics work director suddenly left after being in the job for a few months. The city manager wasn't interested in replacing him right away. The public works department essentially split in two, the highway department and the water and sewer departments. Each were headed by a superintendent. Peter Goewey was promoted from truck driver/foreman to the superintendent of the highway department. Brian, a civil engineer, was hired as the water and sewer superintendent. He offered little resistance to the highway department's long-time practice of using water and sewer department resources to maintain the highways. This is fundamentally a misuse of funds since the water and sewer departments are self-funded with fees to their users. The highway department managers justified it as a quid pro quo, equally sharing their resources, which was not true. Brian soon took a position with Cold Regions where he received twice his present salary. I took over his superintendent position.

The highway superintendent, Peter Goewey, barely graduated high school. He admittedly did not like math and could not write reports, delegating it to the well-educated and experienced department secretary. He did no long-range planning. He told me that he had to see who showed up for work before deciding the tasks for the day. He explained that he could not schedule things because the workers would call out sick if they did not like the task. I was his opposite. I respected the professionalism of the water and sewer system operators. They appreciated having scheduled days in advance. They took the good with the bad. I did not have the call out problem that the highway department had.

When I took over as the water and sewer superintendent, there was a crucial sewer line replacement project in shut down. The Mansfield Project got its name from the street it passed through. It brought sewer from a mostly residential area, down a steep bank and under an earthen railroad bridge sixty feet deep. When I took over as the industrial pretreatment coordinator, the city was under notice by the United State Environmental Protection Agency (USEPA) and faced fines because the sewer line was leaking into the adjacent brook. The engineering firm and contractor stopped work when the contractor's boring operation under the railroad went off course and the engineer feared the collapse of the railroad. The boring technique was done by a large motor and auger, like a giant drill. As the drill progressed, a steel sleeve was pressed into the earth behind it. It became apparent that the contractor was removing more earth than the steel sleeve would fill. The void would destabilize the railroad.

I met with the engineer and reviewed the contracts for the engineer and the contractor. I was looking to see what options the city had. I focused on the project completion date in the contract. It was rapidly approaching and had a clause to fine both the contractor and engineer responsible for each day over the deadline. I saw this as the City's only recourse to regain progress on this project. The engineering firm was very worried about their reputation and became more vigilant. They contacted a tunneling company from South Carolina. They came within a few days and quickly took over the former boring project and completed the fortified tunnel. The engineering company shared the additional cost with the city. Another utility contractor was hired to complete the remaining project.

Russ Davis was the foreman immediately subordinate to me and my greatest asset in planning. He was good with the details for the weekly schedule. He helped me to identify and prioritize the future needs. I inventoried the equipment, documented its condition, and its expected time of replacement. I sought the same information from the water and sewer plant operators. I shared my information with all the water and sewer employees and valued their ideas, so everyone had input into planning. I was able to plot out the needs and anticipated costs for ten years. From this plan, we could plan major infrastructure improvements well in advance. When the city manager asked for our capital improvement plans at budget time, he immediately rejected my ten-year plan. He explained that the city council members only wanted one year because they had only three-year terms. In reality, it was the City Manager who cared to only focus on one year at a time. I presented only the first year with the City Council. Peter Goewey had no such plan. He prepared his capital improvement plan by replacing equipment that was broken down more than it ran. He decided which streets to pave based mostly on political influence from his favored members on the city council. I spent many hours developing a thorough plan while Peter Goewey spent less than an hour.

I soon challenged how the Highway Department often helped themselves to the Water and Sewer Departments' vehicles and equipment. Often, they would have our equipment when we needed it. Peter Goewey was not responsive to releasing it. These were separately funded organizations. The Highway Department is financed directly from property taxes. The Water and Sewer Departments were financed from user fees. These were not necessarily from the same people or organizations. Large water and sewer users would not want to pay these high fees knowing it was being spent on the roads, especially since they also paid property taxes that funded highway maintenance. I felt the strong ethical responsibility to spend the resources as the regulations intended. An equal sharing agreement is permitted, but that is not what was happening. It came to a crisis one winter day when I had a water main break. I told Peter Goewey, the highway superintendent, that I needed my dump truck that he was using to plow roads. He told me that he needed it and that I would have to rent one from a local contractor. I refused, replying that he should rent one and that the water department was entitled to its own equipment. I warned him that I would call the city manager to inform him that we are unable to repair the water main because the highway department refused to release our equipment. We compromised when he gave us another truck. It was not ours but it allowed us to repair the broken water main. Since this incident, I insisted on our truck be fitted always with the tailgate and not the sand spreader. My rationale was that there was no warning to a water main break. There was sufficient warning for snowstorms to make the conversion for snow removal.

Peter Goewey increased his passive aggressive tactics to interfere with what I was doing. He targeted my schedule that was posted in the meeting room. The first, most obvious action was a day we had a contractor to replace a large, underground water valve. It required very large tools and equipment that we did not have. It was a one-day, thirty-thousand-dollar project. Our part was to excavate the valve before the contractor arrived. When we went to the site, the highway department's grader was parked directly on top of this valve and no one was around. I was furious and confronted Goewey. He said that they were doing ditch work on that street and would be moving the grader soon. I asked why this street, now, when he knew my schedule and the commitment to the contractor. He said it was just some ditch work and they would be moving it soon. They moved the grader but we were already behind schedule. The contractor had to wait, costing us more. The highway department never did any ditch work on that street.

Goewey continued with his passive aggressive tactics of interfering with our operations. We had planned to upgrade the water line on Congress Street. Congress Street is in a neighborhood known as Beauregard Village. Goewey decided to pave this neighborhood the same summer as our water project. He wanted our crew to mark all the water and sewer utilities, which are the sewer manholes and water shut off valves in the neighborhood. The reason to do this is for the paver to work around these utilities. It included all the main lines plus all the lines to all the houses. It took a crew three days to do all the markings. The day before the paver arrived, my crew coated all the sewer manholes and water valve covers with grease to make removing any accidental covering with pavement. When the paving company started paving, I noticed that they made no provisions for all our markings, paving over them as if they were not there. I approached Goewey. He said that it was only a one-inch overlay and we could dig out our utilities afterwards. I asked him why he had us waste three days marking them. He smiled and walked away.

As this Beauregard Village paving continued, I saw them paving Congress Street just two weeks before we planned to dig it up. I went to Goewey, again. He gave me the same justification, "It's just a one-inch overlay." I asked him if he was crazy. Certainly, he knew how the public would take this. I told him to put his one-inch overlay somewhere else. We would pave the street properly when we finished. He refused and paved the street. Goewey thought that he would get negative public opinion against me. He was too simple-minded to realize the public would not see the difference. I went to the city manager.

When we met with City Manager Bob Jackson, he realized how bad this would look to the public. Goewey had little in his defense on the wasted asphalt and contracted labor. He then said that there was a "Shit Happens" bumper sticker on the sewer crew's utility truck. I recognized the immature diversion tactic and expected the educated city manager to respond accordingly. Instead, he got upset with me and told me to get it off right away. I was dumbfounded, but I would not retaliate by complaining about the sexist posters displayed in his maintenance department. Instead, I recognized that the city manager lacked the leadership skills to resolve any controversial issues and was looking for an opportunity to end this meeting. The bumper sticker was just an opportunity to avoid making an unpleasant command decision. The meeting ended without resolution.

I worked on many projects that fortunately did not require Peter Goewey's involvement. The River Road Sewer Extension had been considered for several decades. It was where the city planners wanted industry to develop. There was plenty of city water but no sewer. It was mostly on a state highway and only a short section of city streets. It also crossed a railroad, required approval from multiple state agencies, and used federal funds. Goewey was way out of his league in understanding the engineering required. He barely graduated high school, couldn't do math and couldn't write an intelligent response to high level government agencies. City Manager Bob Jackson, who professed to being a chemistry teacher in Ohio, could not understand the chemistry. I did many capital improvement projects including the upgrading of both the water and sewer plants to meet the increasing federal standards. I was successful working with these engineers and obtaining approval from the city council using my science and management education and experience. Two colleges and army service were great experiences for me.

Ethical conflicts with the city manager continued and increased in severity. It was at a city council meeting that a city councilor asked about the sewer rates. I had been working with the public works committee on a rate study and it was obvious that we would need to raise the sewer rates soon. The councilor asking the question was on this committee. He liked setting up the city manager in gotcha questions.

In the past, the city hired an engineering firm to do rate studies costing several thousand dollars. I decided to do it at no additional cost. With the improvements I made to the water plant and its staffing, the water rates were going to be good for several years. Bob Jackson responded to the councilor's inquiry with an assurance that our sewer rates were fine. He called on me to confirm it. I reluctantly told him that we were working on revising the rates.

The next day Bob Jackson called me to his office. He had an evaluation of my performance, which he had never done before. Across it was written in bold letters, "Follow my lead!" I asked him if he wanted me to lie. I reminded him that three city council members were on the public works committee and they knew the answer to the rate question. It was also in my reports that I submitted to him and forwarded to the council. He said that it was not this one time but he could not provide other examples when I asked. Jackson also complimented me on my expertise but criticized me for being "Brutally honest." I realized that Bob Jackson's dominant skill was charming and manipulating people. Expert data and reports were his weaknesses. He was not as bad as Peter Goewey, but he was not much better.

I was getting the message that Bob Jackson wanted me to compromise my ethics. I could not do as he wanted. It felt like a stab wound into my very being. I would not compromise my integrity nor would I succumb to the backstabbing tactics of Peter Goewey. Some management mentors say that you must beat the passive aggressive person at his own game. My ethical standards conflicted with this practice. Jackson and Goewey brought much stress upon themselves with their multilayered manipulations. They had to remember to whom they told what lie. I only had to recite the truth, listen to others' concerns, and do my best to coordinate their various objectives. I would rather change jobs than compromise these values.

Things were not going well for me. It was reminiscent of my army experience with Sergeant First Class Short who told me to go sit in my office and let him handle it. The lieutenant before me complied and it did not go well for him. The water superintendent before me also did I for Peter Goewey and his predecessor. It was not in my personality to allow such unethical conduct.

Peter Goewey's trivial passive aggressive tactics continued. Bob Jackson obviously felt more comfortable with Goewey's unscrupulous style over my brutal honesty and he "Laid me off." I sought a lawyer. Nearly two years passed before we settled. I was not after money so much as to expose these wrongs. When the truth emerged soon after settling, the city council fired Bob Jackson. Peter Goewey soon followed.

I felt it necessary to reflect on my ethics. I had conflicted with police officers and their administration. Now, I have conflicted with city administration and deviant passive aggressiveness. Was I wrong in my ethical stance? I concluded that I was not wrong. It is a corrupt system that operates to preserve the status quo. It served the people within it, not the people who should be served. The ones who funded its operation.

During this time, I decided to fulfill my promise to my favorite high school teacher, Daisey Hronek. I had told her that I wanted to be a math teacher like her. Through college, I found that teaching math would be too boring. I wanted to teach science. I contacted the New Hampshire Department of Education. I was hoping that I could be certified based on my commissioned army experience, as the army had told me. Their response was that I had to complete a program and referred to Keene State College. I met with an advisor and they had no abbreviated programs. There were no specialized programs for someone who already had a college degree. I decided to pursue a second master's degree in environmental science with teaching certification at Antioch University.

Teaching

ON THE FIRST day of a teaching fundamentals class, I watched the instructor walk down the hallway to our classroom. She had long black hair and a long black dress. She was carrying poster board under one arm and a box of markers in her other hand. My first impression was that she looked like a former flower child from the sixties. She stopped at the doorway, looking at us seated in the typical school desk arrangement facing the blackboard at the front of the room. She motioned with her arms as she continued to hold the poster board and markers. She said, "Make a big circle with lots of room in the center." We moved the desks and sat back down. She walked to the center, dropped the posterboard and placed the box of markers on the floor.

She took attendance to confirm that we were all in the right class then gave her instructions. She wanted each of us to divide a poster into four sections. In one section, she wanted us to draw a picture representing ourselves at six years old. In the other sections, we were to draw a picture of ourselves at twelve, eighteen and mid-twenties. My classmates sprang into action, anxious to do the task. I was completely out of my comfort zone. First, I do not draw very well. Second, my childhood was horrible. I could only remember difficult times that I did not want to share with anyone. I knew that I wasn't going to be able to avoid it, so I tried hard to remember pleasant times, which I could not. I decided to display some general things that I did at each age, such as swimming and my pet goat. I used only stick figures. My pet goat, Herbie, looked more like a deer.

When we finished sharing, the professor explained her purpose for this activity. She explained that even though we were teaching older children, we need to remember what it was like as a younger child. The older children we teach will have had experiences that affect them as our experiences affected us. I appreciated the concept well and felt moving out of my comfort zone was worth it. I knew the academics of child development. This activity brought a realization and understanding of the experiences that motivated or hindered students. It also helped us recognize how our childhood experiences could influence our relationships with our students.

It was refreshing to be back in the academic world where ethics and ideology flourished. I completed the program early and did my teaching internship at Stevens High School. My daughter Susan was in my class. She made me promise not to call on her. Immediately upon completing my internship, I got a job teaching earth and space science at Springfield Vermont High School. I never studied earth science directly, only as it applied to biology and environment science. Class sizes were huge, thirty-three to thirty-six students. I was glad to see an opening at my alma mater the following year. I taught biology and agricultural science at Fall Mountain Regional High School. It felt good to be back home with many of the teachers still there from my time as a student. I felt validated to be among people who valued education and had high ethical standards. It was also good to have my friends' children in some of my classes. Having sat in these very chairs as a student, I had a connection to all the students.

I knew from my own experience as a student that the typical homework assignment of reading a textbook and answering questions at the end of the chapter does not work. One only searches for the answers without processing any information. Reading aloud during class is even worse. Students are too focused on getting the word pronunciation and emphasis correct. Any error would be immediately corrected by the teacher. Making a mistake while reading in class is terribly humiliating. Each time the teacher corrected, we felt stupid. The teacher's emphasis and tone often made it worse. While one student reads, the other students are reading ahead in case they are called on. They are not listening to what is being read. Students learn nothing. It is a colossal waste of time. After I completed reading a section aloud, I knew that I was safe from being called upon again. I was free to daydream. Fill in the blank and short answer worksheets are not much better. They are glorified word searches. Find the phrase in the textbook, then complete the sentence. Too often assessments are focused on trivial details and overlook the underlying concept. Meaningful demonstrations and participative activities are far more beneficial. Activities must challenge the students' natural curiosity. Most topics can be reduced to a fundamental concept that can then be connected to the many trivial facts and prior learning. Unfortunately, administrators are too focused on classroom management of behavior when evaluating teacher performance. Reading aloud from textbooks gives a superficial appearance of classroom control.

I reflected on how far I had come and who I had left behind. My sisters graduated high school but my brother had not. I was the only one to graduate college in my family and now I had three college degrees. Kay had a three-year clinical diploma from Concord Hospital School of Nursing. It was an intensive three-year program that focused on clinical nursing but was not a college degree. I always felt that it was sufficiently equivalent to most college bachelor programs. Certainly, it was far ahead of any technical program.

We did not make educational demands of our daughters. We simply expected that they would want to go to college. My oldest, Mary, was the second person in my family to get a college degree. Susan followed two years later. For many years I was the only one with a master's degree. Eventually, both daughters got their masters' degrees. This established a family tradition that would continue. Both grandchildren went to college. None of my siblings' children and only one cousin went to college. Several nephews, nieces and cousins did not graduate high school. The difference between us is how we view the value of education and its benefits. Similarly, all my siblings and cousins have divorced or failed relationships. Kay and I remained dedicated to our family with our solid relationship.

I worried that I would parent the way I was parented, which we humans tend to do. My siblings all had kids and were parenting much like my mother did with total emotional and physical dominance. I relied heavily upon my education and knowledge about child development. I watched with pride as my daughters progressed through the developmental stages that I studied in college. We had many hours together while Kay worked every weekend. I must admit that there were times when the diaper smelled bad and I checked the clock to see how long it was until Kay got home, but knew I had to change it anyway. As they grew older, we went on nature walks. They enjoyed it like a scavenger hunt to see what they could find. We enrolled them in day care mostly to develop their social development.

We had no problems with discipline. As I learned in college and additional readings, relationships are what is important. Children know when parents truly care about them. We all want our children to have a healthy diet. We encouraged them to eat their vegetables to grow healthy muscles. When they are very young and asked if they had eaten enough, I used to say, "Let me check your muscles." I lightly squeezed their biceps and I would determine that two more bites of broccoli or corn were necessary. She happily took the bites and removed her plate. Years later when I mentioned this tactic, Mary paused in thought and said, "You tricked us!" I replied, "It worked," with a smile.

Bath times were fun especially during the winter. They dried off in the living room by the fireplace. Our fireplace irons show the silhouettes of two women. Mary and Susan used to back up to the fire, wrapped in their towels. They lifted their towels to expose their bare butts to the fire, posing like those silhouettes until they got warm. Then they covered themselves with their towels, ran and jumped on the couch, laughing and giggling. I brushed their hair after they got into their pajamas. We watched Disney shows and played games until bedtime. I carried them to bed and had our special moment for discussion. These remain the best days of my life.

I frequently brought them swimming in the public pool. We eventually built our own pool. They wanted to roller skate. I cringed at the bullies and worried they would get rundown, so I learned to skate with them to be the bully blocker. They wanted to learn to ride a bike. They always wore helmets, knee and elbow pads. We started on the lawn where it was safe to fall and made our way to riding around large factory parking lots when the shops were closed. I never brought them onto a public street. We had the perfect place for sledding in the winter. I kept them close to be safe. I had recurring nightmares of Mary being struck by a car, which compelled me to be hypervigilant.

When I got a full-time teaching job at my alma mater, Fall Mountain Regional High School, it was like a heartwarming homecoming. The building was much the same with a few changes. Some of my former teachers were still there. The most noticeable change was in physical education. We climbed ropes, used a trampoline, parallel bars, etc. All those were now considered too dangerous and a liability. The former equipment room was transitioned into a weight room. I found it very much contrary to lifelong health education. It showed students that they had to be a member of a fitness gym to remain healthy. You had to pay for such memberships and travel some distance from home. I worried about the transmission of disease in these close quarters with people touching the same things and breathing hard near each other. Having come from the army, I knew conditioning drills and running. These were free and could be done at home and free from contagious diseases. Sometimes education takes a wrong turn because it is more convenient.

The Fall Mountain homecoming feeling went beyond the school and teachers. I knew the parents of many of the students or someone in their families. I had a connection to the entire community. Unfortunately, a contentious relationship developed between the teacher's union and the school board. Fall Mountain teachers were paid far below the state and national averages and the school board was unsympathetic. They tried cutting back on many benefits, especially healthcare. The union chose a work to rule position. We would do only what were required to do by contract. In a show of unity, we walked in together at the beginning and the end of the contracted times. I did not like this. I take great pride in my lessons and they require a lot of preparation time.

The Newport High school principal, Barry Connell, unexpectantly called me. He wanted someone who could teach biology, environmental science, chemistry, and physics to upper-level students. He lamented that students graduating from Newport did not study science in college. He offered me a substantial increase in pay.

Soon after I arrived, the Newport High School band director ran off with a former eighteen-year-old student, leaving his wife and two children. A parttime semiretired teacher was arrested for driving while intoxicated in the school parking lot after striking a parked car. A biology teacher refused to teach a freshman physical science class because she had never studied chemistry or physics. I could not understand how any credible biology program did not include at least chemistry. I asked her how she answers students' questions about chemistry. She replied, "I read them what's in the book." I understood how Newport students were ill prepared to study science in college. I also wondered about the ethical standards at this school.

I found that the other science teachers had a heavy reliance on the textbook.

Teachers who focus so intently on the textbook heavily rely on the supplemental materials, otherwise called worksheets. Some put them together in "packets." These turn into word search activities. Find the statement with the corresponding terms in the textbook, then fill in the blanks. We developed word recognition skills but did not learn the underlying concepts. Students learned nothing. The science laboratories were in disorder. Old student projects occupied much of the space.

I could not understand why teachers are extensively educated in curriculum and concept development but rely upon a textbook and worksheets. We can research the national and state standards and develop our own curriculum, lesson plans, and assessments. The first years kept me up until midnight preparing for the next day. In time, I had a curriculum that was easily modified and improved from year to year. One veteran colleague, Gene Grumman, said it well, "I never teach a class the same way twice." This is admirable because no class is the same as another. A teacher best prepares one's students by adjusting methods to meet their needs while focusing on the concept.

I disagreed with my colleagues when it came to deducting points for late work. I felt that the grade should reflect the student's understanding of the concepts as defined in the standards. Lateness is a separate matter and should be dealt with separately. Granted, teachers do not have a lot in their toolbox for this. We can call home and keep students after school or during lunch. It is always best when we can encourage students in positive ways in recognizing timely accomplishments. Deserving praise from a teacher with high standards helps students' self-image.

It did not take long before I began to understand the relationship between the principal and the faculty. The social studies teacher, Mark Mayo, across the hall from me was often involved in shouting matches with him. The anger was obvious. The topics were more obscure. I could identify with Mark's passion for his curriculum while Barry was trying to change it.

At the first progress report submission, Barry came to my classroom. He leaned into the door and was holding some papers in front of his chest as he spoke. "We do not give 'tween grades here." I told him that I did not understand. "You gave a sixty-nine to John (name changed). You need to change it to a seventy or reduce it to a sixty-eight." I was a bit stunned by this generalized intrusion into a typically teacher autonomous practice. Besides, it was only a progress report and not a grade of record. For grades of record, teachers often review the students' performance against the standards and make warranted adjustments. Never have I reduced a grade. This committed me to change the grade to seventy, even though I felt it was not deserved. John was not a motivated student. The grade of D might help him realize that he needs to work harder at his studies. As I expected, it was difficult to motivate John to perform better after the progress report. He replied with "I got a C in this class," as he refused to do any work. John ended up failing the class. He was among my few students who failed, which was always for not doing the work. Parents justifiably demand explanations on how their student went from a C to and F.

My greatest conflict with Principal Barry Connell was over attendance. The Newport School Board had a strict attendance policy. If a student missed more than ten days that were unexcused, that student would not receive credit for the course, regardless of the grade. It was difficult because the student had to remain in the class, even though there was no chance of passing. These students were often disruptive.

Teachers took attendance in the grading program. After submitting it, only an administrator could change it. Since the grading program occasionally crashed, I kept a separate record. I discovered that Barry Connell was changing my submission from absent to present. It was well known among the students that one student saw no reason to come to school because he was earning money selling drugs. I worried that Barry Connell was unknowingly making me the student's alibi for drug dealing. If the police report criminal involvement during the time he was supposed to be in my class, a lawyer will use my attendance record to avoid prosecution. If I were ever subpoenaed to testify, I would bring my own records and explain that the school's records were unreliable, even uncreditable.

Barry Connell was also spiteful towards behaviorally challenging students. I had a difficult student who rallied at the end of the semester and passed my class. The following year I saw him coming out of another teacher's biology class and asked him why. He told me that he had failed mine. I told him that he passed and that I would advocate for him. He did not want me to challenge it. He thought that it would bring other wrath against him and did not mind taking the class again.

I left Newport after two years and took a position as the Sullivan County Court Diversion Director. I enjoyed working with youth offenders to avoid the court system. Once involved with the courts, it is very difficult to get free of it. It did not keep me as busy as I like to be, so I found an online teaching position with the Virtual Learning Academy Charter School. As funding for the diversion program became uncertain, I took a position with the Sullivan County Department of Corrections. I started as a corrections officer and moved into case management. I enjoyed helping people as they transitioned from jail. Most found jobs, a place to live and restored relationships with their families. I found satisfaction in helping these people while maintaining a teaching opportunity. I also taught some chemistry and environmental science at the community college. My extensive and diverse education and experiences gave me a lot of flexibility in employment.

My two grandchildren spent most of their weekends with me from infants to adolescence. I enjoyed every minute. It was like returning to the best days of my life when my daughters were young. The daily rituals were the same, doing everything from chores, planning meals, evening entertainment and bedtime. We went on hikes, picnics, day trips, and even spent a weekend in the White Mountains. I was confident in my parenting abilities, allowing me to enjoy our strong relationships. I was also very careful to respect my daughter's parental authority.

I gained some more insight into addiction while working with court diversion and county corrections. Some had very difficult withdrawals. After the withdrawal, I asked if it was enough for them to stay away from alcohol and drugs. All said that it was not going to stop them. They added that they feel normal only when they are using their drug of choice. I tried to understand their compulsion to their preferred drug. I once used an analogy. One potato chip would not hurt my diet. Two are OK. I ate more, deciding that I would exercise a little extra. Finally, it did not matter how much I ate. I knew it was wrong but continued regardless of the harm it was doing. The addicts agreed with this analogy.

Most spoke about their dedication to their children and spousal relationships, which seemed genuine in the early phases of their incarceration. Their families called, wrote, and visited with them. I watched their transition from being worried about their loved ones to an increasingly more self-centered posture during their incarceration. The longer the men were in jail, the more selfish they became. They began demanding money in their commissary as their families struggled financially. I heard parts of conversations about how the inmate pressured the visitor to neglect her and the children's needs to make a deposit into his commissary. Commissary was used to buy snacks, soaps, deodorant, music players, writing and other supplies beyond the provided hygiene products. Commissary turned into a black-market trade within the jail. They shared their commissary for favors in and out of jail. Drugs smuggled into jail could be sold for many times their street value. Money was often transferred outside of jail as they continued their drug business.

The first time I saw the line form at med call was surprising. It seemed like more than half of them needed some sort of medication. There were those who needed medications for valid medical reasons, but they were few. Most were taking psychological medication. I learned about the general categories in college. During the day, many took some sort of stimulant. The superintendent was against medications such as suboxone to reduce the cravings. The psychiatrist relied heavily on antidepressants such as Wellbutrin. In the evening, many got a sleep aide. It is a constant problem in jails and prisons to prevent misuse of these medicines. They may try to "cheek" them, hiding them between their teeth and cheek or under their tongue. The nurse and corrections officer jointly confirm that the medication was swallowed. A liquid form of the medication was used, when possible, to eliminate this problem with a known offender. Cheeking them could be profitable. Drugs can be sold in jail. Addicts have no reservation about taking a drug that was in someone's mouth. Some medicinal effects can be magnified by crushing and inhaling it. Without their prescribed medications, drug users self-medicate. Sometimes, they can trade or sell the prescribed medication and buy greater amounts of street drugs.

Frustrating for me was many people's inflated dependency on medication. I am not totally against medication, but I believe that it should be uncommon. Most of the people in jail and foster care take medicine. It seemed like a crutch to me. It was convenient to excuse bad behavior on the lack of the medication or its improper dose. Medication may dull motivation or reduce impulsiveness, but it does not cause the behavior. Drug users need something or someone to blame, like my mother did.

I worked hard to transition inmates out of jail. I found that having good family support was the greatest asset and indicator of their success. They needed meaningful employment and a place to live. If the family could provide a dependable place to live, half their needs would be met. Continued support from support groups and proper medication was also helpful. It also required a great deal of motivation. For many of us, our family needs are a motivator as they were for them. Unfortunately, the addiction is so powerful that they will sacrifice their families' needs. They still said that they were good fathers. I could understand how some families felt it necessary to sever ties to the inmate. I always tried to repair these relationships because I knew how important they were to everyone. I could relate because my mother neglected our needs and how important her beer was for her. I was trying to sever my relationship with my mother.

I recognized this brainwashing to protect the addict from my childhood. My mother repeated many times that she was a good mother. My younger siblings believed it throughout their childhood and adulthood. The vast amounts of the very limited money went to buy her beer while we wore shoes that were falling apart and clothes that did not fit. One young man's story resonates with me. His pregnant girlfriend always came to visit. He boasted about his masculinity and fatherhood. Having two kids in Pennsylvania and two others in Florida was evidence of his masculinity and paternal powers. I once interrupted his moment of bragging with how could he be a good father to kids across the country? He replied, "What? They know who their father is." I responded, "I tuck my kids into bed every night" and left the conversation. This person eventually left jail, then committed several bank robberies. He is now serving a lengthy prison sentence as a career criminal. Perhaps he still believes that he is a good father.

I was very disappointed when I saw someone return to jail. When they left, they had a job, a place to live, and restored family relationships. Some of the problems were that they had minimum wage jobs due to their low level of education. The rent became due. Their budget was too tight and could not pay the rent. Unfortunately, they knew how to make some money quickly. While doing so, they tried a little bit of their wares. A common excuse was that they stopped taking their meds. Medications do not prevent criminal behavior. The overpowering needs to satisfy their addiction and its high cost led to their criminal behavior. The coming off medication took the blame off and placed it upon an intangible source. Putting blame on their probation officer was another way to shift the blame. I saw this as the equivalent of blaming the police officer for the driving under the influence charge for being overzealous. Addicts believe their own lies.

RECOVERY FROM AN ALCOHOLIC'S COLLATERAL DAMAGE

I am saddened by another person's story. Bill was twenty-eight now. I first met him when I worked for the Claremont Police Department. His father had retired from the navy then from the Claremont Fire Department. Norm was working as a part-time parking code enforcement officer. Fourteen-year-old Billy came to meet him at the police department when he got off work. Billy was a likeable, friendly young man. Now he was in jail for dealing narcotic drugs. He described how hard the addiction was for him. His mother was dying from cancer. She received home hospice and each family member took turns standing by. When Bill took his turn, he saw his mother's narcotic pain killers. He described how hard it was for him not to take his dying mother's narcotics. He quickly interjected that he never did. It reminded me of how my mother's compulsion drove her to steal all my college money. Bill's love for his mother helped him resist his powerfully addictive urges. My mother had no such consideration for me. If anything, she felt a right to take my earnings because she was my mother.

Bill had a six-year-old daughter who came to visit with her mother. Bill had separated from her mother years ago. The girl's mother had full custody but recognized the value of her daughter's relationship with her father. Bill was a skilled machinist and could earn enough money to pay for her child support and buy her additional things but spent it all on drugs. He had a job as a machinist when he left jail. He got an apartment near his employer in Manchester. It seemed like he was going to be successful this time. About a month later, Bill called me when I was home one evening. He said that he needed to borrow eight hundred dollars for a security deposit on an apartment. I knew that he had an apartment when he left jail last month. I also knew that eight hundred dollars was the typical amount paid for his drugs. All that aside, I would never loan money to a former inmate, even one I knew as a child. I politely declined Bill's request, citing my own financial obligations. Bill graciously accepted my decision. My heart sunk deeply when I hung up the telephone. I knew that Bill was back into his addiction and in decline. His health, family and freedom will suffer.

All humans are clever. It has been our greatest asset as a species. We can review and construct plans in our minds. In jail, when they sit around all day with nothing to occupy their thoughts. Some plot ways to get around the limits of their confinement. Some challenge the rules. Others violate the rules to avoid detection of wrongdoing or try to defend their actions. Transitions are more successful when correction programs keep their participants busy. I saw this prankster trait in industrial work environments where workers complete mindless tasks. I also see it in schools when students are not intellectually challenged. These are the same skills alcoholics use to perpetuate their condition.

Living in the community, I often cross paths with former inmates and students. It tests my memory on how they knew me. Did I know them as a student? Was it someone I arrested, a former inmate, a former classmate, or something else? When our eyes met, I could immediately determine how well they were doing. If they were doing well, they called me and we would quickly catch up on their lives. If they were doing poorly, they would turn away and pretend not to notice me.

All addiction is horrible. As a child, I was most familiar with alcohol addiction in my family. From preadolescence, I knew how much mother's beer drinking cost all of us. Our welfare benefits were meager but we were in absolute poverty with the money that she diverted to buy her beer. She felt she deserved it for what she had been through and continues to suffer. She blamed my father, who she drove away. I recognized the commonalities among addicts and the power it had over their lives. They all justified their addiction, placing no blame on themselves.

In college, I learned what was known about chemicals' effects on nerve synapses. Alcohol tends to slow down nerve transmission through these connections. Drugs can slow it down, speed it up, or cause signals to generate on their own. The mechanisms were not well understood then and remain so presently. When working with psychiatrists for our foster children, they selected a treatment medicine from a variety of options. Next, they adjusted the dosage increasingly higher to discover its benefits. If they could not achieve the desired results, they would try a different medication. I remain skeptical about this "science" in that it is mostly guesswork and trial and error. My ultimate bewilderment is how much our society depends on drugs. How often do people get special treatment because they were "off their medication?"

We humans try to make sense of this crazy world we created for ourselves. We naturally seek symmetry, patterns, routine, and consistency so that we can predict and control outcomes. Our primary desired outcome is to be safe. Other things necessary to survive follow. When we do not have this control, we get very anxious, and try to bring things back to where we can manage. Food, shelter, and companionship are some desired positive outcomes. Avoiding unpleasant things is a negative motivator. The direction one takes to avoid a negative motivator is far less specific than motivation towards a positive goal. Negative motivation can lead to some unintended negative outcomes. It is much more productive to work towards a positive goal than it is to avoid a negative condition. Fear is perhaps the strongest negative motivator intended to assure survival in critically dangerous situations. It is often used by many leaders. It is the worst possible way to motivate people or even to train animals. When motivated by fear, we lose our rational thoughts and focus only on immediate survival. Positive goals involve rational, long-range thinking.

Some leaders use milder forms of control with information. Withholding broader knowledge or goals keeps the leader in control. Some will share what they decide is the smallest portion of the information that a person needs to accomplish the task. Many of us have attended routine meetings where the agenda is given at the beginning of the meeting. Competent, confident leaders seek to include the knowledge and experience of their followers. These leaders share the known information and current goals. They solicit feedback and welcome suggestions. They send out the meeting agenda in advance. Competent leaders want people to be prepared for the meeting and welcome changes and additions to the agenda. Leaders too insecure in sharing information and control will lead organizations to no greater than themselves. The greatest organizations recognize the value of each of their members and encourage them to exercise their knowledge and skills. Our strength as a society has always been our diversity. This is true throughout the biological world.

We also need to identify our limits. A foster child's therapist once asked me, "What is your red line" I asked her to explain. She wanted to know what behavior is the worst that we would accept in our home. If the behavior became worse than this red line, we would ask for the removal of the child. I thought for a moment and responded that I would not tolerate behavior that hurts another person in our home. Our discussion clarified that if the foster child hurt someone outside our home, we would likely continue with our efforts to retain stability for the child.

The reason she asked me this question was followed by a warning. This child would escalate his behavior to find out how we would react until we reached our limit. His history was to destroy placements when he did not get his way. She warned that he was going to test us to our red line and maybe a little beyond it just to discover how much he could misbehave and remain in our home. She added that he would seek this red line and repeatedly test it. It was going to be a rough ride until he finally settled into more reasonable behavior. There are foster kids who give up on the placement and smash through the red line to move to another placement. This way they have control over the placement failing and did not feel like a victim.

I later learned about behavior management techniques during specialized training. Life Skills Crisis Intervention (LSCI) sought to identify circumstances and behavior that preceded the misbehavior. By addressing the feelings that manifested in the behavior, one would have a better opportunity to modify the behavior before it escalated. I worried when this was applied to assaultive behavior. When discussing the child's feelings, one must be very careful that one is not providing justification for the assault. I stand firm on my red line. There are no excuses for assaulting someone. The assault is wrong. Responsibility must be centered on the aggressor. Whatever led up to this can be addressed but in such a way that the aggressor retains full responsibility for his or her actions. Understanding my mother's alcohol addiction and others' drug addiction helped me to place the responsibility for behavior on the actor.

I learned about "criminal thinking" with therapists in correctional institutions. The techniques used in Life Skills Crisis Intervention could help expose the criminal thinking in an aggressor. The work on the circumstances preceding the assault is intended to expose the criminal thinking and redirect it. Criminal thinking is thought processes that justify criminal behavior. Most of the LCIS practice that I have seen provides a level of justification that the child will seize upon.

I also learned about Positive Behavior Intervention and Supports (PBIS). It simply rewards good behavior. They concept is that rewarded behavior will be repeated while unrewarded behavior will extinguish. Responding to undesirable behavior could be a reward, negative attention. Rewards can be for short or long periods of good behavior or a single act. It works well when the rewards are meaningful. The rewards must be relevant and the child must perform identifiable good behavior. If the rewards are too easy to attain, they will learn to feel entitled to the reward without really earning it. Rewards can be simple praise, a level of monetary allowance, later bedtime, special time with a favored adult, or a desired activity. Stickers or check marks on a paper chart are meaningless unless they earn a relevant reward.

I must wonder. How did so many behavior management systems develop? Why does one have an advantage over another in different settings? Aren't humans all the same? What is the underlying concept to all these systems? Could it be because someone developed a program to earn a doctorate, then tried to use it to make money? All these systems or programs involve motivating behavior. We can never completely understand the psychological processes and the emotional influences on the behavior but we can define the behavior well. I refer to my science education. Science is measurable, quantifiable, testable, and repeatable. It involves two identical groups when one can be a control group. The experimental group receives only the one change that we are trying to measure. This is impossible with humans. We are too complex. Additionally, most experiments upon humans would be unethical. For instance, you cannot deprive a group of vitamin C to prove it will cause rickets, poor bone development. We must wait for a group that has a vitamin C deficient diet to reach that conclusion. Again, humans are too complex. It is likely vitamin C is not the only deficiency. Human data can never be scientifically pure.

Teaching effectively to a wide variety of students is difficult. New Hampshire education standards limited the number of students in science laboratory courses to twenty-four for safety reasons. Of those twenty-four, I wondered how many went home to an alcoholic parent, like I did. I expected at least one or two in every class. I assumed nearly all came from families that used alcohol. As I taught over the years, I found a few of them had parents in prison or had served time in prison. Some students were supervised by a juvenile services officer because the student had committed a crime and is on probation. Some were under the care of child services. A few were in foster care. Some had been in residential programs. With so much disruption in their lives, they often had gaps in their education. Most were behind in the language arts. Reading and writing are the most fundamental topic students must master to be successful. Others lagged in their math knowledge and skills. Both these skills are essential to understand science concepts. I was strong in math but weak in reading and writing. I did not improve these skills until I was in college. It left me at a disadvantage with my peers until I improved these skills. Unfortunately, I found most of the students who were far behind in these essential skills preferred to give up. It was easier for them to say that they do not need school than to look stupid trying to improve them.

When I worked in corrections, I found a greater sense of integrity among correctional officers than I found with the police officers. Unfortunately, I found a similar sense of superiority among the corrections personnel. As a member of the treatment side of corrections, I found myself working against the security side of corrections. I once heard a corrections officer tell an inmate that he needed to shave, saying "You can't get recovery without shaving?" I couldn't be quiet. I asked him to explain. He said, "They have to learn the rules." So, I asked, "That means everyone with a beard is a drug addict?" This corrections officer had a beard. I saw this in foster care, too. Placements create an artificial environment. Compliance with rules for the smooth operation of the program is used to predict compliance with rules in the greater society. I believed that it was a false indicator. It proved only that the person could manipulate your perception of their behavior. Programs are beneficial when they teach the value of routine and structure in one's daily life and transition that responsibility onto the person. Program inflexibility can be worse than the sudden release from it.

There was a corrections lieutenant who constantly lectured everyone. My grandmother described these people as having the gift of gab. He made it nearly impossible to get a word in, and when you did, he summarily dismissed any opposing view. The few times I got his attention, I tried to get him to understand Mikey's Philosophy. "If you want your words to count, there must be fewer of them." He could not understand how much people just tuned him out. I grew more frustrated with him when he increasingly removed job search privileges for trivial things such as a bed made without crisp hospital corners. He was a former navy boiler room enlisted man with little rank. I was a commissioned army combat officer. He barely graduated high school yet felt superior to educated professionals. He is one to say, "You don't need a college education" and belittled people who had one. He could never understand what Saint Michael's College did for me. Mikey's Philosophy also states that "No well-educated person ever said their education had no value." This lieutenant seemed to get pleasure in undoing the things I helped inmates accomplish. He did many passive aggressive things. He would never realize that his incessant speech was overly aggressive. It is very difficult to express one's ideas with such an unreasonably controlling person. I checked into retirement and realized that I get just as much money as working. I could collect my pension and work elsewhere, which I did. Avoiding a narcissist is the best strategy and one I practiced well by avoiding my mother. Dealing with a narcissist is much like dealing with an alcoholic in denial.

Returning to teaching was difficult with three college degrees, decades of experience, and being highly qualified in all the core sciences. It put me at the top of the union negotiated pay scale. A school district could hire two inexperienced teachers for the same amount of money. I continued teaching with an online charter school and I did some short-term teaching for desperate school districts, some adjunct community college, online, and private school instruction. It feels good to remain among educated, ethical professionals.

Foster Parenting

KAY AND I had built our dream home to share with our two wonderful daughters. I was working as a police officer during this time. I saw many families that were living in conditions like my childhood. I had sympathy and tried to facilitate services for them. These families were distrustful of government agencies, just as my mother was. They trusted the police even less, fearing an arrest that would disrupt their family even more. Most had a minimal education and found it difficult to find a job that would meet even their basic needs. Some, like my mother, did not want a job and relied entirely upon public assistance.

There was a prevalence of domestic violence, which was often how the police became involved with families. It is true that domestic violence occurs at all levels of our society, but it is the children in the lower income ones that are most affected. They are the ones least likely to seek or accept assistance. The laws improved. Police could arrest someone now when there was probable cause that a domestic assault had occurred within six hours. Evidence often included red marks or bruises and an oral statement about who caused these injuries. The intention was to prevent the violence from continuing when the police left. If we did not have sufficient evidence for an arrest, we could use protective custody for up to twenty-four hours. Protective custody is to protect the individual or another person. Typically, the person was intoxicated and we kept them until they were sober. Another tactic was to convince the aggressor to spend the night with other family or a friend. I preferred this option because it avoided the liability of injury to the agitated and uncooperative individual. Most accepted this option over lockup. Disturbing to me were the conversations I had with the ones that I was taking into protective custody. These men explained to me why they were angry at their mate. They seemed to expect my understanding because we were of the same gender. I firmly shut them down by firmly saying, "No one deserves being hit." What also bothered me is when I made the arrest for a violent assault. Six weeks later when the case was heard in court, the couple united and testified the police were wrong. I found more success in convincing the woman to bring the charges. It seemed that fewer of these cases were dropped.

I understood well the effects these domestic violence environments had on the children. They are being taught that violence is acceptable, even necessary. "Spare the rod and spoil the child" has a deep history. Many say, "I was spanked and turned out OK." Comments like, "He hit me for no reason" justify violence if there is an acceptable reason. I saw my mother brutally beat my father several times. He did not even defend himself. I suffer every day from a traumatic brain injury that affects vision in my right eye and a collapsed sinus from my mother's brutal discipline. Similarly, alcohol and drugs were equally normal in a troubled relationship. Perceived unequal sharing of the alcohol, drugs, cigarettes, or money were often the reason for the arguments. Children saw that using these substances was a transition into adulthood, which they did at a very early age.

It was understandable that the older children would run away from such a household. Compounding their reasoning was that they felt entitled to have similar partying and sexual relationships among their peers at a very young age. I was quite successful at finding runaway youth because I understood their home life. I had another advantage as I substitute taught middle and high school on my days off. I already knew many youths and understood why they also had trouble in school.

I first met Joey when he was eleven years old. His biological parents never lived together. His mother was an alcoholic, had only alcoholic friends, and lived in substandard housing. Her discipline style was overly permissive. Perhaps Joey was better able to make decisions than his mother but they were still poor decisions. Joey could come and go from home as he pleased and liked to smoke marijuana. Joey's father lived in a nicer home, provided him with nice things including a four-wheeler but was overly strict. Joey's mother signed over legal custody to his father because she could not handle him anymore. Joey's father was overly strict and violently enforced his rules. Joey was often beaten. Sometimes stripped naked and beaten. Joey often visited his mother on weekends, which his father reluctantly agreed knowing Joey would be unsupervised. Joey failed to return to his father after one of these visits. His father reported him missing. I found Joey walking along the sidewalk with his cousin and returned him to his father.

Over the next three years, Joey often ran away from his father. I was getting to know his family and friends very well and they were getting to know me. It was easy to find him. I started with his mother. She told me where she thought he would be. If he was not there, that person would suggest other places. In a short while, I would find Joey and bring him to his father.

As I routinely patrolled my beat one day, the juvenile officer called me on the radio to meet him in front of the police station. He came out with Joey reluctantly by his side. Joey was now fourteen years old. The juvenile officer put Joey in the back seat and got in the front. He leaned towards me and said, "Go to the Chandler House." The Chandler House was a small, short-term residence for adolescents. It was named after Wells Chandler, an attorney who advocated for a local residential facility for children. The idea is to keep children in their home community to minimize disruption.

We brought Joey inside together. The juvenile officer brought the necessary paperwork to the Chandler House staff. I knew Joey well and could see that he was very angry. He refused to talk to me, which was unusual. When we got back in the car, I said to the juvenile officer, "He's not going to stay there." His response was, "Good, then I can lock him up." This would be the state facilities in Concord or Manchester, New Hampshire. I did not like how the juvenile officer treated children. He did not graduate high school, having only a GED, Graduate Equivalency Diploma, the minimal education acceptable to police. I had a master's degree and studied much child development. I felt that Joey was being harshly prosecuted without being offered supporting services. This seemed to be a common practice with this juvenile officer. If the child did not show the respect he wanted, he treated them harshly while ignoring the needs of others.

As I predicted, the Chandler House reported Joey missing three days later. As usual, I found him a short while later. When I radioed that I had him in custody, the juvenile officer told me to bring him directly to court. He asked me to stay with Joey to make sure that he did not run away. Joey never ran from me. I would easily catch him if he did. The juvenile officer was a heavy smoker. He would not be able to run fast enough to catch him.

As I listened in the court room, there was much discussion on what to do with Joey. His public attorney argued that he should be returned to the Chandler House, but the Chandler House refused. The judge rejected requests to return him to his family because the juvenile officer opposed it. The judge also did not want to lock him up for running away. Only the violent ones should go to locked facilities. If there was no alternative, she would have no choice. It seemed like the juvenile officer was going to get his way. She looked about the court room and said, "Is there anyone here that would take him?" Her eyes swept back and forth across the court room and stopped, looking directly at me. She repeated her question while fixing it on me. I felt uncomfortably on the spot. I knew that Joey had some good points and sending him to "juvey jail" would do more harm than good. I agreed to take him. She looked at the child protective worker and asked if she could approve it. She said that she could issue an emergency foster care permit and follow up with the proper training and certification. I called Kay for her approval and our foster care experience began.

Joey was a difficult child and initiated us into the greatest challenges in fostering a troublesome child. Joey would get off the bus and not go into the school. When I brought him and made certain that he entered the building, I could drive around back and catch him coming out the back door. Joey, like many children with disrupted education, hated school because he was so far behind his peers. He did not want to look stupid. It is better to be a bad kid than it is to be a stupid kid. Joey ended up being placed in an Eckerd Family

Service program in Colebrook, New Hampshire. He completed the yearlong program and we sponsored him through it, coming home more frequently towards the end. The program did not graduate him at the end of the year. They said that they wanted to observe his behavior in the community for three more months. This hurt Joey. He felt that he had earned something that was taken away. He was angry at the program and seemed to give up. I felt that Joey had been addicted to marijuana, even though many experts said that it was not physiologically possible. I disagreed but we agreed that Joey was at least psychologically dependent upon it. Feeling cheated and wanting revenge, Joey decided to seek out old friends and get stoned. We lost our chances with him after this. He was almost eighteen and the system, the courts and child services, did not want to waste any more services on him. I reported him missing and no one went to look for him. It was difficult for me but I did not look for him. I had hoped to see him and convince him to come home. I heard nothing until he got arrested for burglary as an adult.

Joey's family had many similarities to mine. His mother was an alcoholic with no desire to change. The family blamed others for their demise and had no desire to improve themselves. Most members of my family graduated high school but only I went to college or served in the military. No one in Joey's family graduated high school. Joey lived with his mother and his father was mostly absent until the last few months before coming to our family.

There were some profound differences between Joey's and my family. Joey was one of five children. None of Joey's siblings shared the same two parents. Each parent had three children. Joey had two siblings with whom he shared his father. The other two with his mother. Joey lived with his older sister and younger brother. He hardly knew his paternal siblings who lived in another state. My siblings and I shared the same parents.

In Joey's scattered family was a personal value upon sexual relationships. Attraction to and involvement with the opposite sex was a measure of one's personal value. Joey's family members were all sexually active at an early age. The younger that one was sexually active, the greater his or her value. Joey's mother once boasted to me that Joey got his first blow job under the stairs to their apartment when he was three years old. An older girl pulled his diaper down to perform the act. Our family discouraged and strongly controlled our relationships with the opposite sex.

After he was with us for a few months, I learned more about how Joey's family culture had conflicting values around homosexuality. They seemed to tolerate homosexual individuals but strived not to be identified as one. Joey was dating a girl and deceived us about their activities. We thought that they were dating in public places. We even gave him money for the movies. When I learned that he was in a sexual relationship, I expressed my surprise and concern. Joey answered, "We have been dating for two months." After a pause, he added, "I'm not gay." In Joey's world, a relationship with the opposite sex must soon become sexual to prove one's sexuality. Sexuality is a significant component in an individual's personal value.

Life is getting very complicated as we are expected to respect others' choices for pronouns referring to them. It seems to be a personal demand to recognize their nonconforming sexuality. Why has one's sexual preference become so important that I must make major adaptations? My interaction with people has nothing to do with their gender or sexual preferences. I very much want to show respect to everyone. This expectation and my limited memory are driving me to avoid using pronouns. It is a set up for failure. I learn a lot about that person's personality on how they react to my failure to meet their demands. I must wonder. How they feel about the assigned genders to nouns in the French and Spanish languages often spoken around me? I remember my grandfather, who spoke a dialect of Canadian French, often referred to objects as she and he. I realized that these corresponded with their French gender.

Applying my education on Darwin's evolutionary, I could see some logic in a species survival. The success of a species depends upon its ability to transfer its genes to a new generation. The most competitive individuals and species were the most successful. Being the first to mate leads to the first to produce the next generation. As a species, they would not want to waste limited resources on individuals who did not mate to produce offspring. This is why some cultures abandon imperfect babies in the jungle.

I considered how this primitive logic threads through our larger society. It fuels the hate groups who do not share their values such as sexuality, religion, income, housing, and education. Joey's lower class sexual relationships encouraged unprotected sex at an early age. Larger groups discriminated against mixed marriages or relationships. Whole nations fought over resources, such as land. This has been happening for thousands of years. The Old Testament Bible documents wars for the Holy Land. When are we going to realize that working together with our diversity is the best way to assure our species' success?

Joey's family subculture allowed adult choices at a very early age, well before children could manage the responsibilities. I realized that the adults delegating the permissiveness also made poor decisions. The adults placed their own self-worth on their sexual prowess. Decisions on tobacco, alcohol and drugs were also in this category. Joey was allowed these adult privileges and was making decisions as an adult in this subculture. Openly smoking cigarettes was a strong signal to others that he was independent and could make his own decisions. Joey was unable to make good decisions but sadly he was better than his mother and most adults around him.

Joey's concepts of sex roles were profound. Kay came home one afternoon upset with herself for losing a twenty-dollar bill in a parking lot. I acknowledged that she was upset and let her process it as she does with similar disappointments. She complained aloud about herself to herself. Joey came over to me and quietly said, "Aren't you going to bitch her out for that?" I replied that I was not. He added, "But you worked hard for that money." I explained that she worked hard for it, too, and that she earns more than I do. He still thought that I was neglecting my responsibility as the man of the house.

In Joey's family, older children, even preadolescents, participated in adult parties as equals. Joey especially liked marijuana. The adult family members found him skillful in finding it among the friends and neighbors who shared it with him. They thought that he was cute and charming. Joey justified his marijuana use as being "natural." He did not understand my response that arsenic was even more natural because it did not require cultivation. Aside from the few swigs of beer my siblings took from my mother, alcohol consumption was forbidden in my family. Drugs were considered evil. Only my cousins used marijuana as did their father, my uncle.

Though there were some contrasts, the underlying substance use, denial, and protected family secrecy were very similar and dominated social connections. No one in either of our families was interested in change. If it was necessary to establish blame, they blamed people outside the family, especially the police. As he grew older, Joey was no longer able to obtain his marijuana with his youthful cuteness and was expected to pay. He started financing his addiction with odd jobs, stealing jewelry, and eventually forging checks. His criminal activity eventually caught up to him. He was ordered into a residential treatment program from which he ran away. He eventually went to prison as an adult. As with all his placements as a youth and as an adult, he immediately returned to his prior ways. Any counseling or therapy he received during these placements was ineffective. We twice helped him transition from jail, then decided that we are only enabling him to maintain a lifestyle that we did not approve.

Joey graduated high school and earned an associate degree while in prison. It seemed like he was being well prepared during his incarceration. Unfortunately, every time he was released, he soon went back to his old ways of using marijuana and committing burglaries to pay for it. Joey has been in prison more than he has been free. Joey was never violent. Joey operates well in the prison structured environment. It confirms that residential programs are artificial environments with little connection to the real world. It is not a reliable indicator of successful transition into the community.

Our second foster child came as a referral from the same Eckerd program Joey attended. Mitch started his weekend visits and immediately connected with our family. He was a wonderful older brother to my two daughters and took his relationship with them seriously. Mitch was amazing. I would leave work expecting that I would mow the lawn, only to find Mitch had it done. He sought out opportunities to do chores. I found myself competing with him in order to do my fair share.

Mitch came from a different child services office than the one through which we were licensed. His case worker reviewed his file with us. He was in state custody for sexual assault but it should have been unfounded. The charge brought against Mitch was for shoving snow down the front of his friend's pants when they were playfully wrestling. Something that I might have done to my brother. The complaint came to the agency through a neighbor. Neither Mitch's nor his friend's family were concerned. They decided to make it founded so that they could take custody and get him out of his home. His mother was also an alcoholic. Unlike Joey's father and my mother who were dominant, Mitch's mother provided no effective supervision. She needed help with her own care. Mitch's father was deceased.

After Mitch was well settled into our family, we got a call from our local child services office. They wanted a meeting right away. At the meeting were our licensing worker, her supervisor, and a supervisor from the Concord main office. They learned about Mitch's charges. They did not seem to know the details. Kay and I were puzzled by their lack of knowledge since Mitch's social worker was so thorough with us. They wanted us to reject Mitch from our home. I began sensing some animosity between the district offices. They did not like another district using their homes. Of course, we refused to ask for Mitch's removal. In turn, they restricted our license to "child specific," which prevented any agency from placing another child with us while Mitch was with us. We appealed and lost in a power-played hearing. Mitch's social worker feared for her job and would not advocate for us.

We were happy with our family arrangement. Mitch was an ordinary teenage boy with typical testing of the rules. We are proud of him and the man he grew to be. He developed a good relationship with a young woman and has his own family. His children consider us their grandparents. The agency supervisors were wrong because they had no interest in getting to know the children as we foster parents do. Contrary to what they say, they consider foster parents as subordinates and not equal members of a caring team.

For many years, Mitch participated in family celebrations. We were a part of his growing family. While waiting for Thanksgiving dinner to be served, he said something quite profound. We were admiring the view out our front window. He said, "someday, I want to be rich." I agreed, "Me, too." He replied, "To me, this is rich." His perspective reminded me that we all identify success based on our individual experiences and ambitions.

Joey had a son. Like his father, Joey never lived with the boy's mother. Joey tried to establish a relationship with is son after one of his releases from prison. His mother was reluctant but eventually agreed if I supervised. Carlton was eight years old when I met him. He and Joey met a few times until Joey violated parole and was sent back to prison. Carlton's mother's fears were realized. She did not want Carlton to develop a relationship with Joey just to be let down. Kay and I were fortunate to be accepted and continued a grandparent relationship and Carlton spent some weekends with us. That relationship continues into his adulthood.

Due to our strained relationship with the social service agency, we went through a period with no foster children. The only thing that mattered to us was that we knew that there were children who needed a place like ours. We were resolved by knowing that it was the arrogance of the people in the agency. Our real-world care was vastly more successful than any of their artificial experiences. Eventually, they were desperate.

Luke was a fifteen-year-old child sexual predator. He liked four-year-old boys. The treatment programs were all full and he was on a waiting list. He could not go to a secure facility with other boys due to his predator status. The court was being forced to send him back home where he would most certainly offend again. His method was to invite these little boys to his room and play video games. He quickly groomed them into being his victim. His mother saw nothing wrong with what he was doing. She felt that he was being a good friend to boys that needed a friend. Our daughters were older than Luke and he was not interested. The agency asked for a week. I replied that a week often becomes four months. I knew and respected the exhausted social worker sighed when she said, I just want to get through the week. We reluctantly agreed to the placement that lasted four months.

Even though I had investigated and arrested sex offenders, I had never seen one so intent as Luke. He seemed to live, eat, and breathe seeking an opportunity to offend. Trying to understand him was difficult. His social worker told us that he had a working intelligent quotient of sixty-four. I found that he had a limited vocabulary but he understood everything if it was presented at his level.

There were other safeguards in place. Luke was transported to a private school in a Claremont School District van. There were other children in this van but Luke sat separately. At school, he was not allowed to have any money because he attempted to seduce a student at school using money. He was required to use the restroom alone. Luke frequently complained about these restrictions.

Luke came with a large remote-controlled truck. He played with it in our driveway. Unlike his home in the densely populated city, we were great distances from our neighbors. It was easy to supervise him as he played with his remote-controlled truck because our neighbors were far away and blocked by forest trees. Luke played with the truck until the battery was exhausted, then he went to his bedroom to charge the battery. He played with his video games or worked on his language programs on his laptop. He had no internet access.

I soon discovered a pattern to Luke's using his remote-control truck. Though we could not see our neighbors, we could hear them. One neighbor has small children and we could hear them playing. Luke operated the truck more energetically so that it made more noise when we heard the kids playing outside. I realized that he was trying to get our neighbor's children's attention.

The social worker called frequently as the weeks went by. I asked her about the remote-controlled truck. She verified my suspicion. Luke operated the toy on the quiet city street. When a small boy became interested, he would let him ride on the truck. When the battery was exhausted, Luke invited the boy to his room to play video games while the battery was recharged. This was how he groomed small boys and he was trying to attract our neighbor's children. I sent the truck home to his mother.

As the weeks turned into months, Carlton wanted to come for a weekend. He was thirteen years old now so I thought he would be safe. Our living room is large with an open kitchen so we could monitor their contact. I agreed to let him visit but told him that he must not be alone with Luke. Carlton's visit went well. Luke sat beside Carlton briefly to see the handheld video game Carlton was playing, then Luke got up quickly and went to his room. Carlton came to me and said, "Luke has a lot of money." I asked him to explain. He demonstrated how Luke showed him a bundle of money. Luke had eight dollars. He held it close to him in a roll to make it appear to be much more. Carlton also said that after he showed me the money, he said that he had a laptop in his room. I thanked Carlton for telling me and told him that he did the right thing, reaffirming that he cannot be alone with Luke.

This was a huge awakening to me. I was less than six feet away and yet Luke managed to make this proposal without me noticing. I was learning firsthand the deviousness and persistence of a hardcore sex offender. I decided that Luke could not have any money at our home like with school. I also sent the laptop back to his home. He protested that he used it for a speech program but I remained firm. He could not have any means to lure children while he was at our home.

These sex offenders seem to have an addiction at least as powerful as any alcoholic or drug addict. Like addiction, his means to support the addiction were kept secret. Neither he nor his mother saw anything wrong with what he was doing. His mother thought that he was being a good friend to his four-year-old victims. Luke insisted that he was only showing boys "how to have a good time." Luke justified his addiction and his mother enabled it.

Life was growing more intense with Luke. He called his mother every day at 5:25 PM. I gave little attention to what he told his mother. What little I heard seemed to be repeated many times during their twenty-minute calls. He always told his mother what he had for meals. One time he caught my attention when he said that dinner was fifteen minutes late. We regularly varied dinner depending on what the family was doing. Another time it was far more serious. "I talked him out of it" got my attention during one of these calls. I waited for the inevitable restatement. Luke explained that I challenged him to a fight and invited him to the front lawn for the fight. He talked me out of it. It concerned me on many levels. The ridiculousness was the least. A person with an intelligence quotient of sixty-four is not going to outsmart someone with two master's degrees. I was also concerned about the many false reports made against foster parents. Mostly, I was afraid that his mother may show up at my house with a shotgun to protect her little boy. I called the social worker and told her that the four months had passed and that she had to move him as soon as possible. They managed to find a place for the next weekend, then he went to the residential treatment program.

Two years later, I noticed Luke working at the McDonald's drive-through. With a brief calculation, I realized that he was now eighteen years old and would have aged out of the system. Once the money stops, these "caring" residential programs abruptly discontinue services. As much as state and private agencies say they care about the children they serve they ultimately care more about their agency. Bound by confidentiality, I hoped that his treatment was successful.

A few days later, I noticed Luke pacing back and forth in front of an elementary school as I drove by on my way home from teaching at the high school. I struggled for a bit then decided confidentiality be damned. Childrens' well-being was at stake. I went to the school resource officer. I explained to him my predicament. He agreed to watch Luke for a violation of the disorderly conduct statute. Hanging around a school with young children when you had no business with the school would be a cause for public alarm, which is a violation of this statute. I also warned the school resource officer that, if they got a report of abuse from a young child, to treat it as credible. Small children often do not understand their abuse and cannot express it with their limited, innocent vocabulary.

It did not take long before the police had a report. Surprisingly, it came from a fourteen-year-old boy. Luke had invited him to play video games, then touched his groin while he was focused on the game. With the information I gave to the school resource officer, the police were able to locate his treatment program. The psychiatrist expressed his concern and gave a dire warning. Luke did not respond to treatment and regressed in their program. The psychiatrist feared that Luke might escalate to killing his victims. The last thing I heard was that Luke was committed to the New Hampshire State Hospital.

I had to wonder. What is it that one human being can prey on another in such horribly vicious ways? Is it just a deviant expression of the behavior I saw in alcoholics and drug addicts? They supported their addictions at the expense of their families. I wondered if there was some harm done to the complex chemistry of nerve synapses that compelled this behavior like what nicotine does. What seems to connect these addiction behaviors is a powerful human behavior drive. We treat alcohol, drug, and sex addicts and offenders with programs of varying intensity. These treatments have limited success. Many drug addicts attend several programs before finding success in one.

In trying to make sense of addiction, I thought of it as a compulsive disorder. There is something about the substance that is attributed to a compulsive need. During my environmental biology studies, I learned about behavioral drives such as hunger and sex. Hunger drives were necessary for the survival of the individual. Sex drives assured continuation of the species. I noticed in some that their addiction was an even stronger drive. Could it be that the addiction drive replaced other drives? It seemed to be on a spectrum. At the far end of the spectrum, the addict would not eat, preferred drugs over sex, and lost any parental instinct to care for their children. They drove away their families. Fortunately for some, someone cared enough about them to contact emergency services and get help. Those lower in the spectrum were always on a roller coaster ride with the ups and downs and near crashes. Their families ride another roller coaster by their side, connected with a bungy cord. As the addict's roller coaster goes in one direction, the bungy cord stretches and eventually snaps the family's roller coaster in the addict's general direction. Both can fall off track into a crisis.

Many of us have compulsions. Some of us compulsively seek order and consistency. We cannot relax until certain things are in order. I have noticed addicts in recovery have a new or increased compulsion to do something. Cleanliness and neatness seem to be common. Some take up new ventures such as health groups, yoga, painting, writing, and many more. In biology, we call tis replacement behavior. If the replacement behavior fades, the undesirable behavior is likely to return.

I noticed that my compulsions tend to ones that oppose my mother's practices. We grew up in a dirty, cluttered house where many things did not work. It was always an apartment with the lowest rent. Much of the time we had only three rooms for the five of us. For several years, we went without water when it froze in the wintertime. We had to bring water from a public fountain once used to water horses. Door hardware, especially the locks, often did not work. We heated with wood that was mostly my responsibility. I was the first one up every morning to build the fire. Our car never started when it was cold. It often broke down. Passing state inspection was our greatest worry. When repairs were too costly, we bought another fifty-dollar car. My adult house is the opposite. It is modern, plenty of space, and everyone has their own space. Our kitchen and living room are a large open space with a cathedral ceiling and a fireplace. His room is larger than most of the apartments where I grew up. All house repairs are made immediately.

Daniel came to our family when he was sixteen years old when his current foster placement failed. We knew him from when he spent two weeks respite with us while his regular foster family took a vacation. He was polite and charming. We did not understand how his placement failed, but we were used to boys with failed residential placement so it was unimportant to us. Problems with Daniel slowly emerged.

As was often the case, Daniel had problems in school while we had minor problems at home. Daniel had a poor relationship with his teachers. He was disrespectful and often claimed to know more than they did. He started cutting classes and going to friends' apartments. One of my rewards to help motivate teenagers was drivers' education and eventually a driver's license. I expected responsible behavior before I could trust them to drive a car. Daniel completed defeated me with no interest in driving, "My friends will take me anywhere I want to go."

We allowed Daniel to grow his hair longer. He started using makeup. He dyed a section of his curly black hair bright red. He grew his fingernails long and painted them bright colors. He wore fingerless black gloves. He started dressing in only black clothes. He darkened his bedroom and arranged some irregular objects on the floor. He proclaimed to be Wiccan. He eventually refused to comply with any curfew, coming home in the early morning. He neglected his hygiene and smelled horribly. He was revolting against all adult authority. His social media posts were alarming. He described people who had a right to live and those that should die. I searched his room and found a two-foot-long, very sharp dagger.

As things grew worse, the school brought a truancy petition. He was placed in a nearby group home. He refused to do any family reconciliation work. The court ordered a psychological assessment, which was the most revealing I had ever seen. It brought clarity and understanding to me. The psychologist reported that Daniel had "an emerging narcissistic personality disorder." He reported it as emerging because the diagnostic manual identified it as an adult disorder. I learned about Narcissus from my liberal art studies at Saint Michael's College. Narcissus set out on a journey to find the most beautiful person to choose as his mate. He searched long and hard and could find no one. When he stopped to drink from a stream, he saw his own reflection in the water and fell in love with himself.

I was compelled to research this disorder. A narcissist believes he or she is the only one who is important. At first, it seemed to be like an addiction but it was much more. The narcissist discounted the value of anyone who did not serve his or her desires. I saw the connection to his social media posts. The only people who deserved to live served him.

No one has found any physiological cause for narcissism. The popular belief is that narcissism was learned from one's early caregivers. That would be Daniel's birth mother who was in now prison. There was no effective treatment. Treatment recommendations were to persistently confront the narcissist with the reality of his distorted views of his superiority. Advice often given to those in a relationship with a narcissist was to get out of it. Narcissists could only tolerate another narcissist and for only a short time. Daniel had no interest in returning to our home from his residential placement. He aged out of the system and moved to the Midwest.

I learned the value of relationships with Weston and his psychologists. Weston lied most of the time. When I told his therapist that I had to stop the common courtesy of believing Weston until I learned otherwise. I had to treat what he said as a lie until I had evidence to support that he was truthful. The therapist's response was "Ouch!" She went on to explain that Weston valued our relationship. He wanted so hard for us to like him that he said what he thought would improve our relationship. The truth was irrelevant. Weston said what he felt would strengthen our relationship. Truth became irrelevant to him at an early age, living with his schizophrenic parents. His father saw demons in people and went to prison for attacking them. His mother heard voices and saw witches in mirrors. Weston very much wanted to please his mother and agreed that he also heard the voices and saw the witches. Weston did not actually see and hear these things. He learned to lie about it to please his mother so often that the truth did not matter.

I grew up in a house of lies to protect the alcoholic. Weston spent his early years learning lies to protect his mother. The therapist explained that Weston was severely abused by his father who literally bounced him off walls and other heinous acts. Weston remembers none of this. He has it block deeply inside as a coping mechanism. If it every comes out, he may have some serious reactions to them and may not be able to cope with it. The brain can do some fantastic things to protect itself. My ability to turn off the pain of pulling my hair and tune out voices seems trivial compared to what Weston was doing.

A social worker we knew and respected pleaded with us to take Dillon. Dillon was seventeen years old a recently released from jail. His parole officer was about to send him back to jail when his current living arrangement failed. The social worker said that he was an ideal prisoner. I later learned that he spent most of his time in solitary for fighting. I also learned that he nearly beat to death one of my former students. As he got out of the social worker's car, he said that he gets along well with everyone unless they disrespect him. Since everyone is respected here, I did not see a problem. Later, I learned that his definition of disrespect was different from mine. Dillon felt disrespected when he did not get his way.

Dillon demanded respect. Respecting him was a given but that was not what he expected. He had a jail mentality that respect meant that you subvert to his demands. He had other jail jargon such as calling his sleeveless T-shirt a "wife beater." I explained that language was not allowed in my home. He seemed confused but agreed to call his T-shirts sleeveless or tank top. This foster child exerted his desire to do as he wanted and eventually threatened me. Within three days, he was challenging me to a fight. We were frustrated when the police and the social services refused to help us. I demanded his removal but the agency had no alternative placement. The parole officer would not violate him because he now had a place to live.

I even petitioned the court that refused to accept my motion because we were not parties to the case. We were caught among the two battling state agencies and a violent person. We were trapped in a world of confidentiality. I called the governor, which apparently was a breach of confidentiality but it got results. It took three weeks to finally get this violent offender out of our house. It ultimately ended our thirty years of foster care.

Dillon and Joey were similar in their definitions of respect. Both required submission to the alpha male in the home. Dillon violently enforced his beliefs. Joey much more gently manipulated his desires. Both were firm in their resolution for respect. My mother demanded respect for her decision to drink beer. She enforced it upon us with as much force as required and without regard to the injuries she caused. All seemed similar in that they will never change their views. My efforts proved futile.

During our thirty years as foster parents, we fell into a specialty as a place for teenage boys, most who failed at residential placements. As challenging as these boys were, we stand by our statement that the most difficult thing about foster parenting is dealing with agencies, public and private. They think that they have all the answers. They demand that we be "part of the team" while treating us as subordinates. The foster parents are expected to follow the treatment plan in which they have little or no input. The social worker is the sole author and evaluator of the treatment plan. The foster parent is threatened with removal of the child if they do not follow this plan, which was often elusive. Though courts often seek our presence and allow us to speak, we have no legal standing in the child's placement and the services they receive. Even the court has little direction over the foster placement of the child. The court places the child in the State's custody. The State often places them where they want. The court would not know about a changed placement until the next review six months or a year from the last review.

The public does not understand fostering the challenging boys in our care. Foster children have learned to cope in varied and difficult environments. The public expected instantaneous improvement when they were in a caring family. This was rare. Mitch was the only one of more than forty children who responded this way. It was most common that boys tried to change our home to meet their comfort. They were used to arbitrary chaos and tried to recreate it in our home. The chaos diverted the adults' attention so that they could have the freedom they sought. Joey often said, "You're not listening to me!" I explained, "I hear you. I do not agree with you."

The police were the least understanding. Once, when reporting a runaway child, the responding officer handed me the form. I was expected to sign it to verify the information. It was the same form I used as a police officer. It has a phrase saying I agree to go get the child when they find him. I had some children that fantasized about running away to the opposite side of the country. I crossed out the part that says I will go get the and wrote in DCYF (Division for Children and Family Services) will go get them. One officer was hoping mad at me. He threatened to arrest me. I tried to reason with him. The child ran away from me, what makes you think that he will return to me. Do you expect residential placement staff to go get the child? We have the same license. When he continued with his rant, I asked what charge he would bring against me. He said child neglect. I replied, "Good luck with that." The child is not in my legal custody. It lies with DCYF. The officer found the child a short while later and brought him to my home.

I filed a complaint with the state attorney general. The Claremont Police violated the state law that required no one shall have any policy or procedures that discourages the reporting of runaway children. Threatening to arrest foster parents discourages them from reporting missing children. I got a call from a Claremont police captain a few days later. He said that they now realize that foster parents do not have to sign the form and that they would have the social worker sign them. He amended the department policy. Not surprisingly, this was an empty promise. He said it only to close out my complaint. Months later, I was presented with the same form for another missing child. I made the same correction with no reaction from the reporting officer. Years later, DCYF had supervisors on call. Foster parents were to report missing children to them and they would report them to the police.

Transitions from residential placements never went well. Residential placements have an artificial environment. The artificial structure of residential placements had little correlation to the real world in our home. A clean break was much more effective for us. The slowest transitions were with the boys who were doing well. The programs were still paid while the child was with us. They could continue their public funding while we met the child's financial needs.

I grew increasingly pessimistic about residential programs. They claim to create these artificial environments that prepared children for the real world. They speak of learning to follow their unique rules that exist only in the residential program. As I looked more into their rules, I realized that they were designed for efficient and peaceful operation of the program and not life in the real world. Residential programs claim to prioritize the child's needs but in realty the program's design is for its own success. Like other institutions, they had their own jargon. Success in a family is based upon its stable relationships, in contrast to the rotating staff schedules and staff turnover in residential programs.

Residential program isolation from society is like the alcoholic home in which I grew up. We had rules that protected the alcoholic and hid any problems from authorities. Mother even had her own jargon adapted from her limited recall of her childhood Canadien French. It compelled me to study the French language. I learned my mother's expressions such as "Vien sit," "fem la boush," and "mo Dee," were "viens ci" come here, "fermes la bouche" shut your mouth, and "mon Dieu" my God. We understood and were held to strict expectations about what we shared with anyone outside the home, even our friends.

As a case manager for transitioning inmates, I had similar criticisms about our corrections system. Rehabilitation is the foundation of the system. It is called corrections because it is supposed to correct criminal behavior. Jails are also an artificial environment. The only redeeming value during the punishment period are the treatment programs. Often, inmates leave jail to go to a drug and alcohol treatment program. Sometimes they go as an alternative to jail. Unfortunately, these are operated much like the adolescent programs with which I was familiar. Like jail, theirs is an artificial environment with rules to maintain the placement and secure funding. Their redeeming value is the treatment clients get while there. Like adolescent programs, the finances drive the program success. I learned about the success rates of these programs. One's first addiction treatment program was rarely successful. Many people I worked with described attending treatment several times. They may have been rejected in earlier programs for rule violations. Drug treatment was much more difficult and always involved medication to be successful. I wondered about some of the medicines that seemed little more than substitutions for the illegal drugs. Often, the recovering person supplemental their medication with illegal drugs. All these programs involved some sort of aftercare and group meetings such as Alcoholics Anonymous.

I am troubled by the increasingly popular trend to medicate to improve behavior. The proliferation of medicinal treatment seems to have replaced personal responsibility for one's behavior. The blame for their behavior can be placed on a chemical need for medicine. "I did not take my meds" or "He's off his meds" can often be heard as an excuse for criminal behavior. I do recognize that there are some mental health needs for medication. I cannot accept that the criminal behavior was due to a missing medication.

I support medication to help recover from addiction. There are some medicines that will cause physical illness if one takes the drug or alcohol, such as antabuse. The people with whom I have worked that use this method often fail. The medicine does not treat the underlying drives so they simply stop taking the medicine. Sometimes, psychiatrists will prescribe a combination of medicines that attempt to treat the underlying psychological condition, medical conditions with an anti-abuse medicine. A medical treatment program must have a progressive plan to reduce and eliminate the medications. The most effective treatments seem to be with as few medicines possible with therapy and a support group. Multiple support groups seem to increase success. Supportive family connections are at least as effective as any medication. Nothing works unless the person is motivated to recover.

I had an interesting conversation with an inmate. I knew Charlie when I was a police officer and he was a young teenager. He was a heavy marijuana user. We often saw him walking the streets late at night. He was easy to identify with his tall, thin building and very long, straight hair. Sometimes I would pick him up when he was reported missing or if I found him out very late at night. He stared blankly into my eyes as I spoke to him. Charlie always cooperated and said nothing as he got into the police car. His father always met us at the door. Charlie walked past his father and down the stairs to the basement. I had no other involvement.

Charlie came onto my case management list. He was serving time for his involvement in a methamphetamine lab. He was in his thirties but looked much older. The drugs were taking a toll on his health. I was surprised to hear Charlie speak coherently and thoughtfully. Charlie expressed his opinion well. He fully intended to return to his drug use. He felt that his use only hurt himself and it was no one else's business. Charlie would not accept that the meth lab in that apartment building was an extreme fire hazard and left hazardous chemicals exposed to children. He would not accept any responsibility for the meth lab because his roommates, not he, were involved with it.

Charlie stated a position in which I could agree if it truly did not harm anyone else. If Charlie limited his use to marijuana and stayed home when he used it, it would only harm him. However, even as a teenager, Charlie ventured out into the public, placing others at risk.

Transitions from adolescent residential programs and adult treatment programs were difficult and filled with uncertainty. They transition from highly structured, artificial environments to real world uncertainty. I remember the words of one of my daughter's classmates spoken in the jail's recreation room. He was advising a young man recently sentenced to jail and worried about how hard it was going to be. My daughter's former classmate said, "This is easy. You don't have to worry about what you are going to eat, where you're going to sleep, and have a place to be out of the rain. Being out there is hard." He was describing how hard it was to be released with little or no support.

Similarly, foster children who age out of the system will almost certainly fail. They have less support than people transitioning from jail and often no support at all. Many are completely left on their own and doomed to failure. We allowed our foster children to remain and even return to our home as they needed. I understand that some foster parents could not afford to do this. They were restrained like the residential programs that needed the funds to operate. We always provided our foster children with the same things and opportunities as our children. We spent twice what they paid us.

Transitions from treatment programs and jail are difficult because the overly structured environment dissolves into chaos. People transitioning from an alcoholic's home similarly transition from chaos and rules that serve the alcoholic to an unknown environment for which they are ill prepared. Foster children are uncomfortable in the structured foster home and try to create chaos that seems more normal for them. Aftercare programs try to help with these transitions by extending some structure and supervision. Their success relies heavily on the participants willingness to submit to the program's rules. As with the placement, inflexible group programs' rules serve the program more than the individual. I have also seen changing definitions of success to improve the program's statistics. Some participants enroll in several programs with improved success. They found one or more Alcoholics' Anonymous or drug recovery group that they liked. Therapy with medication also helped. The regular meetings and drug testing also helped. Returning to jail for a probation violation, failed drug test, or another crime stopped any progress they were making and required them to start over.

I had the motivation and good fortune to go to college. I learned a lot about the real world that my family and demonized. I also learned about the support my peers had from their families. My family tried to prevent me from going to college. I needed the strength to deny their criticism and overcome their obstacles while focusing on my studies. My greatest motivation was that I did not want to live the same life as my family. My family descended from what was a normal middle class to extreme poverty driven by alcoholism. College helped me make the break by learning what was known about the physiology of addiction even though it is not fully understood. The psychology of addiction remains varied and elusive.

Inmates transitioning from jail had varied motives. There were some who boldly said that they had no intention of changing their lives. They felt that authorities unjustly intruded into their lives and they should have the freedom to live the way they wanted. This group took no responsibility for the danger they presented to others and the laws intended to protect them. Their crimes included illegal drug sales, thefts, burglaries, driving while intoxicated, and operating highly flammable and toxic methamphetamine labs in an apartment building. They did not understand the toxicity and fire hazard of the meth lab and believed it presented no danger to others in their apartment building. They often said that they drive better when they are stoned and dismissed the police report about their erratic driving. This is the strong denial I remember from my mother.

There was another group that understood the harm they had caused and truly wanted to beat the addiction, but they found the temptation too powerful. I learned more about it when I brought a frightening news article about fentanyl in street drugs. Many people were dying from accidental overdose. Scott was very honest with me. He said, "When I hear something like this, I get excited because that is the good stuff. I want to get some of it." Risk of death was irrelevant. He understood that it was possible but he knew how to be careful. These addicts act as though they are better than pharmacists or doctors. They use crude methods to control doses and inject their drugs but still feel safe because they are smart. They did not care about the risk. I described the very sophisticated equipment that I used in college which was required to measure the tiny lethal dose. Their crude methods could never do it. Even if they had the sophisticated equipment and skill to use it, the actual concentration of the drug was unknown. They still wanted it. Their addiction was so powerful that they recklessly risked their lives without regard for anyone else. They denied or recklessly ignored the risk.

The last group had the fewest members. These people were determined to beat their addiction and they succeeded. Their determination was so strong that they would likely succeed even without treatment, but they still agreed that treatment helped. Their motivation was usually for their families, especially for their children. They admitted that they could never do it for just themselves. They still struggled with the addiction that haunted them throughout their lives. Some returned to using it several times. Each time, they were able to succeed again using the methods that worked for them. Some struggled with low-paying employment and supplemented their income with drug sales. Perhaps they could resist the use of their product but the temptation would overpower them. I once used an example that my group of addicts agreed was a good analogy. I am on a diet and I see a bag of potato chips on the kitchen counter. I resisted the temptation for several days. One day I decided one chip would not hurt anything. Once chip is not so bad, I will have two. Eventually I exceeded my daily calorie intake because I ate too many. One person added, "By eating the whole bag," to explain what happens to the drug addict.

I agree that drug and alcohol addiction cross all classes of society and education levels. My work with transitioning inmates from jail were those with less education. This lower level of education limited their job qualifications. Most could only get low paying jobs that were insufficient to support themselves alone. Supporting their families was impossible without additional public assistance.

Addiction is a powerful force. I remember my sister and pouring our hearts out to my mother when I was ten years old. We finally gathered the courage to approach our mother and plead with her to stop drinking. We all cried and Mother promised to quit. I was elated and went outside to play in celebration. A few minutes later, my mother approached me with my sister behind her. She said, "You know, once I start drinking, you know that I cannot stop." I did not know nor understand that she could not stop. I only knew that she did not stop. Mother continued, "I spoke with Cilla and it's OK with her. I just need one more six pack and then I will quit." I looked at Cilla and could see her face communicating what I felt. My heart sank in my chest as I knew pouring it out earlier was all for nothing. I realized that my mother would never stop drinking.

When working in a county jail, I learned a lot about an inmate subculture. They purposefully created their own jargon and definitions to deceive their caretakers. They had a wholly different set of values. All inmate groups adhere to this often-distorted subculture in jail. A primary value is that one did not "rat" on fellow inmates. If you did, then there would be consequences. Common places to carry out revenge were in the shower or on the inmate's bunk. On the bunk, several enforcers pulled the blanket over the victim and all beat him. They called this a blanket party. In the shower, the shower curtain was often the means to conceal the identity of the assailants. Friendships and gang memberships were established for mutual protection.

Gangs grew from this survival concept and became the basis for the gang wars in and out of prison. Oddly, correctional officers were seldom targets of retribution. If an officer was hurt, it was usually unintentional. Gangs protected its members like families protected each other. It seemed that the most dedicated gang members were those who lacked support from their families. They had ways to display to which gang they belonged. Many had identifying tattoos boldly displayed on their neck or face. Some were more discrete on hands, or arms. Other signals cold be a turned-up pant leg, left or right. It could be an offset hat, sleeve, or even a hand in a pocket to signal their allegiance. A bandana and how it is worn could also be a signal. It is strange to me that my grandfather's snot rag could be used as a gang symbol.

Inmates earned badges of honor like rites of passage. It seemed to replace missing the normal rites of passage in their lives. Acceptance into a prison gang could be a major rite of passage. A "real tattoo" is one that was done in prison. Sanitary methods and tattoo pens were absent, making these tattoos difficult to attain. An inmate could elevate his status by revenging a subculture violation that was committed outside or inside prison. Status is gained by acting on behalf of a friend. The highest honor was in beating up a sex offender, especially a child sex offender. Ironically, even sex offenders can earn this status by beating up another sex offender. This is especially true if the offense was upon an adult woman and the other one offended upon a child. Status was gained by serving federal or state prison time over county jail time. These subculture rules create a hierarchy. The ones with the most and greatest honors were the leaders. A subordinate inmate was the leader's soldier who would receive commands to carry out the leader's wishes. People who operate prisons are aware of this hierarchy. They often use it to control the general population. They manipulate it by transferring inmates to different cell blocks or jails. Ultimately, jailers' priorities are to have a smoothly operating facility. Rehabilitation of inmates is secondary. This is also true about any juvenile residential program. Many juvenile detention workers were former prison guards. Many parole and probation officers were also former prison guards.

Prisoners develop a distorted sense of respect. It was more a system to avenge perceived disrespect. One could disrespect another by simply not agreeing with him or failing to follow his wishes. Their hat and shoes seemed to be a part of their identity and any transgression against them was disrespectful. Any historical transgression against one's family, girlfriends, former girlfriends, or property was disrespectful. The consequences of disrespect were often brutal.

Many saw little wrong with their drug and alcohol use. Both were often smuggled into jail. Tobacco was also smuggled in. These items became a pseudo-economy. It was currency to manipulate other inmates. Legitimate commissary, snacks, etc. purchased through a vendor, was used to manipulate peers. A hierarchy of power existed and violently enforced.

Few were truly interested in rehabilitation. They only complied to get parole. They used the increased freedom to maneuver around the parole officer and his or her drug testing. After being called in for a drug screen, they knew that they would be safe to use drugs for a few days before their next call. I understood this determination because I learned it from my mother. She denied any alcohol misuse or addiction, therefore it was not necessary to change. Like my mother, these transitioning inmates denied and disregarded any harm done to their family. Like many who are arrested, they blamed their criminal activity on the overzealous police or parole officer.

Working with foster children, I found many similarities to jail inmates and juvenile residential programs. Maybe my childhood experience in a home distorted by alcoholism and my education allows me to see these similarities. Both have an artificial environment with rules, standards, and expectations found only in their programs. Both believe that compliance in their artificial environment are indicators of success in the community. They share the distorted values of the prison subculture. People who operate these facilities have the same priority to serve the organization first. Finances are most important. It is their job security. They refuse children who require expensive services. They are constantly seeking means to charge services to Medicaid and other providers. Most frustrating to me as a foster parent is their slow transition and after care programs. They delay the transition and any aftercare program as long as possible and continue billing providers. They even sabotage transitions by encouraging the child to return to the program rather than work to commit to the new community placement. We were far more successful with children kicked out of a residential program than one who slowly transitioned. The one's who were kicked out knew that they had to adjust and learn how to be successful in our home and the community. Our greatest challenge with these children was school, another organization with an artificial environment and intensely focusing on the organization's needs over the child's.

Triggers and Coping

Many people who suffer from previous trauma expect others to avoid their triggers. Perhaps it is an effect from my childhood conditioning, but I do not want to inconvenience others to satisfy me. I feel it would be selfish for me to impose on others for my sole benefit.

Triggers often brought back unpleasant feelings. Some were very strong, especially those the disregard the safety of others. I could feel myself in the back seat of my mother's car, cringing down between the driver's seat and the rear bench seat. My fingers were laced behind my head and my face between my knees. When someone threatened to punch another person, I could sense my mother's large body above me and feel her backhand strike my face. The worst thing that I felt was how my mother still had this control over me even when she was not around. Like I conquered the pain of her hair pulling, I decided to conquer these feelings, too.

Throughout my life, I wanted my mother to stop her drinking. She refused to even accept that it was a problem, therefore would never consider changing her alcohol use. The best that I could do was to shield my family from her. She defeated me every time. She was always drunk when she came to my house. She knew that I would not let her in so she came while I was at work. Seeing her car in my driveway was an intense trigger. When I walked in and our eyes met, she did her characteristic throat clearing, pulled at her blouse, lifting it off her chest, and said, "I have to go now." These were all the little indicators from when I was very young. How she performed these were signals to how much she had to drink.

We were about to build our dream home. I was determined to refuse to allow Mother to come to it, even bringing trespassing charges. She died in a car accident. The autopsy confirmed that she was intoxicated. My sister, Cilla, said it best. "At least she died happy." I was something we feared most as children and felt that it was inevitable as adults. We were only surprised that she was not the driver. Mother's influence over me persisted even after her death.

I listened to therapists who helped people identify their triggers. Triggers could be very harmful to their clients' socially accepted behavior and their important relationships. Most of the conversation was on suppressing and controlling the emotions they elicited. Therapists taught their clients how to avoid these triggers. It often extended to the people around them to avoid triggering their emotions. I learned that my triggers were unavoidable. I felt that my triggers were my concern and not for family or friends. I turned them into opportunities to process the emotions that they triggered, become stronger, and gain control over them. I am very fortunate to have such and understanding wife and children. I could gently tell them how and why certain things reminded me of my violent childhood. They did not fully understand the feelings they triggered in me and I wanted to shield them from those experiences. Sometimes, I could use a trigger to help educate my children on the hazards of drinking alcohol.

My mother's death freed me from her physical intrusion into my life. All her psychological effects remain. There are many triggers that bring her back into my life. The most dominant trigger for me is anyone consuming alcohol. I immediately feel stressed when I see people drinking alcoholic beverages and beer is the worst. I found myself looking for clues in their behavior that might resemble my mother's state of intoxication. I needed to know how intoxicated they were so that I could be prepared to protect myself. I was even more alert when my children were with me. My go to coping technique is avoidance, just as it was as a child with my mother. I can control alcohol's influence over my life by eliminating it. I still worry intently about my descendants.

My mother tried grooming us to take care of her. I chose to care for my family. I do not want them to have to worry about caring for me. My grandmother accepted that family cared for their elderly. My greatest honor is for my children to care for their families as I cared for them. I do not want to divert any of their efforts from caring for their families as I cared for them. I am proud to continue to help them throughout their lives. I let it be their choice and never a means to control them. I may give welcome advice and always respect their decisions.

I do not go to bars. I occasionally go to a restaurant that has a separate bar but stay clear of it. I cannot help periodically looking toward the bar to watch for any behavior to indicate intoxication. We arrive early for dinner and leave immediately after we finish. This way I avoid seeing neighbors and friends with any significant alcohol consumption. We attended a few employer holiday parties then decided that we did not want to see our colleagues' behavior when consuming alcohol. We preferred to maintain professional relationships and avoid work-related social gatherings.

As a police officer, I found myself amazingly tolerant of disorderly, intoxicated people. During domestic disturbances, I listened to both sides and negotiated compromises. I learned from my Pepperdine master's degree that people who could make their own plans are more likely to make them work. A plan that is placed upon them is often doomed. My police colleagues dictated solutions with the threat of jail. They closed their demands with, "I don't want to be called back here." They almost always were called back by the original neighbor. Often there was a struggle and the person was charged criminally. These officers were often hypocritical with their own alcohol consumption and behavior. Many had domestic squabbles and drove intoxicated expecting brother officers to have their backs.

If there was evidence of an assault involved in the domestic disturbance, I explained why I was obligated to make an arrest. Most of the time, the assailant voluntarily surrendered because he felt I was treating him fairly. If the situation did not involve an assault but it was clear that it would escalate, I negotiated a means to separate them for the remainder of the evening. Most of these men would rather go to a friend's house than spend the night in jail. The times I needed to forcibly separate them were rare. A common reason to take one into involuntary custody was when they returned after agreeing to go to a friend's house. I did not argue with them. They could argue forever about their degree of intoxication and behavior. I simply explained that they violated our agreement and now they were coming into protective custody. Most surrendered peacefully. If they intensely resisted protective custody, I charged them. I let the prosecutor know that I was very willing to drop charges if they were reasonable when they sobered. This reasonable treatment along with maintaining individual respect made it much easier to settle any future involvement with them.

My most fearful times were riding in the car with my intoxicated mother driving. I started police work with a passion to find and arrest people who were driving while intoxicated. I knew how dangerous it was and wanted to make everyone's life safer. I could not find any when I looked for them. I found them when I least expected. They caught my attention when they made sudden corrections in traffic. If they made a second sudden correction, I began my evidence collection to include in my report. I did not wait too long to stop them. My greatest fear was to watch them collide with another car with a family inside. I wanted to protect children because there was no one to protect me. The information I collected included the field sobriety test. It always puzzled me that the vast majority agreed to this voluntary test until I realized that they were alcoholics in denial. They all expected to pass and be on their way. I made note of other behavior and speech besides the official sobriety test. I could not report every word and selected representative phrases. I described their clumsiness while handling ordinary things such as their wallet and what they said as they struggled with it. I took note of nonsense statements. I continued noting similar details all through processing their arrest, including how clumsily they dialed the phone for someone to come get them. I always sought to make the process as safe as possible by taking immediate control of the car keys. I remained prepared to support them if they fell. A few became violent but were easily controlled in their intoxicated state.

I wondered sometimes how I was able to be more tolerant than my fellow officers while remembering the terror I felt as a child. I attributed it to the times that I had no control over what my mother did to me when she was intoxicated. As a police officer, I now had nearly complete control over what this person could do to me. If they placed me or another at risk of harm, I could take physical control of them. I was still in my top military combat readiness. From this level of confidence, I was able to remain flexible in determining the safest alternative. I understood that they were triggering me but I had also learned to maintain self-control from a very early age. I felt benign concern for the adults who were with the intoxicated person. They could avoid or escape their involvement if they chose. I was more protective when children were involved. I was also aware how a woman could be trapped in a relationship. It was the opposite in my childhood. My mother dominated the relationship and controlled my father. He escaped by abandoning us. There was no societal support especially for men then. Now, I could refer a woman in a harmful relationship to helpful agencies. We have wonderful support services but they only work if she wants them.

I could tolerate working with intoxicated people when I was a police officer and it was my job. I had the power to bring it to a conclusion at any time I felt that it was necessary. I am far less tolerant of intoxicated people as a citizen. I will quickly divert their focus and leave. I choose not to attend functions that serve alcohol. I have often offered our home with its pool, large yard and house as a place for colleagues to socialize outside of work. Never have any taken up the offer when I add that it is alcohol free. "Well, that's no fun," was a reply that remains in my memory. It gives me a hopeless feeling that alcohol is so important that most members of our society can never free ourselves from its harm. Why has alcohol become so essential in our social relationships?

Another trigger for me is when someone says that they are good parents, as my mother often did. Good parents do not feel the need to convince others. Good parents are always striving to do better. The intensity of this trigger varies. It increases in intensity when the parent is drinking. It brings me back to when my mother told us that she was a good mother and her kids would never go without like she did then she drank from her beer bottle. We lived in dire poverty because of her alcoholism. I am most triggered with mothers that are grossly obese like my mother. They shout commands to their child while sitting and make no effort to participate in the task they demand. These self-proclaimed good mothers exert their authority over their child with insults and threats. I never needed any discipline with my children and grandchildren. If they were not accomplishing a task to my satisfaction, I helped them. I focus on participation and avoid criticism. We celebrated together upon its successful completion. When I hear these self-proclaimed good parents, I try to model my methods while realizing they will never change.

Giving animals special consideration over the needs of a child is another trigger for me. My mother was willing to risk our safety for an animal. She almost killed us all one time trying to avoid a woodchuck that ran out in front of the car when she was driving on the interstate highway. She swerved hard and momentarily lost control, fortunately regaining it. She was sober. If she had been drinking, I am certain it would have ended in a catastrophe. It did not turn out so well for the woodchuck. She hit it anyway. At least we survived.

When the barn roof fell in at Bemis Farm, my pet goat Herbie was trapped inside. Mother sent me in to rescue him. She expected me to do something she would not. She also was unable to do so due to her gross obesity. I was only ten years old. I crawled through, over, and under the broken beams and materials laying in all directions. The door to Herbie's stall was hopelessly blocked under the massive beams. I went into the adjacent stall and pulled boards off the wall separating the two stalls to make an opening. I dragged Herbie by his collar through the small opening. I partly dragged and sometimes lifted Herbie over the labyrinth of fallen beams, boards, and roofing. Any one of these beams could have moved or fallen, bringing the remainder of the barn down on top of me. I knew then that my mother felt that my safety was worth less than the life of a goat. This became evident again when she later sold the goat to people who intended to butcher it. The eight dollars bought her enough beer to get drunk. I am triggered whenever I hear or see someone allowing or expecting a child to risk injury on behalf of an animal. The pet adoption commercials bother me because they use the same language as child adoption agencies to "find a forever home." There are many children deserving of the forever home. Using the same language seems to place animals with equal importance as a needy child. I will contribute to children's organizations more than animal rescue efforts.

My mother's name, Lilly, is a trigger. I struggle when I have a student with a similar name even though it may be spelled differently. I cope with it knowing the importance of the child. My daughter named her cat Lily. This was a little more challenging for me, hearing my mother's name in the home where I was determined to keep her out. My coping came from the love I had for my daughter and how it reminded me to identify and separate my feelings from hers. Every time she called her cat, it reminded me that she was more important than my feelings and to protect her from my horrible experiences with my mother.

Senseless arguments are another trigger. I very much encourage civil discourse but when it descends into an argument that is going nowhere, I get triggered. When the argument lacks logic and becomes unreasonable, I end my participation. If I am only an unintended spectator and I cannot leave, I may ask for clarification of their positions. I hope to either direct them to a compromise or truce. My position is that disagreements are opportunities to learn about the other's position while reexamining mine. I begin with the belief that the other people disagree with me because they do not understand. My responsibility is to teach them. Sometimes disagreement is a cultural difference. Dialogue could be a rewarding discovery of different cultures. Arguments of facts may be that one does not understand the information or they have incorrect information. When these arguments of facts have stalled, a verifiable source or more research is required. It is best to pause the argument until the accurate information is found.

An argument in which I refuse to participate is that marijuana is better than alcohol. One evil is never better than another. They are both evil. I hear many justifications such as marijuana is natural. Does that mean fermented alcohol is unnatural or artificial? I ask, "Why does the Cannabis sativa produce cannabinoids, the active ingredient in marijuana?" It certainly is not to benefit humans. Only a narcissist would believe nature exists to benefit humans. It is much more plausible that the plant produces cannabinoids as an insecticide. It is the same adaptation that tobacco plants produce nicotine.

I accept that there are medicinal benefits. All our pain relievers, sedatives, antibiotics, and many other medications ultimately come from a natural source. All medicines should be taken in a prescribed dose. None are intended to be used, as they say, recreationally. I object to the idea of recreational use as applied to mind altering substances. Recreation implies a beneficial activity. I believe such overuse is not beneficial. I define overuse as using an unprescribed substance or using a prescribed substance in amounts greater than prescribed. We struggle to find an acceptable language. Any nonprescribed use of any substance to the level of causing or risking harm is misuse. I have been challenged to argue that marijuana is as natural as consuming food items. This is nonsense. We must consume nutrients required to maintain our bodies. There are no alternatives to nutrients that are essential to our survival. The are always alternatives to needed prescriptions. Intoxicants are not necessary to anyone's survival. I suggest a college course in nutrition and refuse to participate any further in such arguments. No one can win an argument over purposeful ignorance. I accept that if they want to use these substances, it is their choice. There is no need to rationalize its use.

Bullies are a trigger. They find it easier to drag others down rather than improve themselves. Similarly, I cannot tolerate taking advantage over another person. I will always intervene for the underdog. I personally cannot be bullied. It feels like the hopeless conditions I suffered from my mother, grandfather, and school bullies. I will stand my ground regardless of the risk. No one can dominate me with physical threats. I am confident in my military training and especially my judo skills.

Some foods are triggers for me. Those times my mother was sober enough to prepare meals, her cooking was terrible. My mother always put globs of margarine and salt on everything she cooked. She forced me to eat peanut butter sandwiches with chunks of butter too cold to spread in our poorly heated home. She made a horrible, greasy shepherd's pie. Vegetables were always boiled and poorly drained. They were so soggy that water flowed on my plate into the other foods. She always served us, to assure fair and adequate proportions in her distorted standards. We had to eat everything on our plate or suffer violent consequences. Protesting could bring a whack on your head with the serving spoon. It was even more unappetizing to be served with a spoon that had been in contact with my brother's dirty head. Even though I knew that it was pointless, I asked Mother to skip the butter in my peanut butter sandwich. Her immediate response was, "No! I make them all the same." My request to make my own sandwiches was also summarily rejected. When in my school lunch, I could eat around the chunks of margarine and discard them. At home, I was forced to eat them. We rarely ate at the table. We ate on foldable trays scattered about the living room. Mother ate with her plate heaped with food closely under her chin as she shoveled huge fork loads of food into her mouth.

Poorly clothed children, silencing or ignoring a questioning child, unsafe cars, and cluttered homes are lesser triggers for me. My mother had an odd habitat of puckering her lips and holding the with two fingers pressing them to the side of her face. She did this at irregular times and whether she was drinking or sober. I once asked her why she does this. She replied that it feels good. I tried it and it felt uncomfortable. It is very rare but sometimes I notice someone doing this. It brings an image of my mother to my mind.

Birthdays are triggers for me. Birthdays are a major milestone in any child's life. It is a time to recognize physical and emotional growth. Many families have markings on the wall to chart the child's increasing height. New privileges and responsibilities are rightfully earned. During my childhood, birthdays were of little consequence. If we wanted a cake, we had to bake it ourselves. Even this depended upon whether we had the ingredients to make one. My paternal grandparents dependably sent birthday cards with money. My mother took the money "to buy food for the family." She added that it was not fair for one child to have money while the others did not. Whether she used it directly for food or beer was irrelevant. If she had not spent the welfare money on beer, we could have the money for ourselves.

My birthday is of little consequence to me. I prefer not to celebrate it. I am thankful when my family does something for me, but I would rather celebrate them. Cake and ice cream are good because everyone enjoys it. Whenever someone gives me a gift card, I try to use it in such a way that they or the whole family benefits. Celebrations of my children's and grandchildren's birthdays are big events. Lots of family, friends, decorations, and many gifts fill our house. I have always done something personal for each of them. When my daughters reached twelve years of age, it became very challenging. Since then, I have always bought flowers. I look for their favorite colors and a practical vase. Unless he asks for something specific, I give a video game gift card to my grandson.

If there was a privilege to be earned, she gave it to my brother at the same time. If I protested that he was a year and a half younger and should wait, she rebutted with she was not going to treat us differently. It was her form of justice focused on equality, not necessarily fair. Ultimately, it was easier for her. There were few privileges to earn with my mother. I gained all the responsibilities and my brother had few.

Most people I know who have psychological triggers avoid them. Teachers are often expected to compensate for students' triggers. Perhaps it is ingrained into my psyche as a small child but I do not expect others to treat me in any special way. For a long while, I just suppressed the emotions triggered. Eventually, I began evaluating the circumstances in which I felt these triggers. It is not possible for the people around me to fully understand how such things affected me. It is unreasonable to expect them to avoid seemingly ordinary things just for me. As a child, the adults in my life taught me that my emotions did not matter. I was already conditioned to keep my emotions to myself, which was also a trigger. I decided to take a new approach. The triggers became an opportunity to heal old wounds and for me to become stronger.

When I felt a trigger, I kept my focus on the present while still realizing that I am recalling an unpleasant memory. I refused to allow it to affect those around me. I studied what emotion it rekindled, why, and how it was doing it. The trigger is mine alone. I chose to recognize that memory and analyze why it just got triggered while continuing to interact with the present events. This tactic grew easier the more I practiced it. I began with the lessor and more frequent triggering events. My daughter makes an excellent shepherd's pie. I enjoy it but it brings back the memories of my mother's horribly greasy shepherd's pie. Rather than suffer in silence with a memory of my mother's awful shepherd's pie, I compliment or praise my daughter's shepherd's pie and enjoy it. My daughter's response is my therapy.

Perhaps because my mother used it so much, I rarely use margarine or salt and use them sparingly when necessary. We steam or microwave our vegetables instead of boiling them. They are not soggy like my mother's. We always have our meals together at the dinner table. Family members serve themselves from the food placed in bowls or pans on the dinner table. Each dish has its individual serving spoon, unlike my mother who used the same spoon for everything, mixing the foods. Her logic was that it all ends up in the same place anyways. Now in control, my family chooses which foods and the quantities each person wants. We enjoy each food in any order we wish. The meal is celebrated together and not seen as a burdensome obligation the way my mother did it.

I still feel no pain when someone pulls my hair. It was a victory over my mother's abuse. She could pull my hair all she wants and it would never hurt me. Unfortunately, I still suffered the unpleasant strain against my neck, which was unpleasant but tolerable. The best thing was that it negated the controlling pain she intended to place upon me. Realizing that I could overcome physical pain, I decided to extend this skill to control these triggers.

I let the triggers bring back the feelings I had as a child. I could remember each in minute detail. In college, I learned that painful memories helped organisms to survive. If something hurt, we learned to avoid repeating the mistake. Similarly, we remember when something tastes good because it was likely very nutritious. Avoiding the painful stimuli ensures one's survival. If we suppressed that memory, we may repeat that behavior and risk our safety.

As these triggers arose, I began sorting them according to their intensity. Unsurprisingly, the more intense ones were the more life-threatening ones. These included driving while intoxicated, other reckless driving, assaults, especially strikes to the head. Any alcohol consumption was an intense trigger as I had learned that a little consumption always continued into heavy alcohol consumption. Whenever my mother was intoxicated, we suffered emotional and physical abuse.

Long periods of criticism whether directed at me or another person is a strong trigger for me. It irritates the old scar from the many times my mother and grandfather criticized me for hours at a time. These people do not realize that their intended target has tuned them out. It is a protective instinct to shield one's self-esteem from this barrage of unflattering rhetoric. I have used the response, "If you want your words to count, there must be fewer of them" with little success. It seems those prone to lengthy lectures cannot reform just like an addict. Similarly, for meetings to be most productive, have an agenda planned well in advance of a meeting and solicit attendee input into the agenda. Ideas are better developed when people have time to research and process them. Otherwise, it is a one person show with limited feedback.

I decided to accept the triggers as psychological scars. I could not erase them any more than I could erase the physical scars my mother gave to me. I can use these triggers to heal and become stronger with the emotional scars. I hope to be able to help others heal from their triggers.

Recovery

ONE THING I learned about working along with professional therapists and psychologists is that they never agree with the best course of action. I am confident that some will object to my methods. When I consider my accomplishments and compare them to my siblings and other family members, I realize that I have done just fine.

My journey cannot be yours. There is no right way or wrong way. Recovering from an alcoholic's damage is not a straight path nor is it one with a finish line. Restarts are accepted, expected, and infinite.

I know of a technique to name what affects you. It reminds me of Father Couture's teaching at Saint Michael's College. God refused to give Abraham his name. If he had a name, he could be controlled. I do not see much value in naming something within myself. Many people know my name. I do not give them the ability to control me.

I believe that I can recognize what triggers my feelings that have roots in my childhood. The physical and emotional injuries partially heal and will always be a part of me. The effects are far too complex and deep to identify with a simple name. Triggers can bring out very different emotions at varied intensity. I can recognize these emotions and not let them control me. I can also analyze them and their effects to build strength for me and my family.

My grandmother was the family matriarch. She was the anchor that tied the family together. Thanksgiving was always a big function at her house. She eventually grew too old to continue this practice. Our connections were limited to visits. I wanted to continue the Thanksgiving celebration my grandmother did for the family in her honor. Without my grandmother, I would have no contact with my cousins.

Kay and I built a nice home, far better than any home I lived in even when my father was with us. It has a large, open kitchen and living area to host large family gatherings. As my grandmother's health faded, we provided the site for family gatherings, especially at Thanksgiving. It lasted only a few years, until my older sister's health faded. She became limited to a nursing home. We siblings drifted apart. I remained connected to Priscilla. We visited and spoke regularly by phone. She was a good resource for me to process our old emotions.

Visiting my sister, Priscilla, in the nursing home elicited mixed feelings. It maintained a valuable family connection. All the mean things we did to each other as children seemed to bind us together now. We were proud of our families and how we emerged from the nightmarish childhood. I worried about how our visits almost always brought up some angry feelings towards our mother. Were my visits causing more harm than good? It also pained me to see my morbidly obese sister deteriorate to the point that she could not get out of bed without assistance. Her health descended to the point that a mechanical lift was required. Each time I returned home to my active life, I thought how I would not want to live like Cilla. What kind of life is that to be totally dependent on others? She was once a strong parent but now helpless. Her obesity and years of heavy smoking had taken a toll on her body. I do not want anyone to have to care for me. I am the provider to my family. I will not be a burden to my family. I felt guilty thinking that way about my sister.

The day following a visit with my sister, my niece called me to tell me Cilla had died. Priscilla's cling to life was very delicate. Like my other two siblings, she is paying a heavy price for the many years of smoking. We knew that if she fell asleep without her CPAP (Continuous Positive Airway Pressure) on, she may never wake. She was prone to falling asleep during the day. She was often dozing when I arrived to visit.

I felt sadness and guilty relief comparable to when I learned that my mother had died. Both their deaths came as I feared. Cilla died due to her rapidly failing health. Mother died violently in a car accident we expected. Mother could no longer intrude into my life. Cilla was released from her burdens. I was saddened that both took with them a connection to our family history. Both required my financial resources for their funerals. While Mother was mostly an unwelcome intrusion into my family, Cilla was always a great support for me. Her death was a great loss for me. I let her go knowing how frustrated she must have been confined to the nursing home that she knew she would never leave.

With my childhood family separated from me, I felt alone with my past. I focused on my immediate family. Kay and I remained busy professionals. My daughters grew to be intelligent, college educated, independent professionals. My two grandchildren are well on their way through college and a profession. My mother and grandfather worked to keep the family dependent upon them. I enjoy being a contributing parent and grandparent while supporting their independence. We were told what to do in my family. I inquire and seek opportunities to support my children and grandchildren. I can be proud how they are a sharp contrast to my childhood family who did not go to college and remained laborers. Their lifestyle has profoundly affected their health and limited their lives. They all became prematurely disabled. Their health severely limited their retirement activities.

Most would agree that we strive in a safe environment, when we do not have to focus a lot of our attention and effort on being safe. Our world must make sense. We want routine with its predictability. We seek symmetry and rhythm in our surroundings. I find validation in these needs when I read about fictitious characters. Even with them, the story creator has developed some rules and limitations even in the most powerful characters. Count Dracula would die in the sunlight or with a wooden stake through his heart. He could not enter your home unless he was invited. Such stringent rules for an imaginary character. Even when there is no reason to have rules, we make them up. It shows me how much we need rules to help us function in our complex world.

There is a spectrum for order in our lives. At one end of the scale is complete chaos. There are some people who thrive in chaos. We saw it with foster children. They felt safer in chaos because it kept the focus off them. There are others who create chaos so that they can be the ones to take control and be the rescuers. There is another group that creates the chaos so that they can play the victim role. Victims get less blame, therefore less accountability.

I learned to deal with the chaos by refusing to deal with it. I say, "I can handle a crisis because I do not accept the crisis." The crisis is not from my doing and I will not let it become my responsibility. I remain calm, leave responsibility where it belongs, let it play out, and take minor actions to move the situation into a more favorable direction. From this calm perspective, I can better direct the situation. I accept control only in a very rare, real emergency. Assisting others to move progressively to control their own situations is far more effective in the long run. Otherwise, I could spend a lot of time and effort putting out fires that I did not start.

At the other end of the spectrum of order, life is completely dominated by the patriarch or some social organization. Dominating social organizations could be a cult or a cultlike religion. At this end of the scale, the family is limited to the will and ability of the patriarch or organizational leader. Anyone who attempts to do better with be quickly reprimanded. No one is allowed to be better than the head of the family. My grandfather was a perfect example of this for me.

I do not have a consistent method on how I handle domineering control freaks. Most often, I let them ride their false chariot knowing it will eventually crash. If I cannot avoid them, I will ask questions about their objectives. I try to leap over the one-up-man-ship details that strokes their egos by asking them to define their expected outcome. Most of the time, they cannot clearly define their goal. I then ask them to think about it and let me know when they are certain. Sometimes they move the goals. I will call them on it and ask why the goal has changed. I will also expect them to differentiate what they expect from me and what must be done by others and especially them. Eventually, deadlines are due and the tyrant will allow compromise and more rational delegation of tasks.

Occasionally I encounter a control freak that uses fear to motivate and control the people around them. Fear is a powerful motivator and one that is impossible to control. Fear is a primal survival reaction of fight or flight. Human reason is abandoned and the animal instinct to survive takes over. If avoidance is not possible, I will confront this person directly. I refuse to be bullied and I refuse to standby while another person is bullied. A person who leads with fear does not expect an intellectual response. It is usually easy to redirect them with intelligent replies and questions. My diverse and excellent education is my greatest asset. Unfortunately, one must always be prepared for any violent response from a person who uses fear. It is unfortunately a popular parenting style. Children are threatened with spanking in many households. It results in children less prepared for adulthood.

Flexibility lies between these extremes. When flexibility is towards the side of chaos, it is still mostly chaotic and produces an insecure environment. When flexibility is closer to the highly ordered side, it is most secure. The benefits of growth can best be achieved from this position. From flexible security, one is free to take some risks while being able to rely on a secure foundation. The protective parent can help the child process what did not work and what can be done to better assure success. No one can, nor should they try, to control everything.

I am quick to notice when I see people taking things to unnecessary extremes. Like shining army boots. The shine indicates that there is enough wax to protect the boot. A spit shine takes it to an extreme in a game of one-up-man-ship. "I am a better soldier than you because my boots shine more." I could never please my mother and grandfather regardless of how hard I tried. They kept moving the goal posts. Sometimes the expectations for quality of the result changed. Other times it was the method of how to perform the task that changed. It may have taken me too long other times. There seemed to always be a reason why I could not be as good as they are. People with such a drive to perfection tend to be insecure. Perfectionism shelters a fragile ego and uncertainty. A domineering perfectionist lacks the confidence to accept anything outside his or her direct control. I can deal with them by refusing their demands and find satisfaction in what I accomplished.

I find it easier to deal with perfectionists than what I call slackers, a term from my army days. Slackers always have an excuse for failing to perform. It is never their fault. The excuse is their way of pushing the problem onto someone else. I must first avoid the urge to solve their excuse. My drill sergeant firmly said that excuses are one's failure to identify and eliminate an obstacle. Your excuse is your problem, not mine. My struggle is to get them to see that they do have control over the excuses they present. If they are unable to control a specific obstacle, an alternative pathway is likely possible. One must identify the desired result and find the motivation to accomplish it. Slackers are most likely to give up trying.

For alcoholics, they must first accept that there is a problem. My mother never admitted to having an alcohol problem, so there was no convincing her to change. As one recovering from the effects of my maternal alcoholic in denial, I must first accept that I have acquired certain traits. This is why I welcome my triggers. I need to recognize them; then determine why and how they affect me. Some traits are desirable. Others can be intrusive and destructive to my ability to function at a level that I desire.

I did not realize that I treated my anxiety about transitioning from home to college with long walks and self-reflection during these walks. I found motivation by assuring myself that if anyone can do it, if it is humanly possible, I can do it. I just have to have the motivation. I lost the motivation to go to medical school as I learned more about the personalities of the students and the instructors. There was too much arrogance and sense of superiority among them. It was not a world in which I belonged. I was determined to finish college. It was perhaps the most significant decision in my life. I found some of the same arrogance and superiority in the army. I would be constantly in conflict called competition with West Point Graduates.

I enjoyed the high ethical standards in college and in the army. During my childhood, my mother constantly lied and made false promises. She taught us to lie to teachers and social workers about our home life. My grandfather never lied but his standards and expectations were always changing. My grandmother was my only family mentor with consistently high ethical standards. Her standards were perhaps too high in that minor infractions were sins that could commit one to hell for eternity. I found it difficult that one could erase these sins by simply confessing them to a priest and saying a few prayers as penance.

RECOVERY FROM AN ALCOHOLIC'S COLLATERAL DAMAGE

During my childhood, it was necessary to evaluate my mother's mood and state of mind as it changed with her level of intoxication. Out of necessity, I learned empathy. Empathy is very different from the sympathy my mother expected from us. When she was feeling sorry for herself, she expected us to also feel sorry. Sympathy is feeling the same way. Empathy separates one's feelings from those observed in another person while understanding their feelings. I could not feel the sympathy my mother demanded. Being able to identify her feelings made it easier for me to avoid her wrath when she thought we lacked sympathy for her. I keenly analyzed her moods to be prepared for sudden and often violent changes. My strong empathy skills came at the expense of knowing my own feelings.

Buddhism's mindfulness that I learned in college helped me. I was learning to use the coping skills I used with my mother on myself. First, I paused to objectively evaluate my surroundings. Some things affected my feelings while others were benign. I sorted these out and focused my awareness on what was affecting me. Unlike with my mother, I could take time to process my surroundings. With my mother, my safety depended upon quickly analyzing the surroundings even before getting off the school bus. From where the car was parked to her location in the house and even the smells. Second, I looked inward to identify the emotion or combination of emotions that were affecting me. By connecting what is around me that is affecting my feelings I could gain some control. Finally, I evaluated the importance of what was affecting me. I used my standard evaluation guide, if it will not matter five years from now, it is not so important for me to seek immediate resolution. If it is that important, I will keep my focus on the five years from now. Even if I deem it to be important, I have five years to make any necessary changes. As much as I need to be in control, I am also a great procrastinator. I do not need to resolve it now.

My need for control is directly related to feeling safe. I prefer a position in a room where I can monitor the whole room. I especially need to know when someone new enters the room. I also need to have a route to leave the room. If it is blocked, I feel my anxiety sharply increases. Where I park my car matters. I feel vulnerable when entering and leaving my vehicle. I park at the far end of a parking lot, mostly to avoid congestion of people and cars. I plan for an easy departure, or as I jokingly say, "I plan my escape." I feel the greatest anxiety if my vehicle is blocked. I am certain that these needs are founded in keeping track of my mother when she was drinking. She would storm into the room a dispense her brutal justice. Though I could not escape, I could brace myself for her beating.

I realized that my anxiety was directly related to things that I could not control. The less control and the more meaningful the situation, the greater the anxiety. A more direct way to control the anxiety was to gain control. If I could not gain complete control, then lessening the importance of the circumstance helps. When my anxiety remained high, I found new releases since taking long walks were no longer feasible.

Physical activity helps to release some of the anxiety. Cutting, splitting, and stacking firewood was physical, readily available, and produced a benefit to my family. It reduced our heating costs and provided a warm, comforting fire in the fireplace my whole family and guests could enjoy.

Running provided me with a good release while maintaining good physical conditioning. It had another additional advantage that no one could interrupt me during this time. My phone provided motivating music and I also set it to not disturb. Any messages would receive an automatic reply that I would return their call when I have completed my run. Only my closest contacts would get through the filters I set.

Gardening was another outlet for me. It connected me to a more positive aspect of my heritage, my grandparents' farm. It also produced healthy results that my family could enjoy. While gardening, I listened to the birds and other wildlife, which was also relaxing.

Though I have maintained a gym membership, I rarely use it. Those times are for the indoor track for a run. I found little value in weight exercises. It cannot simulate natural body workings. Working with firewood not only meets strength training, but it also produces a result with economic benefits. I value the conditioning exercises that I did in the army. They are all founded on natural body movements, unlike weightlifting. I use them when I have not done other physically demanding activities.

I found one caution about using physical activity to relieve stress and anxiety. If I used an activity to relieve anger, I found that returning to the activity when I was not angry would rekindle the anger. I had to retrain my thinking while doing that activity. Most of the time during physical activity I am thinking about planning my day or week. Sometimes I plan a project. Resolving and planning daily activities dominate my thoughts during physical activity.

When my mind goes to undesirable thoughts during physical activities, I listen to music. I usually listen to music when running or conditioning drills. When I find my mind regressing to negativity, I focus more on the lyrics. The music I listen to is intense with heavy beats and mostly from my college days. Perhaps this music brings me to the most influential time of my life and the time I escaped my family's entrapments.

Dealing with stress when I cannot leave a commitment such as a meeting, I developed several techniques. Held over from my childhood is the ability to tune out the presented and escape into my imagination. Massaging my palms with my thumbs helps me remain focused on the presenter. Changing positions and applying pressure to my breastbone is another method. This technique directs my attention to my breathing. Slow, steady breaths with comforting pressure help me refocus.

There were many times during my childhood that we ran out of necessary supplies. These even included the essentials such as bread, milk, and toilet paper. Invariably, we ran out of things because my mother put off buying them when her priority was having her beer. Kay and I developed a system to provide for our family. We always had a back up for things we use. For instance, when the ketchup bottle was empty, there was always another in the cupboard. Whoever removed the backup from the cupboard wrote it on the grocery list.

My anger is something that I can control directly. I consider the source of my anger. It is always from the actions of another person. I rely on my education to evaluate the person and their actions that caused my anger. Most of the time I can attribute it to their ignorance or arrogance. My preferred option is to dismiss it for karma to resolve. Ignorance and arrogance will always feed the karma cycle. If the person is persistent and unavoidable, I seek an educated, more sophisticated response to defuse the anger missile aimed at me. A person who lacks a factual or rational basis attacks character. The personal attack is irrelevant to the argument. I can also end the conversation with an invitation to resume it when the other person is able to separate personality from the facts. This satisfies my need to have some control over my situation. I keep it in perspective with my guiding concept, will it matter five years from now? If the answer is yes, then it is worth resolving. If it is not going to matter five years from now, then it is best to abandon the argument. I retain the control that I need.

I learned to evaluate my research sources in college. I extend this concept to working with people. Their education level is my primary evaluation. I can then adjust my communications to their understanding. If they boast a college degree, then I want to evaluate how they earned it. Not all colleges are equal and not all degrees are applicable to our conversation. I also find a distinction among what I call integral and composite degrees. An integral degree is one that was earned from the beginning to the end in a coherent degree program. Composite degrees have credits transferred from several sources, several different colleges and maybe some credit for life experience. Composite degrees do not have the same value as a degree whose components have direct connections. I rarely share that I have three integral degrees from three reputable colleges: Bachelor of Arts from Saint Michael's College, A Master of Business Administration from Pepperdine University, and a Master of Environmental Studies from Antioch University. Two of these colleges have religious origins. Coming from a family with little education, I feel capable of communicating on most levels. Mostly, I try to share my knowledge of a topic as I do when I teach science. When I encounter someone unwilling to accept any views but their own, I realize that my efforts are wasted. I will not broaden their view of the topic any more than I can lift something while standing on it.

So many times, my mother made promises to us. We were happy in the moment only to be disappointed when the promise was not fulfilled. After a while, we learned that the promises were a means to satisfy our immediate wishes. We stopped expecting her to deliver promises. Mother lost her credibility with us. We allowed the promise to be her escape from our reasonable requests. Alcoholism destroys the alcoholic's credibility. Unfortunately, they teach their children that credibility is not important.

Empty promises are often combined with excuses for the present behavior or circumstances. The excuse identifies something out of the alcoholic's control. The promise is designed to satisfy the child's wishes when the excuse is no longer present. Most of Mother's excuses were based on financial limitations. She denied many of our requests. It did not take Cilla and me long to realize there would be fewer monetary excuses with less beer. We were still in our preteens when we unsuccessfully tried to get her to stop drinking. My mother's misdirected funds to support the family has been my strongest motivation to avoid using alcohol. Mother's beer feels like a great waste of money that I could use for more important things. It also makes it hard for me to spend money on myself. I prefer to spend money when it benefits others in our family.

It is very hard for me to make promises. It is important to make promises to the people you love to build a trusting relationship. Promises can be implied or they can be specifically planned. The implied promises provide for the person's basic needs. These I can easily do. It follows my commitment to become a parent, which was not easy for me. Before promising something special, I must be certain that I can deliver it. I make no excuses for failure, so I put a great deal of effort into making certain that nothing will interfere with fulfilling my promise. When there is some doubt, I try to set an intermediate time or goal to reevaluate the situation before making the promise. I can offer an intermediate goal, a specific time, or an alternative to the request to let my family member know that I feel their request is important to me.

Doing things for my family is my best coping mechanism for the things that my mother neglected. I remain keenly aware of how my grandfather dominated the family and kept everyone dependent upon him. My mother tried to condition each of us into various roles to care for her. I want to provide for my family while teaching them to be independent from me. A method I use with my adult children is to have them decide as much as possible. I may offer suggestions when I see their struggles but I always respect their decisions and support them as needed. I respect their independence. I continue our relationship with the patience and understanding that began during their childhood. I strive to support their independence. My greatest concern is that I will leave them with unfulfilled promises.

Unlike my grandfather and mother, I do not try to control or interfere with my daughters' lives. I remain present to always assist them. I was rewarded with time with my wonderful grandchildren when she asked me to "watch the kids" when they were young. I am immensely proud that they are in college and support them as much as I can. It is a great motivator to abstain from any alcohol so that I am fully available all the time. My mortality will someday end my direct support but I am satisfied that they are very capable of meeting their needs and their children's needs. They will miss the daily love I show and the little things I do for their convenience. They will not miss me because they need me to do something for them.

Closing

JUST LIKE SOBERED alcoholics, I realize that I will always be in recovery from the harm done by my mother's alcoholism. Alcohol's harm is deeply rooted in every individual and family with an alcoholic or former alcoholic. Healing leaves scars. Some scars are debilitating. Resiliency helps with motivation with the ability to adapt being the greatest strength. Since I could not erase its effects, I decided to find a way to use these mindsets advantageously.

The times that I struggled to meet impossible expectations of grandfather and mother developed a strong sense of reasoning. I tried unsuccessfully to make sense of their demands when they made no sense. When many others would just give up trying, I sought many alternatives to explain the irrational demands. I managed to find some order in classifying and categorizing their irrational behaviors. This developed a skill to quickly make sense of the real world and led me into studying science. Science had irrefutable facts that could be proven. Though some biological classification systems have conflicts, I am accustomed to functioning effectively in ambiguity.

I deal with the lingering elusive perfectionism from my grandfather and mother when I encounter it from others placing similar demands upon me. I remind myself that I do not have to meet their definition of perfection. What is good enough for me does not have to meet your expectations of perfection. It is most likely that what is good enough for me exceeds your perfection.

The successes that I achieved in science contradicted the conditioning from my mother and grandfather. I was not the stupid failure who will always depend on them. I can learn and do anything that I choose. I only must be motivated. I felt some personal karma when my studies brought me to a level they would never understand.

I realized that their understanding was much less than mine, but I never thought of them as stupid. They tried to force me to conform to their limited understanding of the world. I escaped their intellectual confinement by coaching myself, "If anyone can do it, I can do it."

Like a high-end functioning alcoholic, I have a few traits that persist. I am always hypervigilant. When in a room with others, I prefer a position where I can see the whole room and especially the entrances. It developed from being on guard to my mother's entrance into the room when she wrecked her violent discipline upon us. I always park my car at the far end of parking lots. The primary purpose is easy exit. I joke that I always plan my escape. It allows me to enter and exit my vehicle when I feel most vulnerable away from everyone. It also lowers the risk of damage from other cars. I can function if I do not get these positions but I will sense a higher level of anxiety. The extra exercise is a side benefit but not a significant consideration.

I accept that we all have our own interpretations of what makes sense in this crazy world. No one has a perfect understanding of anything, large or small. Each one of us distorts reality based upon our experiences and how we learned to find security. I welcome different, rational interpretations. It may help improve my understanding. Individuals can only exist as part of a larger group. Different perspectives contribute to our society's strength. Each group within a society shares some common interpretations that bind them. This is where I often struggle. I have a high sense of ethics and factual analyses. I have changed jobs several times due to ethical conflicts. I avoid people who promote conspiracy theories and morality that deviate too far from a factual, ethical basis. I can accept a hypothesis but it must be proven to be true. Otherwise, we call it "Jumping to conclusions." In terms of the scientific method, the accept their untested, unverifiable hypothesis as a proven theory. I maintain my personal standards and accept the consequences of changing relationships.

I define my own standards as simply as possible so that I can easily evaluate new information and situations. Truth and verifiable facts drive my thinking. It began with my own identity. I separated my identity from my birth family. Born as George Michael Sanborn when my father wanted me to be George Henry Sanborn III and my mother wanted me to be Michael often challenged my identity. I was George when I was with Dad and Michael when I was with Mother or grandparents. By high school, I decided to be G. Michael Sanborn. For the few years following this decision, I wanted to be called Michael, not Mike. When I became more comfortable with my identity, I placed less emphasis on names and titles. I am Mike around friends and Michael in formal situations. G. Michael Sanborn when my full name is required. With the advent of computer systems, I am forced back to sign George as my first name when legal full names are required because G. is not a valid entry.

It is always good to step back and look at what one has achieved. It can be a project such as a freshly mowed lawn, a woodpile for the winter, a well-tended garden, or a clean house. It can also be how my children followed my footsteps by going to college, getting professional jobs, and now have master's degrees from integral programs. Our grandchildren are also on this path. My retrospection could be my college experience or the teacher that convinced me that it was possible. My struggles and experiences have benefitted me, my family, and I hope many others.

I will end by assuring readers. If anyone can do it, you can, but you will not do it alone.

www.ingramcontent.com/pod-product-compliance
Lightning Source LLC
LaVergne TN
LVHW010202070526
838199LV00062B/4466